D0675392

Tom Kennedy died peacefully in his sleep on May 26, 2021. He had been aware that this collection was under preparation and was very much looking forward to holding a copy, as much as he had the two volumes of his final novel. Although this book was not planned as a memorial, to our distress it now will fill that role. But it serves as just one of many tributes to Tom, along with Facebook postings, email exchanges, friends' conversations, and private thoughts.

Tom touched so many people, and a number have offered their memories in these pages. But, as important as he is to us, his own memories of those he knew thoughout his years have sustained him. Although he called *My Life with Women or The Consolation of Jazz* a novel, it can be considered a life story in disguise. As he explains, "Some of this really happened, as memory serves me." Tom's memory served him well.

In "Dear Prudence," jointly written with Line-Maria Lång, Tom concludes, "Before this moment, I have never realized something in all my seventy-four years: From the beginning, nothing at all has lasted; memory is all we have. Memory is all, and all is memory."

It is our great fortune to have our memories of Tom.

Celebrating

Thomas E. Kennedy

edited by
Walter Cummins

with
Renée Ashley
Mark Hillringhouse
Line-Maria Lång
Louise Stahl

SERVING
HOUSE
BOOKS

Celebrating Thomas E. Kennedy

Copyright © 2021 by the contributors

All Rights Reserved

Published by Serving House Books

Copenhagen, Denmark and South Orange, NJ

www.servinghousebooks.com

ISBN: 978-1-947175-54-9

Library of Congress Control Number: 2021939292

Member of The Independent Book Publishers Association

First Serving House Books Edition 2021

Cover Photograph by Mark Hillringhouse

Serving House Books Logo: Barry Lereng Wilmont

Travels with Tom
Walter Cummins

ONCE I REALIZED IT WAS TIME to celebrate more than thirty years of friendship with Thomas E. Kennedy, along with his host of literary accomplishments, I found that many others wanted to celebrate Tom too, and you'll find their contributions in the selections that follow. Reading them, I concluded that happy friendships are all alike, at least at their heart, but that each is unique in its details. That is, the same Tom Kennedy lies at the core, but those of us who shared time with him carry different memories of different adventures.

In this photograph Tom and I are about to set off on one of several January walks through the Oxfordshire countryside to Broughton Castle, home of Lord Saye and Sele. Sometimes it was just the two of us; sometimes we were joined by others. Up a single-track road to the one-street village of North Newington where we turned left and walked out past a sheep pasture, then right onto a path through a wooded area, following it to the large lawn around the moat that surrounded the castle. Our reward for having come that far was passing among the headstones of the local church to the upscale Saye and Sele pub for an excellent meal. One time the chef left the kitchen to apologize profusely to Tom for not being able to serve remoulade sauce. If no one else was with us, we tried to create a legend that we had made the trip on a run, tossing boulders back and forth. Despite Tom's gift for magical realism, we couldn't convince others.

As much as Tom enjoyed our rambles, he was essentially a city person, taking great pleasure in pointing out the homes of famous writers and thinkers—Kierkegaard's apartment off the Coal Square in Copenhagen, Descartes' in Paris, the nearby Maison de Verlaine, a restaurant in the building where the poet died, and where Hemingway and his wife Hadley stayed briefly in the attic when they arrived in Paris. He knows New York City well, the habitats of Allen Ginsberg, e.e. cummings, Henry James, Theodore Dreiser, Sherwood Anderson, Edna St. Vincent Millay, Marianne Moore, Thomas Wolfe, and many others.

He and I devoted a day to a wander through that city with stops at the former Chumley's restaurant, where the wall behind the bar was decorated with patrons' book jackets, to which Tom added one of his own; a drink at Pete's Tavern, where we occupied the booth in which O. Henry wrote "The Gift of the Magi"; ending at the White Horse Tavern, habituated by Dylan Thomas in the last months of his life, on the day of our visit crowded with members of a fife and drum corps from South River, New Jersey.

But I don't want to give the impression that Tom is merely a flâneur. Most of our friendship—like many of Tom's—has involved literary pursuits, critiquing each other's drafts, challenging ourselves to write dueling stories about the same situations, preparing book and magazine issue anthologies, creating online series of illustrated essays about our literary travels and about the strategies writers concocted to support their writing habits. The most significant result of a casual conversation was the creation of Serving House Books, our response to a joint complaint about the many good books and writers that deserved an outlet. Considering reviews and awards, we were right.

And, as others in this collection explain, I am hardly the only friend to have enjoyed literary projects with Tom, and to walk city streets and visit watering holes. Where did he find time to turn out so many books, stories, essays, translations, and more—all of the publications listed on the pages of the bibliography that concludes this volume? For that alone he deserves celebration. But just as much, he deserves celebration for being Tom and a valuable friend.

THIS COLLECTION INCLUDES a Tom Kennedy story, an essay, and a translation; a joint memoir of a trip to Prague by Tom and Line-Maria Lång; selections from interviews given by Tom; memories of Tom from friends in the United States and other countries; contributions from Danish friends (two in both Danish and English versions); reviews of several of Tom's novels; and an extensive bibliography of works by and about Tom.

Contents

A Tom Kennedy Story

OF THE MANY STORIES Tom has published and often republished, I've chosen "Years in Kaldar" for this collection because it has a special meaning for me. It arrived as a submission to *The Literary Review* in 1988 when I was the magazine's editor. I read it with a sense of illumination and discovery, thinking, "He's really very good," paragraph after paragraph. Our other editors were just as impressed, unanimously agreeing to award the story the Charles Angoff Award as the best work we had published that year. "Years in Kaldar" led to a personal friendship, an invitation to Tom to become an advisory editor, and many literary collaborations.

The story, which also received Honorable Mention in *Best American Short Stories 1989* and in the *Pushcart Prize XIII, 1988-89,* became the basis of Tom's first novel, *Crossing Borders.* As the story was for me, the novel was for Susan Tekulve of Converse College an introduction to Tom's talent. This was her reaction:

> I recall the director of creative writing floating Tom's first novel, *Crossing Borders,* across my desk. "Have you read his work?" he asked. I opened the book, read the first page, and closed it. The prose was muscular and controlled, but not too controlled. The narrative voice was so distinct I heard it inside my ear canal. This was the writing of someone at the height of his powers and, as I learned later, it was fiction that cost him more than years to hone. Like the Matisse on my wall, Tom's writing was all bright swirls of color, and his novel was an invitation to contemplate a pulsating portrait of a man living in such existential pain that he burns down his "perfectly acceptable" life with hopes of re-inventing himself and securing a more meaningful existence. I slipped the book into my satchel so I could take it home, and savor it—without having to stop every half-hour to consult with a student over her semi-colons.

Tom had many story publications and magazines to submit to. I consider it my good fortune that he chose us, a life-changing coincidence.

— Walter Cummins

Years in Kaldar

IN THE EVENING, after they coaxed the children to sleep with fairy tales and lullabies, small faces bathed in orange glow of nightlights, Jack and Evelyn Lynch sat in the living room in horse-blanket armchairs on either side of the smoked-glass coffee table, facing the television screen. Lynch took off his shoes and wiggled his toes, yawned, scratched, smiled, and turned his attention to the stack of papers on the glass tabletop. He worked there, glancing up from time to time at the TV, or to say a word to Evelyn, or reach for his drink. He read and took notes on a manuscript he was editing. Evelyn had her research cards piled unevenly on the table so she could work on the coding for her project, but mostly she only watched the television, sipped her coffee, smoked Newports, tapping her ash into the stained saucer beneath the cup. From time to time, she glanced at Lynch. He could feel the heat of her anger. She wanted a fight. He didn't know why exactly, perhaps just on the grounds of general discontent, disconnection. She began to mutter, insult him, and once that started, he knew he could do nothing until she talked herself out and went to bed.

On the screen, Alan Ladd, wearing a flannel shirt, was saying to George Peppard, "I have seen you make grown men vomit with fear."

"Why do you stay here?" Evelyn asked. "Why do you stay with me?"

Lynch looked at her, then at the pencil which he jiggled between his fingers. "This is my home," he said, raising his palm.

"*Your* home. *You. Your. You.* You give us *nothing.*"

He closed his lips. Alan Ladd and George Peppard began to box.

"You know what you are?" she said. "Know what you are? *Paper.* A bunch of goddamn worthless paper."

He nodded, smirked to himself, kept his mouth shut, aware from experience that she would run down in fifteen or twenty minutes if only he could keep from fueling her wrath. Actually, it was not a bad spiritual exercise. And it was interesting to be privy to such negative observations about oneself. She criticized his appearance, his occupation, his family, his character, personality, and general behavior. He listened to the things she said, thought about them. The only danger was if he accidentally listened to her voice itself, instead of just the words; the sound of the voice, the loud, hard, constant substance, the grainy smoked-menthol texture of it could infiltrate his peace, rouse him into her game. Then he would be on his feet, shouting lies, distortions, vulgarities, or worse, concealed truths, things from which he had meant to protect her, things her mother had said behind her back, or veiled slights forwarded by the boss from his wife, or his own observations of how she had conducted herself at some party or function. When these rages took hold of him, he didn't know himself. He paced, grinned malevolently, struck for blood, pain. If she began to cry, he bore down harder. Sometimes he stood watching her, thinking that if she came close enough, he might do something, lash out with his knuckles, the back of his hand, lunge for her, could feel his eyes wide open, fascinated by his own meanness.

But essentially, this was her game. He let her play it alone, waited for her to run down and stomp off to bed. His own game was a quieter one, so quiet he couldn't even hear it himself, though he had listened, tried to, for he wanted to know himself, to be free of blindness.

At last, she rose, glaring, cocked her leg, kicked his shoes from beneath the edge of the coffee table. One skidded into the wall beneath the TV. The living room door whacked shut behind her. He flinched, startled by the sound, then knew he had peace until morning. He cherished these interludes of solitude. (Perhaps *that* was his game.)

First thing he did was switch off the TV (Alan Ladd's face, bleeding from the nose, vanished with a click), spread out his papers. He freshened his drink with a healthy splash of Glenfiddich, filled a dish with peanuts, sorted through his record albums: Morrison, Dylan, Parker, Getz, Vivaldi . . . He chose the Vivaldi, sat again and sipped his malt whiskey, nibbled Planters, wrote letters to friends, contemplated women he had known, meditated, thought about his father, prayed, tried to find a prayer to focus on a power he no longer believed capable of an awareness of men, until he could neither drink more nor stay awake longer. Then he made his bed on the sofa, slept in his underwear with his eyeglasses folded in his hand because he feared being alone in the dark and unable to see.

During the night, he woke to the sound of a slow rain striking the roof gutter, sizzling in the dead leaves across the lawn. Not because he missed her so much as in a lonely panic to deny that this had happened to them, that their life together had grown so strange, he got off the sofa and climbed the stairs to the bedroom, lay beside her in the dark, listening to the whisper of her breathing while he stared at the knotty pine ceiling and contemplated the burnt, strange landscape of their ten years together, the children they had made, the transformation of their feeling for each other from what they had once called love to a relationship stranger than any he had ever known or could have imagined—the intimate hostility of people too closely connected ever to be free of one another, whether or not they parted. No, not connected. Disconnected, like a limb torn loose of its socket, bone grating on bone. He could remember saying to her, "I love you." The words he had held back until he felt sure he meant them. And, "I *do* love you," the extra verb emphasizing the doubt it tried to annul. The word seemed so cheap, the mandatory lie of surrender. The sound of it was like a trap with all its springs of pledge and vow and unspecified future commitment. It seemed a word for people weak with loneliness, desperate to deny that they were sealed within their flesh, alone for all time; he wondered whether this was due to a deficiency in himself.

In the pale morning light, he opened his eyes, watched her lift the white sheet and rise from the bed, her face bruised with anger. The haloed silhouette of her naked body in the narrow parting of the curtains might have been a woodprint, Hopper, a bad mood in its best light. Lynch's eye traced the contour of her breast, perfect curve, the bawdy tilt of her stem. Admiration began and ended in the eye, went fallow in his brain.

He remembered when he had realized he wanted to marry her, a dozen years ago. He had been lying on her sofa, waiting to make love with her while she stood naked by the window of her apartment on 85th Street, rooftops and water tanks behind her. She had been taken from his arms by the telephone, which she stood chatting into while he lay there and admired her body. She stood with one foot on a chair seat, and she probed and caressed the skin of her leg as she talked, looking first at one side, then the other, evaluating. The long soft plane of flesh inside her thigh drew his blood toward his center, his center toward her. He had fancied that he knew the difference between love and lust. He did know the difference between wanting a woman you dislike and lying to get her and wanting a woman you like and not having to lie. But this was more, a more complete emotion than he had yet known for a woman, so lacking another word, he called it by that one, *love*, though still there was the doubt whether it was ever anything more than people just craving the touch of one another. Nevertheless, he had experienced his attraction as *love*, used the word, thought it, buried his mind in its flow and ebb of sound; as he watched her there at the window with the dark city behind her, melded with the sound of her voice speaking into the phone, the whole situation added to the cumulation of what he had already seen of her, which made him see she was the best woman he had ever known in his thirty years, the best woman, all told, likely ever to be available to him. And she was not pink and passive. She was a source of power, enlightenment. He had learned from her, grown stronger from her.

Then she was setting the telephone back into its cradle, crossing the room to him, the light behind her, her teeth in shadow, and he was telling himself to share what he felt with her, *tell her*. "I love you," he said. And to nullify any lingering doubt, again, louder: "God. I *do* love you."

She had taught him, opened him with the prying, agitating tool of her honesty. His friend, Jay, his best man, had advised him: "Listen, Jack. Two things. First, when she tells you you got lousy taste, all she really means is she don't like your tie. And second, with a woman like Evelyn, you might think what you got to do is take down your defenses. *Don't.* Strengthen 'em!"

Yet her truth, her honesty, was illusion, too, insecurity, youthful brashness, a flair for cruelty. Familiarity stripped it of power.

From the straight-back chair, she took the kimono they had bought in the Ginza during more promising times, blue willow branches printed on white cotton, faded now with years of boiling. The print was not unlike what he could see through the parted drapes—white sky, scratchwork branches not yet curved and fattened with spring. He lay in bed and watched her tie the belt; her hands jerked the knot as though to snap a neck.

At breakfast, she looked at him across the raw wood table. "You have egg on your lips," she said, the blankness of her face eloquent with contempt.

Sure as a prophet, he knew this morning, its small range of possibilities, the threat of bitterness, the equanimity, transcendence they struggled to learn and teach each other. Sometimes, rarely, they *met* over breakfast or dinner, wryly affectionate, understanding, knowing how absurd they were, what fools they were, yet trapped in their absurdity, rare moments of closeness. *After all these years,* they thought, shaking their heads. He patted her shoulder, squeezed it; she touched his cheek. The children watched, open-mouthed: *What now?*

More often they fought. Quiet spite. Or hollered, snarled. Or, if the children were awake, they seethed, holding it in, taking succor from the anger which was the strongest passion left between them.

They could not part. He couldn't leave her. The children held them together. He could not upset their world, did not believe in divorce. They stayed together, ten years behind them, another ten or fifteen to go. No doubt they would part when the children were grown (*but how could they really? how could they?*), when *they* were, say, twenty-five, if he and Evelyn could last together that long—otherwise sooner (*but could they ever really?*). Lynch had lost his father at twenty-three, and it had been too soon. It afflicted him that he had never met the man as an adult. Therefore, he wanted to stay as long as possible, to preserve this world of family for his own two kids. Perhaps *this* was his game, his fiction, the void which was not void and held him from the chaos without. But who knew what their next decade would teach them about marriage? Perhaps a marriage had seasons, long periods of dormancy in which it gathered strength to assume another form. Something stronger than passion, strong as that feeling he had known as a boy, welling not from the blood or even the heart, from the soul perhaps. The love for father, mother, for his brother, Jeff. Gone now. Dead as strangers. A few flickers of memory, a few impregnations of his character. No, no, more than that, much more, but still so little compared to this pure feeling, this direct connection with the children, this love he shared with them which would not let him be numb or alien or immune to the world.

Lynch and his wife had not made love in more than a year. The last time had been after a year's abstinence, and had been nothing at all like love. What was it, he wondered, that drove them apart? Truth or illusion? Was it the cool truth in her gaze that turned him away? She was beautiful. Why didn't he want her? Or she him? Why was her body so cold in his sight?

He watched her stub out her cigarette, swallow the last of her coffee, rise, leave the table without a word or glance at him.

That evening, standing behind the ladder-back chair where his mistress sat watching the television, he laid his thumbs along the back of her shoulders and kneaded the muscle there. He relished the stiff, knotted tension, the resistance. Something good lay beneath it for him, like juice beneath a shell.

On the television screen in black and white sparked with blurs of green, Bela Lugosi was saying to Peter Lorre, his Hungarian lips supping on the words, "The soul is eaten. Fifteen years in Kaldar. Skinned alive. Day by day. Minute by minute— . . ."

Lynch bent, placed his mouth against Cindy's ear. "Your body is the only truth," he whispered. It seemed as good a lie as any. He wanted it to be truth. He wanted to allow his passion for women, for a woman, to be the single, irrevocable, irreducible fact. His face turned to them as surely as plants grew toward light. His desire, his will for her was true, the lie irrelevant. He wanted to skin the tension from her. He wanted her will. When he broke the tension from her muscle, he knew the will beneath would flow into his palms. For a little while, he would own her, master her, the expression on her face, the light in her eyes would be things he created from her body. And then he would release her.

His thumbs worked at her shoulders, building slowly, carefully, in force, retreating instantly when resistance flared, the strength of his thumbs addressing the will that tensed the muscle, pressing harder, slowly, gradually taking control.

She moaned, exhaled, her shoulders lowered. He put his lips to her neck. Her head tipped back. Her shoulders moved into his palms.

Later, she lay on her hip beside him and picked gently at the cruciform of hair on his chest.

"Do you love me?" she asked.

"Yes."

"Why?"

"Because I don't love you."

She blinked, thought, smiled. "You're a fox," she said. He watched the teeth of her smile, the teeth and lips, white, good teeth and full lips, a scrap of red meat lodged at the base of one canine.

"And you love me . . ."

"Yes, I do," she said.

" . . . for the same reason."

The lips went slack, closed, tightened. "Cynic."

He was stroking her calf, slim and muscular, downed with pale beige hair that kinked against his palm. She pinched his sideburn and tugged. Through her teeth, she said, "I want to hurt you."

"Why?"

"To make you jump. To drop your face."

"The face I have here is the bottom one," he said.

She looked into his eyes. Her blue-green gaze flecked with yellow and sienna, eyes soft and submissive with something falsely received, ex-traded. That was not the way he liked to own her. That was a way for her to own him. He did not want her to own him.

He said, "That was meant as hard truth, kiddo. *Hard* truth. *Hard.* Truth." As he rolled over onto her and pinned her wrists above her head and watched her eyes change from openness to hurt to glitter.

On one knee before the television cabinet, he spooled the video tape back, triggered fast forward. He saw Lugosi's eyes in black and white with green sparks and let the film play, adjusting the volume down not to wake Evelyn or the kids. He sat in the horse-blanket chair with his bourbon, Cindy's fragrance in his nose. The smell saddened him now, seemed to emphasize the ephemeral nature of everything, even that physical closeness. Here and gone. Flesh against your fingers, lips between your teeth, her will gathered in your palms. And gone. An hour, an evening, a few touches, a fragrance. *After coitus all animals are triste.* She liked his game, he thought. She didn't want to be allowed to love him. She liked it as it was. His control kept them intact, free to use one another, to enjoy one another, the illusion of not—void in void. His resistance gave life and direction to her yearning, his desire to possess gave the framework of strategy to them both.

The green sparks danced in Lugosi's mad black eyes. Lynch spoke the lines with him: "The soul is eaten. Fifteen years in Kaldar . . ." He and his brother Jeff had seen that film together thirty-five, maybe thirty-six years before, a Saturday matinee at the Newtown theater, up over the concrete bridge past the graveyard and the railroad tracks and the river. And those lines had been the mainstay of their repertoire for years. When they had nothing at all to say, they could always fill the silence with a black glare, a Hungarian Gothic accent: "The soul is eaten . . ." Hawk lips supping on the words.

Jeff was three years older than Lynch. Until Jeff was nine or so, he and Lynch had been devoted to one another. Their parents liked to tell a story of how they went out to the theater one night, leaving the kids to take care of one another. A thunderstorm broke out on their way home, and they got back to the house to find eight-year-old Jeff and five-year-old Jack huddled together under a blanket in the dark, arms around one another while the thunder cracked outside, telling each other, "We can't get hurt, so there's no reason to get scared, right?"

"Right. 'Cause thunder can't hurt you anyway, and anyway it can't see us under here, right?"

Lynch rattled the slushy ice in his glass, sipped the bourbon, and wondered how your love for a person could die, vanish. Maybe, he thought, you somehow just lose the capacity to keep it alive. People grew from one another and lost interest in understanding one another. He thought of Jeff's face, could call it to mind in detail, his turtle-like nose, thin lips, his smile, his cool, funny manner, how they once would have lain down their lives for one another, simply because a world without one of them in it was unbearable. And now, somehow, they couldn't bear five minutes alone together. *Why? Is it me?* He thought of Evelyn last night in terminal frustration: "You don't *know! You* don't *know* how you are!" Intriguing him. *Tell me how I am. Give me a hint.* But she could not explain further and, anyway, it wouldn't have helped. They were in disconnection. Nothing they said to or of one another at the moment was valid. They were not even capable of touching one another with their fingers or their gaze without their lips curling, nostrils cocking as though at a bad smell. Disconnection. He thought of the way his son sometimes touched him as they spoke together, unconsciously picking at the hair on his arm or stroking his shirt or tugging at his earlobe, running a finger across his lips. He thought of how his little girl's body clung to him when she was tired or frightened, the fragrance of sunshine in her auburn hair. He tried to remember how it had been to make love with Evelyn, closed his eyes, but smelt Cindy and saw her smiling mouth, lips, teeth, eyes so green, hovering over him in the dusky light, careening rhythmically, endlessly, shifting to the side, to the side, groaning inarticulate questions of pleasure.

On the screen, the shadow of Bela Lugosi flailed with a saber at the shadow of Peter Lorre tied to a rack, flaying the skin from his body. Vengeance for Kaldar. Screams. Mad eyes. Lynch tried to remember the gleeful horror the scene had given him and Jeff all those years before, but remembered instead the night that Jeff predicted their estrangement. Lynch was about seven, Jeff nine or ten. Jeff had been in school for two or three years and had begun to go places without Lynch, to see people Lynch didn't know, to play games Lynch was too small to join. This particular night was clear in Lynch's mind even after nearly four decades; he could remember it the way a person remembers being hit or jumped or thrown down by a car. He couldn't remember the pain, only hollow details, brilliant in memory.

Lynch had been lying in bed, the clean, cool sheets folded over the satin lip of a peach-colored woolen blanket pulled up to his chest. He could smell those clean sheets, feel the warmth from the yellow lamplight, smell the pages of the Superman comic he was reading. Jeff stood beside the bed, barefoot on the wood floor, buttoning his striped pajama top. He looked at his younger brother and said, "You know, Jack, someday, you'll have all your own friends who you'll always want to be with and play with. And me, I'll have all my own friends, too. But we'll still see each other at home."

"Sure, I know that," Lynch said and pulled the sheet up to his forehead so his brother wouldn't see the tears squeeze out of his eyes. But Jeff did see. "Hey," he said. "Listen. I'm just talking. That'll never happen. That'll never happen to us."

They sat at the round glass coffee table, chatting, she leafing through a catalog, he half-heartedly trying to organize some footnotes. On the television screen, a swarthy man with a dark Van Dyke beard was saying to John Forsythe, "I would smile at your agony."

Lynch sipped his coffee. He glanced at Evelyn, at the brochure in her hands. He could see women in spring coats on glossy paper, light glinting off them in white smears. She always dressed so well. Who *for*? he wondered. *Why?*

A tumbler of club soda stood on the table beside her. Lynch experienced *a déjà vu*, recognized the source. When he was a boy, right up until he went into the Army, every night at nine, his mother went upstairs and brushed her teeth, then came back down with a tray of brushes and jars and tubes which she set on the table in the dining room, which was also the television room. Then, while she watched television, slowly, methodically, using all four fingers of each hand, she massaged her scalp for thirty minutes, moving the skin of the scalp against the skull bone, rubbing, stimulating the blood flow for thirty minutes—she timed it exactly. When she had finished that, with the rubber tit on the handle of her Py-Co-Pay toothbrush, she would massage her gums, in between the bases of the teeth, front and side, top and bottom vibrating her hand, moving on, vibrating, moving on, using a round chrome mirror on a wire stand to guide her work. Then she slipped the toothbrush back into its green plastic sleeve, clicked its cap on, and unscrewed the lid from a jar of Pond's hand cream, scooped up a blob of it on her finger-tips and massaged it into her hands, wrists, forearms, elbows—another blob—neck, cheeks, the nub of her chin, her upper lip, forehead, down the top of her nose, her earlobes. Then, her face and arms glistening, she closed up all the jars and tubes and rearranged them on the tray and, when the next ad came on, climbed the stairs with the tray and returned it to her vanity table, after which she came back down again to fill a tumbler with water from the kitchen tap. She covered the mouth of the glass with a pale green plastic coaster embossed with green floral designs. She kept the glass of water beside her bed in case she woke, thirsty, during the night. But first, she would sit at the dining table and watch to the end of whatever was on—*Perry Mason* or *Alfred Hitchcock* or *What's My Line?*—with the glass of water on the table in front of her, her face glistening with a layer of Pond's.

Something about that glass of water had always been repugnant to Lynch. He used to sneak glances at it, watching the tiny, lethargic bubbles which rose in it from time to time, sliding up along the wall of the glass with its pink fleur-de-lis decal toward the pale-green, plastic-flowered ceiling of the coaster across the mouth. She had always seemed to him perfectly oblivious of him or anything else throughout all these rituals, a person devoid of awareness, protected from it by insignificant purposeful motion. But once, as he was gazing at the water tumbler and she was gazing at the television, she said to him, without turning her eyes from the screen, "You might not be so quick to sneer at it if you were dying of thirst on the desert."

On Lynch's twenty-first birthday, his father and his brother, Jeff, took him out drinking with them. Toward the end of the night, Jeff went off with a waitress, and Lynch and his father sat at the bar, while the bartender counted up the take. Lynch's father was pretty drunk. He was staring glumly into his shot glass, eyes fixed, brow wrinkled, the breath whistling in his nostrils. He said, "You know your mother and I haven't had relations in twenty-two years. *Twenty-two* years. They told her another baby'd kill her. And that was the end of it."

It was not until the next morning, as he lay in bed with a head that felt like a kicked-in watermelon, that Lynch realized the significance of the statistic. Twenty-two years. *He* had been their last act together. Little Oedipus. Or, at any rate, when he came out, the door locked behind him. He wondered how any man would allow himself to put up with such a situation. But still he admired them all those years together, staying together. He couldn't imagine them apart. All those years of thirst, drinking tap water for the passion. And it had been important to him and to his brother, he knew that. The glue of their rituals, their self-control. He knew them. They were there. Always. You always got a fair deal from them, and you knew they would always be there for you. If you got hurt, they got upset. You lost, they cared. You won, they smiled. Always. A single, stable base from which to address the world. You knew the soundness of the wall behind your back. That one thing you did not have to doubt.

Palms cupped around the rock glass, he stared down into his drink, the remains of his drink, the deep whiskey he had poured over three steaming cold ice cubes which were now slush in a finger of pale amber. If he poured another, he knew he would also pour a third, and the third would cool the drowsiness from his brain, and he would put on The Doors or Charlie Parker and pour another and contemplate the fact that he was killing himself, but that that was fine because he was dying anyway, even as he sat there and puzzled over his life as it evaporated, as the once long night proved itself as ephemeral as all its predecessors, fading toward a dawn as fleet as all other hours, that emptied as quickly as a full bottle of whiskey.

He poured another, sat in his sturdy armchair, legs crossed, gazed through the parted curtains to the navy blue sky, the black scratch marks of late winter trees and branches imprinted against it, the unearthly high street lamps up above the sunken highway at the next corner, staining the darkness an unnatural pink.

He sipped his whiskey, considered himself, the increasing evidence of the mortality he only now had begun truly to understand awaited him. He was stout now, next year no doubt, or the year after, would be fat as his father in the last part of his life. He was not unlike his father actually. His eyes were bad, too, his teeth, his lower back. His excesses had left their mark after all. His joints sometimes ached. His toe (gout?). A grape cluster of varices swelled behind one knee. His internal organs—spleen, liver, gall bladder, intestines—complained from time to time, grumbled and muttered and bit. Their complaints were earnest, stern pains, needle-sharp flashes, a shot of pain in the rectum which gave a hint of how death would humiliate, with pain in undignified places. Sensations too ephemeral to present to a doctor as symptoms, the opposite of a child's growing pains, perhaps ending pains, advance signals of the last leg of the journey.

He studied the back of his hand: three pale liver spots, roughened, reddened skin, knotted veins, fattening at the blade. His father's hand, the way his father's hand had looked to Lynch when he was fifteen years old. Gone now: father, mother, brother. Gone from him. Now there were the children, and Evelyn who had borne them. He remembered her swollen belly, the arc of her body in a sundress, remembered her on the table with her thighs spread, white belly humped up, while the midwife told her when to breathe, when not, when to push, when to wait. Lynch held her hand, rather made his own available to hers, felt useless.

The midwife, a dark-haired woman with a black mole on the edge of her upper lip, looked up from where she sat on a stool between Evelyn's legs. "Perhaps your husband will wet a cloth and lay it on your forehead," she said to Evelyn. He hurried to the sink, ran the tap over a cloth, wrung it out, patted the perspiration from Evelyn's face, touched the damp cloth to her dry, swollen lips. She smiled at him.

The midwife's voice, strained now, said, "Okay, now you push. Come on, do it now. *Push.* That's it. Good. Okay, now, again: *push.*"

Lynch looked from Evelyn to the midwife to the place between her bent, parted thighs. The midwife took up a shears. He heard the clip, the groan lost amidst other groans, and a slimy scalp appeared, swelling through a wall. Lynch was dizzy. Then the plastic-gloved hands were drawing it forth, turning it, a face, glistening body red and purple and pink, a penis, pudgy thighs, knees, the body lifted free and laid on Evelyn's still swollen belly, the cord yet uncut. His hair was red, eyes open and blue, gazing, startled, embodied, while Evelyn's face, tipped forward, smiled at him, her palms at his frail purple arms, and Lynch stood apart, a pale attendant.

Cindy stood waiting for him at Rockefeller Center, looking down over the railing into the skating rink. She wore a tweed skirt and jacket, tailored, impeccable, skirt just above the knees, slender nylon-sheathed thighs, brown leather shoes with pocked toes, medium heels, pale brown hair clean and long and glistening in the evening light, as taped organ music piped out of the speakers.

Lynch held back, admiring her from the avenue: picture of a lady, hot as a cat. His happiness at the sight of her felt so pure. He wanted only to give and have pleasure of her. Only that.

Some moments lasted. He realized that now. Some moments lasted and were worth their price, were inevitable, cheated time. He sat in the horse-blanket chair, ears sweating in plastic earphones within which Stan Getz blew "Sophisticated Lady," and that moment of admiring her at the skating rink survived itself, reflected in his mind, and he saw himself cross the narrow arcade of elegant shops, past the long planters and water-spouting lips of stone fish, as he came up behind her, saw her jump, then smile, as he touched her shoulder. She turned, and he leaned to kiss her, his hand sliding up under her skirt, and she whispered, *"Jack!"* as his palm moved up against the inside of her nylon-skinned thigh to the warm center of everything. He could taste her lips, feel the smooth, dead nylon against his palm, the rough tweed against the back of his hand with its three pale liver spots, as his palm took possession of her.

"Jack!" she whispered. "Everyone can *see!*"

"Let them eat their hearts out," he said around the spice of tobacco and gin on her young mouth.

Even now he could taste it, drunk, could taste and smell her, see the glow of her pale body on the white sheet in the dark room, the parted thighs, the smile, teeth, the reaching hands, open arms, even as the snores welled up the base of his nose, and his ears sweat against the now silent earphones, and his head nodded forward in sleep.

The smack of curtains opening in an angry burst and Evelyn's voice, muffled, woke him, caught him by surprise. He opened his eyes and heard her words, but could not understand them, saw the glare of her eyes looking down at him where he had slept in the horse-blanket chair. He lifted off the earphones, felt cool air against his damp ears, tried to speak, but his voice was clogged with phlegm.

"Daddy! Daddy!" the kids shouted, racing in through the French doors, across the carpet toward him. His son stopped short, stared, open-lipped. "Why did you sleep out here?" he asked.

"Go and eat your cornflakes," Evelyn said.

"But why did Daddy sleep here?"

"Just *do* as I say."

"For fun," Lynch called after the boy. "Just for fun. So I wouldn't wrinkle my jacket."

"Are you prepared to talk sense?" Evelyn said.

"'Course I am." He lurched forward in the chair, saw he still was wearing his jacket, his tie, his unlaced shoes. A half-full drink stood on the carpet beside his foot. The amp of the tape deck hummed, and sunlight slanted in across the windowsill through the parted curtains, as he coughed and dug into his trousers for his handkerchief.

"I'm taking the children to my parents for a few days," she said. "No scenes. I'll come back Monday and expect you to be gone. Are we agreed on that?"

"No, we are not."

"You've done it this time," she said and stared at him. "You've really done it."

He felt the blood run into his cheeks, couldn't meet her eye. "Meaning what?"

His voice was thick; his tongue ran out to wet his lips.

She glared, her eyes bright with hot anger. "I will *not* be your fool!" she whispered. Then the coldness covered her again.

The breakfast table was set. "Daddy!" his son called out. "Sit next to me, okay?"

"We're going to Gramma's," his daughter said. "Mommy said you were too busy to come."

He looked at them, at Evelyn, at the table, covered with food the way a family's table ought to be—sugar, butter, coffee, cream, toast, cornflakes, a pitcher of juice, napkins, plates, spoons, glasses, a waxed container of milk imprinted on the side with a child's crayon drawing of a cow. He sat down, meaning to explain, persuade, to speak and clarify everything, but as he tried to find the words, something rose up in him that seized control. He lifted his palm, swung, flat-handed, round-house. His hand smacked the milk carton. It flew across the table, sloshed a trail of milk down the wall, floorboards, struck the floor on its side, milk trickling from its spout. He rose, shouting, "*I do not want this . . .*"

"*Jack!*" she whispered. "The children!"

He paused, felt the blood in his face, eyes bulging, saw their faces, their eyes watching him, suspended. He took a decision. They must see this. They must know. That it was not for lack of love or passion or fear of pain. He slammed the flat of his hand down onto the table. The cups jumped in their saucers, and he bellowed out: "*I do not want this to happen to us!*"

He was breathing hard, through his mouth, thinking, trying to think. No one spoke. Evelyn stared. The children moved behind her. The room was still. Lynch always remembered that. How very still they were, his wife, non-plussed, staring at him, his children gazing up in bewildered fear at their father, a man they did not know, as his own mind flashed with thoughts of his own father and mother, the stillness in which they had lived, the standoff they had survived, dead now, gone, all of them, as his lungs heaved for air and his heart banged against his chest.

First published in *The Literary Review*, 31:3 (Spring 1988)

A Tom Kennedy Essay

"I AM JOE'S PROSTATE" marked a turning point in Tom's writing career. After many books—novels, story collections, essay collections—and prize-winning works in dozens of literary magazines, attaining the National Magazine Award 2008 (reprinted in *Best American Magazine Writing*) led to much wider recognition and, eventually, a contract with Bloomsbury for the four novels of *The Copenhagen Quartet* and many reviews in wide-circulation newspapers and magazines.

Tom flew from Copenhagen to New York with no expectation of being chosen. After all, the essay had appeared in a well-regarded but limited circulation literary magazine, *New Letters*, and he was up against Stephen King and essays from national magazines like *The New Yorker* and *Harper's*. Still, he was proud to have been a finalist, and the event would give him an opportunity to visit New York and spend time with a good friend, Robert Stewart, *New Letters'* editor. He wore a faux-leopard-skin pillbox hat to the ceremony, prepared to watch the events and sit among an audience of big-name writers and editors, the hoi palloi of the publishing world. Imagine

Photo Credit: Steve Friedman ©2008

his shock when it came time to announce the winner of the magazine essay award, and his name was called. And there he was moments later on a stage with Bob Stewart and, the trophy presenter, Charlie Rose.

Winning put Tom in a new category of writer, sought by agents and potential publishers. He and *The Quartet* found a new home with agent Nat Sobel and Bloomsbury.

In addition to winning an award, "I Am Joe's Prostate" has the power to make grown men squirm. Later in this collection, Renée Ashley describes her fascination with one man's reaction while hearing Tom read the essay to an audience.

I AM JOE'S PROSTATE

THE YEAR IS 1994. You are fifty years old. It is three domiciles and one wife ago. In the bathroom of your somewhat classy north Copenhagen bungalow, you stand over the porcelain and pee. You have not yet learned the word *micturate.* You are so innocent. Finished, you wash your hands and open the door, startled to find your wife of twenty years' marriage listening there.

She says, "You piss like an old man." She is a physician. She says, "You need to have that checked. I'll make an appointment for you."

Three weeks later, you ride your classic, green, three-speed Raleigh twenty-five minutes north to G_____ Hospital. Through the maze of hallways without a thread or a clue as to what you are about to experience, you find the urology department. An extremely large First Resident with no name plate on the pocket of his white coat extends his extremely large hand of extremely large fingers and mumbles his name. His first name. Surnames here, you will learn, are not offered, delivered only begrudgingly upon explicit request.

With a file under his arm, Dr. Mumble leads you into an examination room, has you remove your pants and perch on your knees on a metal, paper-decked table. Without prelude or warning, he rams a long fat finger up your kazoo.

You bellow, then croak, "Is that supposed to hurt so much?"

"It varies," he says absently, his back to you, washing his fingers at a sink, and continues, "There is a certain enlargement, but not more than might be expected for your age." You wonder what it is that has a certain enlargement. You finally, some years ago, learned about the existence of the clitoris, but still know nothing of the prostate. Dr. Mumble looks in the file—*your* file—instructs you to go to the nurses' station for further instructions. There you are given a large glass of colored water to drink and directed by a woman in white into a long, narrow room where you are further instructed to micturate into an odd-looking steel vase with a slanted, recessed lid. Kindly, the woman in white steps out and shuts the door. You understand intuitively what *micturate* means, recognize it as the word of choice here in the land of white and yellow.

The odd-looking steel vase, however, does not look like something you would *want* to micturate in. Nonetheless, you do so. The slanted recessed lid flutters like a butterfly under your stream, causing a kind of needle on a machine you only just noticed to zigzag along a moving belt of graph paper. When the last few drops have dripped, causing the needle to twitch and fall still, you zip away that of you which most rarely sees the light of day and wonder what to do. You have no further instructions. Perhaps you should just go home. Yes, perhaps that is what you should do.

But the woman in white is waiting outside the door for you. You notice that she has beautiful eyes and very sensuous lips. You caution yourself not to occupy your imagination with such details in your current situation, and the woman in white with sensuous lips turns you over to another of her sort, though larger of build and darker of complexion. She leads you into another room and instructs you to undress. You have never been naked in front of a strange woman unless the object was hanky-panky.

Everything? you wonder, but trust she will say stop at the appropriate moment.

"You can leave your shirt on," she says with a smile, and you think of Joe Cocker and wonder if she is teasing you. There is no name tag at her breast pocket, and she has mumbled neither her name nor her rank. She pats an examination table, indicating that you are to lie there. Face up, you presume. You do as you are told, noting distantly how passive you have become.

She takes your penis in her fingers. *Your penis!* She sprays something into it. You say, "*Ow!*"

"Yes," she whispers and begins to stuff some manner of wire down your penis. You are rather amazed that such things go on so close to the civilized streets on which you until today so innocently dwelt. It reminds you of a scene in an Alfred Hitchcock film. *Frenzy.* It occurs to you that some men would no doubt pay a great deal of money to have a woman perform this kind of act and curse your imagination, turn your eyes away from her lips which are also rather sensual. You concentrate on not noticing the sensation of her fingers touching you, but anyway there seems no real danger that the jaunty head of Eros will poke up here.

She says, "Tell me when you feel the urge to micturate."

You felt the urge to micturate the instant she started stuffing that wire into you. Now you notice that the remainder of the wire is attached to another machine, the nature or function of which you are not destined to come to know.

You say, "Now, please."

She encourages you to stand before another metal vase and says, "You may micturate now."

Nothing happens.

She taps her foot.

Nothing happens.

She says, "Would you like me to wait outside?"

"Yes, please."

She withdraws. Still nothing happens.

When she returns she looks into the empty vase and sighs. "It would seem you didn't really have to micturate," she says.

"I thought I did."

She hums. "Well, we'll just have to try again."

It seems to you this would be an appropriate moment for her to stroke your hair and say, "You poor guy, you, it will all be over shortly, I promise," but instead she says, "Back on the table."

Having finally successfully micturated to her satisfaction, you anticipate release back into the world of clothing where private parts are truly private. Indeed, you are allowed to dress, but are then led into yet another room, instructed to lie on yet another table and left alone for a bit, perhaps to examine your conscience and feel guilty about the fact that you didn't really have to micturate before, but only said so to make her stop shoving that wire in. At length, two women come in, and you are instructed to open your pants. Why does this not surprise you? And why are you not surprised not to know their names or professions? You might ask, but there have been so many nameless people by now that it hardly seems to matter.

The taller, dark-haired of the two women seems to be in charge. She tugs your pants down to your pubis, applies some oil, and lays a flat round metal thing the size of a small saucer on your pubic hair. She slides it around a bit. You notice she is looking not at you but at a screen alongside.

"Excellent," she says. "Your bladder is completely empty. Nothing is left. Excellent."

You ask, "May I go home now then?"

"Won't be long," she says. "Please wait here."

Presently another woman in white enters. "You'll have to take off all your clothes except your shirt," she says.

You wonder about your socks, but think, *Fuck it!* Back on the table, naked but for your unbuttoned shirt, and suddenly half a dozen people, men and women, tramp in and surround the table you are on. No one is identified, but a familiar face appears amidst them—that of the very large First Resident with very large fingers. All things considered, you are glad that you are lying on your back. To put you at ease, he peers down into your face with a terrifying smile and says, "I bet this won't be nearly as bad as you fear."

Then he is inserting a wand the thickness of three or four pencils into Private Johnson while he and the other unidentified people peer alternately at you, at a screen, at you, at a screen.

The wand seems to have been plunged into the very pit of your soul where it is being stirred around. You groan, but it elicits no attention or relief. You cross your arms and groan louder. Someone, a woman, tries to uncross your arms to pin your hands down which seems to you a very odd thing for her to want to do. You decide to make a stand. Your arms are crossed and will stay that way, and you set free all the groans within you, listening with some obtuse comfort to their melody, flooding from your chest in a minor key.

The very large First Resident peers unsympathetically into your face and snaps, "Would you please *stop that!*"

But you and your groans are working together now, at last you have a partner and you will not let him go until that wand is removed from your inner sanctum.

When the thing is out, you lay groggily on the table. A woman in white hands you a pail. "You may have to micturate," she says.

How can I micturate when my bladder has just been pronounced excellently empty? you wonder, but micturate you do. It comes in pints and quarts. You note the level of micturition rising toward the lip of the pail and croak, "Nurse! Another bucket, *hurry,* please!"

At last, dressed again, dazed, you sit in a chair alongside a desk in an empty room, waiting. You do not know what you are waiting for. No doubt you have been told to wait. Thoughts of escape no longer find refuge in your consciousness. You wait. The door opens. The large First Resident appears with the same thin folder under his arm. *Your* folder.

He smiles at you. "Did you have a bad time of it?" he asks.

"It was no picnic lunch in the Tivoli Gardens," you say, but your bravado rings lame even in your own ears.

He sits, opens the file. "Okay," he says. "We can offer two forms of treatment. Surgical or pharmaceutical."

You don't even think to ask treatment for what. Instantly, you yelp, "Pharmaceutical, please." *No incisions.*

"Don't dismiss the surgical possibility," he says earnestly. "It is by far the fastest and most effective." He looks at you expectantly.

"I think I should prefer the pharmaceutical," you say.

"*Pre-cision,*" he says, making a ring of finger and thumb and jolting it.

"With surgical precision we can take the thinnest slice or two, thin as the thinnest salami slices, thinner. I urge you to consider it. It's safe and precise. I'm required to tell you about the possibility of side effects but the chances are *extremely* slight."

"Of . . . ?"

"Uh, impotence. And incontinence. I am required to tell you that. But it is highly unlikely. Unlikely. With this procedure you won't have to be getting up two or three times in the middle of the night to urinate any more."

You say, "I don't get up in the middle of the night to urinate. Only like if I drink a bottle of beer at bedtime."

He furrows his brow, looks at the folder on his desk. "Here it says that you do."

"Well," you hear yourself say, "I am sitting right here and telling you that I don't. So what it says there is not correct."

The very large First Resident juts out his lower lip. He looks very sad. For reasons unknown, you thank him as you slip out the door.

The thirty-minute bicycle ride to your office is not the most pleasant you have ever experienced. Each of the morning's invasions is echoed in every bump and pothole and curbstone that the rims of your Raleigh strike. At the office, your wife phones to ask how things went.

"Everything's fine," you say. "There was nothing wrong with me."

Epilogue

A dozen years, two domiciles, one wife, and no medical problems later, a routine blood test teaches you a new scrap of scientific terminology: *PSA*. The letters stand for Prostate Specific Antigen, but that sounds even more cruelly clinical than the simple, jaunty "PSA." You learn that PSA should not be higher than 4, but yours is 6.9. A follow-up sample shows it to be 12. By now you know what that very large First Resident was talking about slicing like a salami—your prostate. You might have known this sooner if only the *Reader's Digest* had included an article entitled "I am Joe's Prostate" in their talking organ series back in the '50s. But you know now how good your little walnut-sized prostate has been to you all these years, with what joy it has assisted.

Although you have no symptoms—no prostate enlargement, no urinary difficulties, no pain—the elevated PSA alarms your GP sufficiently to send you once again for tests—this time to F_____ Hospital. Here the personnel seem considerably more like human beings than they did at G_____ Hospital. They have names and identify themselves as doctors or nurses, and this time you are equipped with questions and a pad and pen. You write everything down. You are alert to the possibility that they may endeavor to insert foreign objects into narrow hypersensitive places, and you are determined not to allow them to do so. So determined are you that they measure your blood pressure at 160 over 120. But this time, they navigate another canal, through the backdoor with ultrasound needles. You are told that there will be some discomfort but no real pain.

There is terrific discomfort and real pain as well. Each time the doctor positions the needle and aims, watching the ultrasound screen, he says by way of warning, "And . . . *now!*" and something painfully uncomfortable happens somewhere you have never felt anything but pleasure before. You engage in a philosophical discourse with yourself as to the differentiation between discomfort and pain.

First, they take six biopsies. No cancer. Then they take thirteen more biopsies. No cancer. But your PSA has now risen to 15. They take twelve more biopsies. By now, after thirty-one biopsies, you are urinating and ejaculating blood, but still no cancer is found. Your PSA drops to 9, hops back to 12, up to 19, back down to 14, up to 18, down to 13, up to 20. Once your prostate has recovered from all the probing and sticking, you have no further signs of blood in your urine or seed.

But there is a tall, slender, long-faced chief physician there at F_____ Hospital who knows, who *intuits*, that the cancer is there. He reminds you of the policeman Porfiry Petrovitch in *Crime & Punishment*. Or a taller, morose version of Lt. Colombo of the LAPD. They have not yet found it but it *is* there he assures you. He is, in fact, eighty percent sure it is there and fifteen percent sure that it has already spread. But he can do nothing until he has the hard evidence: a cancer cell. He wants to take a scrape of your prostate. He wants to put you into full narcosis (where they stop your heart and lungs for a while and keep you alive by the grace of a machine) and scrape the tiny five percent portion of your prostate where the ultrasound needles can't reach. Then you will come out of narcosis, and he will send the tissue sample to the pathologists for determination of whether there are malignant cells present.

Your ex-wife was a pathologist. She once revealed to you how difficult it is to determine malignancy. Sometimes healthy cells are falsely identified as malignant. Sometimes malignant cells are falsely identified as healthy. She quit practicing because the hospital administration was pressuring her to make too many fast decisions about what was and was not malignant.

This long-faced, morose physician, who is convinced that cancer is present in your prostate, which has otherwise been so good to you for half a century, will then, once he has found the cancer, be able to make a diagnosis and offer treatment. The treatment he urges will be removal of the prostate. All of it.

"You're fortunate," he tells you. "You're still young, and the cancer is very early. You can be completely cured."

Of the cancer that might not be there. Any possible side effects?

"There is a risk, I am obliged to tell you, that the scrape could result in impotence and/or incontinence."

And removal of the prostate?

"That *will* lead to impotence and incontinence. But the worst likely side-effect of the scrape, which is not very likely to occur at all, although I am obliged to inform you of the slight possibility, would be a modest leakage and a possible reversal of your ejaculatory trajectory."

You stare at his long, morose face, his protruding eyes, and you are aware that your own face radiates the meaning of the word *aghast*. "*What, exactly*," you whisper, "does that mean?"

"Well, when you have sex, which you could continue to have quite satisfactorily by the way, you might be likely to ejaculate into your bladder instead of, well . . . outward. But the pleasure would be precisely the same, the sensation."

Incredulously, you tell him, "The pleasure would *not* be the same at all. The whole point of ejaculating is to do it into someone else! You think I'd be happy fucking my own bladder!" For one disoriented moment, you picture *impregnating* your own bladder.

"No need to be facetious," he quietly advises you. "Besides this is all quite hypothetical." His expression clearly is one he learned in a patient management course: Deactivating the Prostate-Protection Reflex in the Recalcitrant Aging Male Patient.

You are invited into another room to watch a video entitled, *Granddad's Prostate Cancer*. In it, a man who has had his prostate removed plays with his two very cute grandchildren, a boy and a girl, twins of about four. He sports a wispy, grey beard and has very tiny teeth; he looks into the camera and smiles a rather silly smile with his tiny white teeth. "My grandchildren think it is very funny that they have just *stopped* wearing diapers and Granddad has to *start* wearing them again." He chuckles.

You are not amused. You definitely do not want to wear diapers. And not that you're such a stud or anything, but you do greatly enjoy waking each morning with some lead in your pencil as indeed you cherish the occasional two-backed beast with your beloved or even the good old honeymoon of the hand. You definitely do not wish to take a permanent vacation to the land where even Viagra offers no hope. You will never willingly ejaculate into your own bladder—which seems to you of a magnitude of strangeness equal to the man in the *Ripley's Believe It Or Not, Volume 2, Sexual Abberations,* who inserted a 75 watt lightbulb into his own colon.

You develop your own future plan of treatment. You will return to the lake. On the east side of Copenhagen there is a lake you love. You love this lake because it is a street lake, in the midst of the bustling city. You have loved this lake from the moment you first spied it, thirty-four years ago. It is called Black Dam Lake, and there is an old Copenhagen proverb: *I'll go out to Black Dam Lake.*

If and when it should become necessary, on a fair and sunny day, you will rent a rowboat from the rental wharf on Black Dam Lake. You will paddle out to the center of the lake, and there you will drop anchor. You will unpack the picnic lunch you will have brought with you in a wicker basket. You will dine on smoked eel and dark rye bread spread with raw fat. Lots of it. And because fish must swim, you will drink cold bottles of beer. Many of them. And iced schnapps in your favorite Holmgaard aquavit glass, many of them. While you dine, you will watch the swans float past like beautiful white question marks. You will watch the ducks and grebes paddle along the surface, and to encourage the seagulls—for they are an important part of your plan—you will fling bits of bread and eel up into the air to get them hovering overhead in an excited, crying cluster.

And then, when you are sufficiently satisfied, sufficiently besotted but not yet incapacitated, you will take the pistol from your belt, place the barrel in your mouth, pointed upwards toward your cranial cavity and pull the trigger. It will be a high caliber pistol and will tear a broad path through your brain, spraying bits and clumps of grey matter upward, which the seagulls will catch in their beaks and gobble down, wheeling over the lake, their gullets full of morsels of your thought and personality so that you will sweep across the lake like a great pointillist consciousness on your way to forever.

Where will you get a pistol?

Oh, you'll get one. By Charlton Heston's eyes, you will!

And how can you be sure you'll be strong and deliberate enough to carry all this through when that day comes?

Well, isn't it pretty to think you might?

Coda

Nonetheless, once again, you sit in a chair before the desk of Porfiry Petrovitch.

"You must choose now," he says. "The number is very high. The disease is present. It may already have spread. I *know* this."

His protruding eyes make you think of the face in an ancient ikon.

You say, "Well, I had a second opinion from . . ."

"I *know* the source of your second opinion," says Porfiry Petrovitch, "both professionally and socially. He is a nice fellow and a good internist, but he is *not* a urological surgeon, and he knows *nothing* of this."

Porfiry Petrovitch is younger than you, but his eyes are stronger, his protruding eyes. You turn your own gaze from them, look out the window behind him at the slate gray sky, toward the door which is shut and unpromising. His protruding eyes never waver from your face. They contain the words that he has spoken, that he need not repeat: "You must choose now." But he has already chosen.

So you nod. The procedure is scheduled. For three weeks you watch its inexorable approach. Then, finally, in the ward, you are dressed in a flimsy gown, being measured for support stockings, checked over like an old car, stuck with needles, thermometers, fed a pill and told it is best you get into bed because you might get woozy.

You note that you feel pretty good. Feisty even. Planning some havoc as a silent orderly rolls your bed out into the hall, the elevator up to the OR where the anesthesiologist looks soberly into your eyes and says, "We have to ask your name, standard procedure."

"My name," you say, "is Porfiry Petrovitch," giving the name of the head of the urology unit. The surgeon, alongside, laughs. "Then we'll cut right in!"

A nurse adjusts the valve set into the vein on back of your hand and the anesthesiologist does something to it, and now you are feeling *very* good. You cannot believe it is possible to feel this good.

"Think about something nice now," the anesthesiologist says.

You say, "I feel pretty damn good," and he whispers at your ear, "Men pay lots of money to feel the way you're feeling right now."

You do not reply. You are completely absorbed thinking about your wife, about how she looked in her aquamarine two-piece swim suit last summer on the beach at Skorpios, the surf frothing around her beautiful legs, blonde, tan, smiling. She is smiling for you with her blue blue eyes, drawing you forward into her gaze, her gorgeous body . . .

Suddenly they're rolling you out again.

"Say, where are you taking me?" Your voice sounds slurry.

"It's over," says a nurse. "We want you down in the wake-up room for a while where we can keep an eye on you."

You open your mouth and hear yourself say, "Dr. No. Ursula Andress." This seems hilarious to you, but no one even smiles. Can they even hear you? Are you dead? Is this death? You want to explain your words but you notice a fly on the sheet, just sitting there, so still.

A while later you notice that you are hooked up to some contraption on which hangs a bag of blood in a clear plastic bag. From the bag runs a tube which disappears under your sheet. You become aware of a very annoying discomfort in the worst of places. The blood, you understand then, is your own micturation. You have been fitted with a catheter. You are given permission to get out of bed. You do so carefully, supporting yourself on the contraption from which your bag of blood hangs and to which you are connected by a long, flexible tube. The contraption looks like some kind of garment rack, and you discover that it is on wheels.

For want of anything better to do, you shuffle out of the room and along the ward corridor, rolling the rattling contraption alongside you, your bag of blood swaying there. You do not like looking at the bag of blood, but it seems wherever you send your eyes, they always wander back to it, recoiling from it again, wandering back. You shuffle the length of the hall, learn how to turn your contraption without causing the connecting tube to tug at your exhausted tugger where you least want to be tugged just now. It occurs to you that all the nurses here are very good-looking, and you advise yourself not to even think about that for a second lest your tugger begin to get untoward ideas.

You begin to shuffle again, back along the corridor. Three men sit around a table, their contraptions parked alongside them as they play cards with a greasy-looking deck. "How come you don't sit down?" one of them asks as you shuffle past.

"Hurts less when I'm on my feet."

"Hurts less when he's on his feet," another man explains to the first as I proceed to shuffle the night away.

Next morning the surgeon comes in to visit. Not Porfiry Petrovitch but the smiling, good-humored fellow who actually did the cutting. "Just to let you know," he says brightly, "that I took three good slices and everything looked fine. No enlargement, no irregularity. It is a good-looking prostate I saw."

"Should be," you say. "It's Joe's prostate."

He laughs as though he understands.

The surgeon returns that afternoon, a nurse alongside him, a dark-haired nurse who fills her translucent white uniform so perfectly that you have to avert your eyes for fear of losing your catheter.

"Is there still blood in his urine?" the surgeon asks her.

"The color of rosé wine," she replies.

You thank her for ensuring that you will never again for the remainder of your life drink rosé wine.

"We don't drink rosé wine here either," she says with a twinkle of regret.

"How do you feel about going home now?" the smiling surgeon asks.

Then you are alone with the nurse. You are in bed. She is alongside. She reaches under the covers. Could this be love? you wonder as she whispers, "Take a deep breath now. I'm going to remove the catheter. I'm afraid I'll have to move back your foreskin first."

"If you try to do that," you say, "we'll be here forever because I don't have one."

"Then take a breath."

You do, and you hear a strangling gargling horror-comic groan contract your throat: *Argh!* You consider that the first person who ever thought to write that sound with just those letters had been through this very procedure.

She holds it up for you to see—a thick pencil-like device with a ragged bulb on the end. She points at the bloody bulb. "That's the thing that hurts coming out."

You have just reached an understanding of what the ugliest word in the language is: *Catheter.* Three syllables of misery. Even worse in Danish: *Kateter.*

It will be a fortnight before you have the biopsy results. That, you know, is when the treatment can begin. The aim of this exercise has been to tenderize you for the real cut.

Two weeks ensue with frequent, fiery micturations. You live in dread of the micturation urge. You have twisted the water pipe alongside your jakes into a pretzel and ground a millimeter off your molars. You sustain yourself by contemplating your hatred of the word *catheter.* You check its etymology, hoping that it is named for its inventor so that you can put a face on your hatred, but find it is built of Greek and Latin word parts that mean something like *passing through.* Every time you grit your teeth and micturate fire you consider the fact that this ugly collection of letters—some of your favorite letters of the alphabet, too, though here organized in the ugliest possible fashion—represents a device which threatens to become a long-term fixture in your life.

There will be catheters, there will be catheters . . . In the room the nurses come and go talking of catheters . . . We have lingered by the catheters of the sea by sea girls wreathed in plastic tubing . . . I should have been a pair of ragged catheters scuttling across the floors of rosé-colored seas.

On the appointed day, you enter the appointed consultation room and shake the hand of the smiling surgeon as well as the hand of the dark-haired nurse at his side. The dark-haired lady. There is always a dark-haired lady. Saying, "Take a deep breath now . . ."

You are motioned to a chair. The smiling surgeon sits, lays the flat of his palm on a folder before him on the desk top. "Well," he says, and smiles. "Nothing. There is nothing."

"Nothing?"

"No cancer. Not even a single cell. I took samples from every corner where the ultrasound needles can't reach. And there is nothing. You have a healthy prostate."

"What happened?"

"Sometimes the PSA is wrong," he says.

The dark-haired nurse nods, smiles reassuringly. "Sometimes the PSA is wrong."

Thus, after two years, twenty blood tests, thirty-four biopsies, the last three of which were surgical, and two weeks of micturating fire, you are sent out into the world, onto the sunny pavement to find your way in a world of health.

What is a man to do? Down the street and on the other side, you see a sign that says BAR. You head for it.

First published in *New Letters* 73:4 (Summer 2007)

A Tom Kennedy Translation

WITH HIS FLUENCY in Danish, Tom Kennedy played a major role in bringing Danish literature to English readers through his translations of prose works and especially poetry, widening the audience for poets of international stature like Pia Tafdrup, Hendrik Nordbrandt, and Dan Turèll.

Turèll, who died young, holds the status of a folk hero in Denmark, and Tom published translations of his work in several magazines, eventually collaborating with the artist Barry Lereng Wilmont for an illustrated edition and with the composer Halfden E for a recorded version of Tom's reading accompanied by Halfden's music.

The poem that follows, "Last Walk throuh the City," first appeared in *Absinthe: New European Writing* (Number 12, 2009); and in book form in a bilingual edition titled *Last Walk through the City/Gennem Byen Sidste Gang* (Copenhagen: Pavillon Neuf Private Press, 2010), with original lithographs by Barry Lereng Wilmont.

Last Walk Through the City
by Dan Turèll

Before I die I want to stroll through the city one last time
let this be my last humble wish
to walk on my feet through my city
through the city of Copenhagen
as I've done so many times before
and I'll know this is the last time
and I'll choose my route with care

and I'll walk down Isted Street or West Bridge Street
and walk down all the narrow sunless side streets with all their shutdown shops
and I'll look at all the junk-shop displays of yellowed curtains and greasy gas rings
and I'll rummage in the book boxes and I'll buy nothing
and not because it's the last time
but because I never rummage in the book boxes to buy anything
but to rummage in them and think how short and strange life is
and I'll look at children playing in the small square stony windblown courtyards
and I'll listen to them shouting to and at each other
and I'll see their mothers lean out of kitchen windows
and call them in when dinner is ready
and out the windows clotheslines will hang with the family's underwear
and it will flap in the wind

and I'll walk through West Bridge's poets' quarter in the gloaming
I'll stroll along Saxo Street Oehlenschläger Street Kingo Street
and I'll stop in someplace in one of the serving houses
maybe Café Golden Rain
and savor a bitter and nothing else
and then out and on
I'll wear my soles thin this last stroll in Copenhagen

the usual alkies will sit there waiting for nothing
the young hitchhikers will stand with their backpacks and their cartons of milk
hurried and harried people will wait for their connections

families will come with suitcases and baby carriages to take a weekend with the family
    in the country
and I'll stand in a corner and be overwhelmed
and not be able to do anything about it and not want to either
just be overwhelmed by all that life and all that swarm
wet eyes without clear reason
and very very distant

and when I have pulled myself together I'll shake the shoulders of my coat
shake the Central Station off as a dog shakes his wet fur
or as when you leave a theater after a movie
I'll light a cigarette and go down West Bridge Street to the Town Hall
    Square
where everyone flutters around between buses and movie houses
and again I'll just lean up against a poster-plastered pillar
and I'll know that here somewhere on these stones lie my whole life and all my
    dreams
just like so many others' lives and dreams

everything is so swift and fleeting
like your last stroll through the city
and I'll walk down the Pedestrian Street like a shadow
and all the way down I'll be accompanied by all my friends
and they will all be ghosts
and no one but me will see they are there but they are
and we say goodbye to everything and each other
and we are not sentimental
but the air is full of something no one knows what it's called or is
and we walk there in silent conversation
and somewhere towards New Square they are gone again
and I myself fade out a little further down

My last stroll through the city is done
and a single shadow less frequents the street—

Dear Prudence

Line-Maria Lång and Thomas E. Kennedy

(Edited by Martin Glaz Serup and Kristian Bang Foss. Danish text translated by Martin Aitken.)

Line-Maria Lång and Tom Kennedy on their trip to Prague

MAYBE IT'S BECAUSE I'VE ALMOST COMPLETELY STOPPED trusting myself that I take as a sign clouds drifting in front of the sun, a white cat's perfectly executed leap onto a garbage can, the little click of a button hitting the pavement.

I'm standing out front of the airport inside the yellow lines of the designated smoking area and have just lost a button on my cardigan. Tom arrives early for everything. One time he was coming over to my place for dinner and I was standing with a yellow towel wound around my hair and a green one wrapped around my body like a sari. Our eyes met through the crack in the door. He walked around the block five times. Since then he's always waited outside in the street until a couple of minutes before the appointed time.

We're going to Prague. I'll be staying there for three weeks to write, but the first four days are ours together, the trip we've talked about for years, before as well as after he developed the cyst on his brain.

The button lies orange and conspicuous on the pavement; I pick it up. The thread is still on, which could be a good sign. I slip it into my pocket and light another cigarette. I call Tom, though I know I'm being overzealous, he's only three minutes late, but I can check with him that I've got the meeting place right—that's my excuse. Did we say outside Terminal 2? Terminal. Terminal. Terminal. But he's already switched off his phone, of course, and it won't be switched on again until he's back home in his apartment in Copenhagen's Østerbro quarter. Tom's old-school about things like that—when he's away somewhere on a trip, he's there and only there. I call again, wondering if I should leave a message, wondering if he's ever going to hear it. I picture Tom in an ambulance, on a white stretcher, breathing the words '. . . but I've got a plane to catch', because that's the way my thoughts work at the moment, too fast, too negative, too dramatic, with no sense of chronology. And now it's the taxi driver I see, the one Tom ordered to pick him up; he's ringing Tom's doorbell, over and over, until at last he looks in through the bedroom window and notices Tom's body. At first he thinks he's asleep. A thin guy with an apologetic, stooping posture trundles a big red suitcase over the yellow demarcation into the smoking area and asks if he can borrow my lighter. I hand it to him; he smells of stale sweat and a musky perfume, turns his collar to the warm breeze and lights his cigarette. Bang, bang, bang. The taxi driver, thumping his fist on the pane. The taxi driver, calling the emergency services. The taxi driver, shouting: He's dead, he's dead. The neighbors poking their heads out of their windows all at once. The stooping guy thanks me and hands me back the lighter in the flat of his hand. The thread has come out of the button now, I can feel it in my pocket. I think about how I'm going to tell Tom's son, how I'm even going to get ahold of Tom's son.

Tom is standing in front of me, straight-shouldered and a testing smile on his face.

'Prague,' he says, and his smile widens.

✳

Her name is Line-Maria, and she is talented, warm, and very pretty. I met her nine years ago at the Danish book fair when she was twenty-eight. She was launching her first book. She comes from a long line of Swedish-Danish artists and writers. One of the first things she told me was that her father had died when she was twelve. It always seemed that was why she had taken to me so quickly; I am thirty-seven years older than she.

Today, we are going to Prague, eighty-minutes by jet south-east of Copenhagen.

✳

He looks so sweet when he smiles, it's as if his face were particularly disposed to it; sun comes out from behind cloud when the corners of his narrow mouth, from their more solemn point of departure, turn upwards. And, talking about sun: sunbeam wrinkles, as I always call them, about his eyes.

He looks lightly tanned, but I always think that. A pair of shades stick up from his breast pocket; he holds the handle of a trolley suitcase with one hand. I always feel such tenderness about the items that belong to people I love—a small trolley suitcase packed by his own hand and almost certainly very neatly, the zippers brought together and centered at the top, the shades that instantly make him so cool when he puts them on, the shirt with its perfectly triangular lapels—maybe even pressed?

I kiss him on the mouth. We are great kissers-on-the-mouth in my family, but I kiss only a very small number of close friends that way; with Tom it's like a tradition now. We kiss on the mouth, when we meet and when we say goodbye.

We show each other the tickets we've printed out, and nod affirmatively.

I first met Tom at the book fair in Copenhagen in 2010. Afterwards, we went out to eat. His posture is as straight as a pencil—even when he's sitting down—it was hard to tell how tall he was. I'm still not sure, but I remember thinking about it that time. But mostly I was taken by his geniality combined with an almost stately reserve, or maybe it was more a no-bullshit form of self-respect. He ordered a triple vodka and had to say it three times before the waiter understood him. I've always thought there was something cowboy-like about men who drank in quantity and without shame and yet seemed to remain so wholly in control.

•

I think it was after I saw some video of Michael Jackson being subjected to a comprehensive search by airport security that my fear of airports grew. And right now that fear seems only to have gotten bigger. 'A byproduct of the imagination', Tom called it the last time we saw each other, because I tell him about my fears—apart from the ones concerning him.

We stand in line for the security check, and that's the worst. Laptop out, belt off—someone touching my laptop is more invasive to me than someone touching my underwear. And every time, I imagine I'm going to be detained and held in some basement room.

Tom is already loosening his belt as we move towards the conveyor. He quickly locates the objects he needs to place in the tray, while I try to conceal my shaking hands.

My fingers grip the cardigan button in my pocket as I go through the metal detector or whatever it is, that unpoetic triumphal arch, monitored by an unsmiling man on the other side. And maybe it's because we're together, Tom's calm making up for my nerves, but somehow I think we manage to look like just a normal pair of travel buddies. We collect our stuff, and my relief at not having said something ridiculous or forgotten about something completely stupid and against the law at the bottom of my bag, something that would set off all the alarm bells and a thousand flashing lights, is immense.

At last we emerge, straight into the Duty Free with its clouds of perfume, its alcohol and lotions, its cartons of cigarettes.

Tom goes through the airport like it's his apartment; he knows where everything is, glances at the departure boards with a conversant air. He has a particular bar in mind where we can sit with a beer. He even knows a place I had no idea existed, where we can smoke. The IPA soothes my nerves. But I'm not relaxed until we're on the plane. The combination of handing all responsibility to someone else and actually flying is joyous—'to rely on the kindness of the pilot', you could say.

•

The driver is holding up a sign that says 'Sir Thomas E. Kennedy' and 'Lady von Lång'. We're standing in the airport in Prague. I ordered the shuttle for us, typing the names into the field boxes on the company's website with a giggle, and now here we are in flesh and blood, cardboard and marker pen.

✳

In a taxi from Vaclav Havel Airport, the driver points out the medieval and seventeenth through the twenty-first centuries Prague buildings. The city is beautiful from an air-conditioned cab, with a curving river and many ornate bridges.

We are quartered a block from one another in Prague 3, she on Kristanova in a small apartment provided by her grant, I in the Marriott Hotel, a couple of hundred meters down Jicinska. She is staying in Prague for three weeks to research golem myths that she will incorporate into her fiction. I am staying for three days, one of the last remaining capitals I haven't seen. A second reason is to show me Prague.

Long after the Velvet Revolution, Line-Maria was introduced to this city by Jan Sonnergaard, a Danish writer who died two years ago at the age of fifty-three. She and Jonas, the man she is living with, were supposed to meet Jan in Serbia. He was a close friend. She and Jonas were preparing for the flight when they learned that Sonnergaard had died of a sudden cardiac arrest in Belgrade.

✳

The traffic is impossible, but the airport isn't far from the city. Our driver has bushy eyebrows and a chirpy little smile on his lips the whole time. He tells us about the city as we drive, talking fast and a lot. He says he's a trained psychologist, but likes to drive. He advises us to watch out with the taxis, they always try to pull one over on tourists, he says, turning his head towards us for a second and raising one eyebrow as if to hit it home to us.

Tom is dropped off at his hotel. We've arranged to meet up later on. I watch him as he walks away: there's a jaunt in his step, though one leg is still rather stiff-looking—it's a year now since he broke it.

As we pull away, the driver asks me why I'm not staying in the same place as my grandfather, and I tell him that Tom feels like family but isn't.

It surprises him. I've seen the same reaction before.

We arrive, and I get out of the car. He raises a bushy eyebrow, lifts my suitcase out of the back and puts it down on the sidewalk.

'We must look after the love we have,' I say.

'So you're not together either?' he asks hesitantly, only to apologize immediately.

I shake my head.

He hands me two calling cards: one in case I need to order his 'transport service' as he calls it, the other if I want to go out and have dinner with him.

A young man greets me. It's his apartment I'm staying in. The walls are adorned with posters of Marilyn. The place reeks of scented detergent, but there's dirt on the electric kettle and in the corner where I leave my shoes. The corner sofa is gigantic; the refrigerator stands directly opposite. He's forgotten to put toilet paper out; the listing description said it was provided, but I don't mention it. The whole apartment is as hot as a sauna. Opening the windows doesn't help, the air outside is still and has the same temperature as the scented air inside. Sweat rolls down my brow. When the guy has gone, I take a quick shower and drape some paper napkins from the plane on the toilet roll holder.

I meet Tom outside his hotel. He's changed clothes and is wearing the shirt I know so well, the one with the chili peppers on it. It suits him—Tom is a man who can wear a hat and wear colors too. We walk arm-in-arm down a steeply sloping street and find a place where we can sit outside underneath an awning.

*

Our first night, we stroll along Vinohradská. It is unseasonably hot in the Czech Republic, even for the height of summer, even when the night sky clouds over. Our outdoor area is surrounded by shoulder-high, wooden patio walls with purple and yellow flowering vines draped over them here and there and a canvas ceiling. A waitress comes over, a blocky, attractive, middle-aged woman.

*

It's all very Czech, everything in shades of green and brown. We order haxe—pig's knuckles—and chicken. Tom apologizes for his speech impediment, it came with the cyst on his brain, the cyst we thought was going to kill him; they said it was growing, only then it stopped. He speaks slower and more hesitantly now. We used to speak Danish together—his Danish was good, and he still understands it, but can speak only English. I don't think about it as much as he thinks I do; to begin with I did, but not anymore, and even if it takes longer now, he still says what he wants to say, and I know the words he sometimes mixes up. Now and again he'll say 'okay' or 'thanks' at odd moments, and I've heard him say a bright 'good morning' too for no apparent reason; I sometimes say it too, to pull his leg, and I think he likes that, the fact that I'm not afraid of it. I've noticed how people who don't see him that often will lean up insanely close (once I even saw one of his friends cup his hand behind his ear and bend it towards him) while staring at him as he searches for the right word. A certain look comes over his face when that happens, a pained little smile of sorts. On occasion I've guessed the word he's looking for, but I try not to guess unless I'm really certain—I can tell how much it annoys him when people cut him off. But sometimes I just know. We have our own little codes now too. Going to the bathroom we call to 'go stare at the wall', and one happy night we cooked up the hopeful expression 'Let there be sorbet'. Similarly, 'Sorry, Bob' came about because we listen to a lot of Bob Dylan together but sometimes have to cut him off in mid-flow when we leave the café in which his song is playing or when we change tracks to listen to one of his other songs. 'Sorry, Bob' is something we can use to convey faux vexation about something we've decided we're going to give a miss.

We might say, for instance:

'Are you going to Henrik's concert?'

'No, I'm afraid it's going be a "Sorry, Bob" from me.'

Back in Prague, we talk about the rain that now drums against the awning to remind me of my father, a drummer: he would drum on plates, tummies and tent canvas—it was as if his entire body were geared just to drum. Anything rhythmic makes me think of my dad. The waitress, a smiling, jovial woman with charmingly protruding ears, puts the vinegar and oil down very hard, though amiably on the table, after which she quickly returns, as if they had been ready and waiting for us, with two large, dewy glasses of beer.

Tom tells me it was when his father gave him a copy of Dostoevsky's *Crime and Punishment* that he knew he wanted to be a writer. But he reminds me that he did not get published until late. He often does, maybe because he wants to make sure I don't assume anything else but that the trouble it's been too is something he still stands by. It wasn't until twenty years after he started that he finally succeeded. That was in 1981, much to our amusement, because that was the year my mother got pregnant with me.

'Maybe you were lucky for me even then,' he says with a laugh, and instead of 'cheers' we say 'good morning' as we chink our beer glasses together. How wild it seems for us now to be in Prague, drinking beer in rain and sunshine—it wouldn't surprise me if a rainbow appeared!

'We did it,' I say. 'Another trip together.'

'Good morning!' and we raise our glasses again.

Tom in Prague

Our first trip was to Washington DC, from where we brought back another couple of expressions. 'The shit', which of course isn't our own, but something we love to say anyway: 'Is he a good writer?' 'Yeah, he's the shit'. And then there's 'I'm hungry for more than cheese', though that's more about me and stems from me opening the mini-refrigerator in my hotel room and asking a literary editor if he wants some cheese, while he, to my astonishment and horror, is already taking off his shirt, slowly and libidinously utters the now famous words: 'I'm hungry for more than cheese.'

Tom is served his haxe (it really does look like pig's knuckles!) and I my chicken and spinach. The menu said "chicken on a bed of spinach", which I thought would mean more spinach than chicken, but the whole thing looks like a big house on a very small lawn.

*

I had eaten haxe in Köln years before with dobbelt-korn schnapps; I remember the two older men, business colleagues, I had traveled with to Köln. The one played piano for our schnapps. I wonder if they are still alive . . .

The clouds overhead burst. The rains come sloshing down. We change tables to be out of the rain which blows in sprinkles beneath the overhang. Finished with dinner, we agree that we should wait out the rain. The cloudburst should cool the heat. We order snifters of seven-star Metaxa. The semi-sweet brandy is good. Line-Maria reaches across the table to squeeze my hand, as she is wont to do, and tells me many things to cheer me, although I am not in need of cheering—despite my recently developed speech impediment—but I am cheered nonetheless.

*

When the plates are taken away, we say 'Good morning!' and raise our glasses of Metaxa, a drink to which Tom has introduced me. I tell him it's getting time for 'me and you taxi'.

*

When the rain lets up, we ask the waitress where to get tobacco at that late hour. She does not speak English other than for the menu items. "Flora," she says. Line-Maria knows where Flora shopping center is, on Jicinska. The waitress performs a pantomime, saying "Escalator," bending at the knees one time. Down once. Line-Maria understands.

We walk in the freshly-rinsed air to Flora. They stare vacantly when I ask for cigars—apparently the Czech word for cigar is different. They do have menthol cigarettes, and I stroll home with Line-Maria, who smokes a menthol, along Jicinska under the trees in the cool night. I kiss her hand at her apartment and watch while she goes in the door.

*

I don't really remember the rest. When I get back to the apartment I'm really drunk. I know we went looking for cigars for Tom, and I can see that we bought toilet paper, coffee, and drinking yoghurt. I get into bed and everything spins. I can't get to sleep. I keep thinking about the water heater, a kind I've never seen before, with a flame that flares up into a little fire in a gray box on the kitchen wall when I turn the water on. It makes me afraid, wondering if it's meant to be that way. I Google it with some difficulty, with one eye shut, 'Water and little flame in box', but find nothing.

I do some of the breathing exercises my doctor taught me. I have an appointment with her when I get home. I've been seeing her ever since what I refer to as 'when I became afraid everyone I know is going to die without warning.' That was after my friend died suddenly in Belgrade two years ago.

*

She doesn't talk a lot about it but I sense she is still marked by his death.

*

The way my dad died suddenly when I was a child.

I breathe in and out. Slowly.

I get out of bed and go and look at the flame in the gray box. It's wide and looks exactly like the waving flame from a Dupont lighter.

I've asked my three oldest friends to write me a letter that I will keep unopened until the event of their deaths, meaning there will always be a goodbye from them no matter what. So that I never again will lose a person so abruptly. Tom took the matter so seriously that he has now written some two hundred pages; he still adds to it. It's the most moving thing that has ever happened in my life.

The cyst on Tom's brain is located in the language center. The first time I saw him after they told him, his novel *In the Company of Angels* had just been published in Danish. I was to read from it at an event in a community center. He told me they were giving him blood thinners following the strokes he'd suffered, and he'd told them, 'I'm going to be drinking some vodka, which is a blood thinner too—so just factor that in.' In writing, his voice was the same as ever. We sat next to each other on two chairs up against the wall. 'It's growing,' he said. 'They want to drill a hole in my head, but I don't want that.' He put his hand to his head. I can never forget that.

*

Next day, we take the metro three stops to the stainless-steel bust "Metalmorphosis," the twenty-five feet tall bust of Franz Kafka, fabricated with fourteen tons of stainless-steel.

*

It's not until he's standing there on the escalator that I realize my stupidity. But I can't apologize yet, I'm too frightened of causing him even the slightest distraction. I say nothing, can think only of how I urged him to 'come on', and him smiling behind me, stepping cautiously onto the escalator, and then that look in his eyes, unnerved and uncertain. Now he stares straight ahead, now he grips the rail, as the posters sail past on the walls and the moving staircase rattles beneath us. It is long and much quicker than the Danish ones. It's such a short time since his leg mended after he broke it, on a staircase on his way down to the trains at Nørreport station. And even if he hadn't broken his leg, you still don't urge a man in his seventies to 'come on' and pile onto a moving escalator. The worst thing almost is that he's shown me a confidence I have failed to live up to. Normally, Tom is good at saying no. He once told me about a time he was asked to do a reading in an inflatable bounce house—it was some kind of concept the event had going. 'No,' he told them. 'It's not going to happen,' he told them again when they tried to talk him into it. But now here he is, standing on an escalator that's as steep as hell, and it's going so fast we can hear someone's bag hitting the joins in the glass walls about three times a second, a scraping, rhythmic sound. I can see his leg tremble slightly. He sees me looking, and I look away, away from his leg, because he mustn't be distracted, he needs to look straight ahead—isn't that how best to keep your balance? At last, at speed, with a glimpse of a movie poster featuring a cat with a walking stick, we are swept safely back onto terra firma. The metro train comes rattling in with a strange smell of kerosene at almost the same moment. Once we're seated, facing each other, Tom says politely but firmly: 'Let's not take the Metro again.'

*

The bust is disassembling when we approach the square, blocks rotating and reassembling to show a likeness of his head and face—much as Kafka dealt with reality to lace it with the surreal in his imagination: So that Gregor Samsa could transform overnight into an insect, or Joseph K could be charged without charges being levied and never know what he was accused of, or give new meaning to "Dear Father."

*

Kafka's great, silvery head is turning when we get there. Being in the city feels so overwhelming, so many new impressions to take in that I can't take it all in, but seeing my great idol dissembling and reassembling like a Rubik's cube in front of me, his face in constant change, still fazes me.

Now, Kafka is in profile, and maybe Tom senses my thoughts—recently I've felt the contact between us to be almost telepathic. He smooths my cheek and says how striking it is to see the city reflected in so many different distortions in the Kafka head's mirrored surface. Very Kafkaesque, we agree on our way to the Astronomical Clock. I keep looking at the map on my phone; although I've been to Prague before, I often get lost—which is also very Kafkaesque, Tom points out, making sure that I'm not sad about being nowhere near the guide I'd hoped to be for him.

*

We find the Old Town Square and Astronomical Clock. The tower was built in 1338, the clock installed in 1410 and rebuilt in 1490. The lapses are as old as me. The clock features the astronomical dial, reflecting the positions of the sun and moon; an hourly show of "The Walk of the Apostles," figures in moving sculptures and a calendar dial with a medallion indicating the month are also represented. The twelve apostles appear from a round hole beneath the lofty clock face. It is under repair, wrapped in scaffolding and plastic.

*

I confess that the ongoing restoration work on the Astronomical Clock doesn't matter much to me—even very small clocks can give me a sense of dread these days.

*

I feel the heat all around me as a stagnant mass of humidity, pressing upon me. I used to like the heat. In New York City where I grew up, the hotter in summer, the better; even in Death Valley, the hottest place on earth, I felt content. Now, I must get into the shade . . .

We take a table outside the Restaurant Blatnice, beneath parasols. Despite the heat, I manage to remain standing until Line-Maria sits. After we have schooners of Urquell draft and after we eat, I suggest to Line-Maria that we take a cab back to our respective domiciles.

Next day again, Line-Maria recommends we be near to where we're staying. Secretly exulting, I link arms with her, perambulating on the hotel side streets. We spot the Restaurant Roma, which has tables on the sidewalk. We sit adjacent to a group of people, standing outside a small bar; a man among them is a guitar-player, starts singing "Dear Prudence."

Line-Maria and I have a history with this song. A year ago, when I was just developing my difficulties speaking—a scan revealed a cyst on my brain pressing against the language center—I was walking in my courtyard when I saw my next-door neighbor, sunbathing in skimpy clothes. I said, "Beautiful day." Apparently, she heard me say only the first word, and I thought that would be an acceleration in my old-man small-talk. She is beautiful, but I pulled together my speech impediment and said, "You are not beautiful. The day is," and heard what I'd said and fled into the building. I told the story to Line-Maria; immediately, she understood it and devised a solution. "Next time you see her sunning, play 'Dear Prudence' for her with open windows, and turn it up for the part: 'The sun is out, the sky is blue,/ It's beautiful and so are you.'"

✳

The sizzling dishes of lasagna are placed on cold white plates; the crust of cheese is crisp and golden, oozing hot béchamel when penetrated by our knives.

After we've eaten, we go back to the café where the guitarist was playing. Unfortunately, he's packing his guitar away; it turns out he was only booked for a vernissage. Some artists are exhibiting their work in the café and now there's a kind of after-party going on, but they seem glad for us to join them: 'Come in, come in,' they say. Maybe they think that as tourists we're loaded with money and desperate to take some unique souvenir home with us.

✳

Line-Maria settles on a plank bench by a tree on the street, with a half-score people seated on straight-back chairs or standing around her. They are old, so

Line-Maria stirs interest: Beauty is youth. I venture inside. The place itself is small and empty but for one woman sitting at the bar. The sixtyish barmaid straggles in from the street. She has some kind of lacy blouse on, revealing her shoulders quite fetchingly. To this seventy-four-year-old man, this sixtyish barmaid is attractive. Ignoring me, the barmaid starts to speak Czech with the woman at the bar.

∗

Tom goes to the bar to order beer, while a young woman with white hair styled like a cotton pad (it looks surprisingly good) shows me the various paintings. The music they're playing in the bar is loud, for although they call it a café it's much more of a bar. I think the music is bothering Tom, he keeps looking around as if for the source of it, as if the offensive loudspeaker might be coerced into obeying him if only he could glare at it reprovingly enough, angrily enough. Now it blares out "I Will Survive", which despite the genre divide reminds me of what might be my favorite piece of short prose by Hans Otto Jørgensen, comprising a single sentence: "You won't bloody die".

When the girl with the cotton-pad hair has shown me all the paintings, Tom is still standing in line at the bar—or rather, not in line, but waiting nevertheless. I can see that he's annoyed. Tom has a very readable face; I know of no one else who with just the slightest of adjustments is capable of altering his expression so entirely—he's got at least five different smiles. The one he's wearing now is almost oblique, one corner striving upwards as if to form a fatigued YES? But from where I'm standing it would look to anyone else like the kind of flirtation of which I know he would approve. The woman behind the bar, a pretty-looking, cherry-redhead, is talking to her friend, waves a couple of times to Tom to tell him she'll be with him in a second, then whispers something to her friend and sweeps her hair forward, though it's rather too short to remain this side of her shoulders. Tom's mouth is becoming narrower and narrower, while her hair keeps falling back behind her ears. I tell him the two women are talking about him, but he doesn't believe me—not even when the redhead points at him. His reaction is to turn around, look out through the open door, and then at me.

I sit down on a bench outside, beside a tree in front of the bar, and try to save a place for him with my bag, but very quickly a man with an unusually pointed chin asks if he might sit down. He doesn't understand when I try to explain to him that I'm waiting for my friend. Nearly all the bar's customers are outside. It's only recently that the law was passed prohibiting smoking in bars and restaurants here, and now everyone congregates outside, improvising tables and places to sit on the sidewalks; in this case some planks have been laid across a fence around a tree to become a wobbly kind of bench. I'm just about to go in search of Tom when he emerges with the beers. The guy with the pointed chin gets to his feet without being asked, but Tom tells him it's not necessary. A moment later, the redhead barmaid comes dancing towards us; she wants a light for her cigarette, even though she could clearly have asked any one of her many smoker friends if she could borrow their lighter. But she wants to borrow Tom's, and I can see how it pleases him. She can barely speak English, but stands for some time in front of us, shimmying and smiling at Tom. And Tom smiles the smile that is my favorite smile of his, wide, with his lips held tight together, which gives him just the slight suggestion of dimples in his cheeks, only ever visible when he smiles like that. And I always imagine him thinking, whenever he smiles that smile, that 'Everything is actually pretty fantastic'.

*

The barmaid comes out, and with a few quick steps, she dances at me, moving her fetching shoulders. I rest my gaze on the see-through part of her blouse. Alas, it is not fated to be because I don't dance and don't speak her language, and it's too difficult to explain that I am interested; the spirit is willing, but the pencil has no lead in it.

When Line-Maria reappears, she says, "I told you she likes you."

*

And we talk about so many artists, and we make the acquaintance of a dog that looks like a thin wolf; we're told it's frightened but that we shouldn't bother it. The dog and its owner know the guy with the pointed chin. He grabs hold of the dog's tail that is tucked away between its legs and lifts it up gleefully in the air; to my surprise it cautiously starts to wag. And I think this is when it hits me, how well Tom is speaking now, he almost sounds the way he used to—I don't even think the people we're with would notice his speech was impaired.

They find it so interesting that we're from Denmark. The guy with the chin says he thinks of our queen every time he orders a Margherita pizza. And Stockholm, our capital city, is so beautiful. I glance sideways at Tom, and we laugh.

*

I feel good about being in the company of Line-Maria, who is popular with these people, which makes me feel I must be quite a debonair old man—or her grandfather. Suddenly, we catch sight of the bar sign: Gallery Bar. We have crashed a private viewing.

*

Again, they're playing "I Will Survive", only now it animates me, not least because Tom keeps dispensing quick-fire wit like the old Tom. But I daren't mention it to him because I have a theory that the self-conscious, perfectionist Tom sometimes makes his impediment worse.

When the time comes to leave, they all wave goodbye and call after us: 'Thanks for a nice evening' and 'Margherita', as well as some stuff in Czech that we don't understand, but which sounds very kind.

We buy a bottle of Bohemia Sekt to take home with us from a bar that's just about to close. Arriving back at Tom's hotel, we take a couple of glasses from his room and fill them to the brim, leaving the rest of the bottle to chill. We sit down outside the hotel. There are lots of people sitting about, but we manage to locate a sofa where only a Japanese man sits quietly in one corner. To start with, I'm nervous we'll be told off by the Marriott's staff for drinking our own booze. I've always been scared of people telling me off. I crawl under blankets whenever I see movie scenes where someone gets caught doing something they're not supposed to.

But Tom doesn't seem to mind. We ride the elevator up and down to replenish our glasses, so no one can tell it's not wine we bought from the hotel bar. But the third time up, Tom brings the bottle back down with him, tucked under his arm, and I put up no fight.

We talk about art and artists, and about how we're both just as dependent on music as on literature, while I shape a little lady out of the silver foil from the top of the bottle—it's something I always do when drinking bubbly in good company. Tom has a little collection of my ladies in his apartment, where they stand side by side, gold and silver. I've told him he needs to buy bottles with some snazzier foil on them. That he needs to think about my ladies' dresses.

'We're never going to get her home though,' I say, handing her to him.

'I'm good at looking after little things,' he says.

*

With the foil, she deftly fashions a miniature dancing woman with long dress, arms and head, complete with breasts.
   "Where did you learn to do that?"
   "Nowhere. I just saw the dancer in the foil."
   The Japanese gentleman smiles and says something in Japanese, pointing at the dancer. We smile our incomprehension, and he says something else which ends with "Arigato." I say, "Arigato." Forty years before, I was in Tokyo and only remember that word.

*

We talk about Bob Dylan and his "Leopard-Skin Pill-Box Hat", the part where he sings, "You know it balances on your head just like a mattress on a bottle of wine", which I love so much. Tom once thought Dylan sang "matchbook" rather than "mattress". We sat on the Copenhagen square they call Kultorvet one time and talked about it, and I was prepared to admit at once that I was mistaken, as I'm always inclined to think when it's a case of fact against fact. But Tom looked it up as soon as he got home and wrote to me: 'You're right, it's a mattress!' The next time we met up, we experimentally, in defense of the matchbook and its rectangular similarity with mattresses, balanced his planner on top of a bottle of wine we never drank.

And now I sit thinking about that leopard-skin pillbox hat Tom had made. I've seen a photo of him wearing it. It was so him.

He gets to his feet to go to the bathroom. His shades are on the table. I didn't see him put them there.

There's something sad about that. Sitting beside his sunglasses. They reflect the light off the glass tabletop. I look at the grey cushion where he sat; it kind of reinflates, erasing all trace of him having sat there. I know those shades so well. I once took them home with me in my bag, because for some reason I had to hold them, and I don't know why, but when I discovered them there, the first thing I did was take a photo of his shades next to mine, temples entwined.

The Japanese man looks across at me and then at my little foil lady. He's still looking at her when Tom gets back. I take Tom's hand as he sits down.

'You know I love you, don't you?' I tell him.

*

The demi-sec is not bad. We speculate in whispers what other people make of us: that I am an evil, wealthy old man, that she is a young, good-looking adventurer. To furnish their fantasies, we hold hands, kiss one another's hand lingeringly, gaze into one another's eyes—which is not painful to me. It occurs to me that it is a bitter-sweet charade, that I am celebrating the things I cannot have, then that I am a lucky old toad that she will play this charade with me.

As if she reads my thoughts, she says, "You know I love you, don't you?" It is a statement that might seem patronizing by anybody else, but not from Line-Maria. I remember the day we met, nine years ago, and I know that she loves me, but say, "I don't know why you do. It's mystifying."

✴

At first he says nothing. He lights up a cheroot and takes a deep drag before slowly blowing the smoke out of the corner of his mouth.

'I don't know why you do,' he says then.

His gaze is kind, genuinely inquisitive. 'I don't know why you do,' he says again.

He makes to light my cigarette, but his lighter has stopped working. The wheel turns, but produces only a spark.

He picks up the little foil lady and stands her on his palm, studies her and pours us some more wine with his other hand. We raise our glasses to each other. 'I love you,' he says slowly, adding: 'You're like a daughter I can flirt with.'

He's said that before. The first time was on the plane on our way to DC. I was offended by it then, but now I grasp what he means. There's truth in it too. By nature I'm flirtatious myself, and when a man I love says the word "daughter" to me—oh, my heart!

'I know you do too,' he says. 'But it's mystifying.'

Again, he's said this kind of thing before, and it makes me sad, or I feel helpless about it, because what does it take? We so often talk about how it's all a matter of chance, who's alive at what point in someone else's life, how fortune conspires to bring people together who feel for each other in special ways. And we've always known we were talking about us. We know it's us. When we laugh a whole night over jokes that appeal so intuitively to us, when he says, 'Let there be sorbet!', we know, we just know what the other one means. As different as we are, we're still from the same planet. We've told each other that. Meet someone with the same gaze, and know he is your friend. We hold everything about each other dear, or at least I do—even sides of him that can be so annoying, like when he suddenly ups and leaves his own birthday party without saying goodbye; it's a side of him that's so closely bound up with another side I would never wish to be without.

But I say nothing. I raise my glass, he raises his, and we drain them both. We hold each other for a long time. His shades have gone from the table. He picks up the rest of his cheroot from the edge of the ashtray and tries to light it, but the lighter is still not working.

I'm both relieved and worried about him walking me home. I'm almost never afraid of real people, but darkness and dense shadows frighten me; street lamps that go out ominously.

It's so sweet of him, but I'm already thinking about him walking back on his own through those steep and dark, uneven streets. There's one spot in particular, where the pavement has broken up and two chunks have kind of come together in a lump where it's so easy to stumble and fall. We reach my front door; he waits for me to find the key. We hug again, and I kiss him on the mouth.

Once I'm inside, all I can think about is the broken-up sidewalk and his leg that only just healed. I wish I could text him. When we meet up in Copenhagen we always send each other a message to say we got home. I stand in front of the gray box and stare at the flame inside. The wide, waving Dupont-lighter flame.

I bed down on the enormous brown sofa in the living room. On the wall above the TV is a big, black clock I feel like taking down. Just before I fall asleep, I realize we forgot the little foil lady. I hope the Japanese man took her.

•

I sit on the balcony, narrowing my eyes so I can see the screen. The sun is lava, and once it reaches me I know I won't be able to see the screen or even sit there for the heat. The sun is lava. It steals towards my balcony, silently approaching, coming ever closer, and I know, I just know I'll need to move—soon. The sun touches my shoulder, and I inch away, inch away again. I'm meeting Tom in a couple of hours. I'm supposed to be writing a sci-fi thing for young adults based on the Golem myth, but my fingers are idle at the keyboard, and now only half the screen is in shade. I can't get into it, it's as if my imagination is broken. The fantasies I try to conjure—a scene from my wedding with me in an insanely glitzy dress, a rooftop dance with

David Lynch—all grind to a halt. But it's also because my imagination is treacherous, it wants to run away with me, dismissing the rule that it must only conjure things up that could actually happen, however unlikely they may be, and I find myself thinking up a party for the resuscitated, those who are so sorely missed, who now jump out of cakes and cry, 'Had you fooled, you delicious thing! We love you! We're here and we're alive!' Or a ridiculous scene I now try to stop, where I walk by graves and blow life into them, the way the Rabbi Loew did in the Golem of Prague narrative. The bones rise up, up, up! They clad themselves in skin and put on the faces of Thor's goats, becoming strong and living people again.

I go back inside and sit down on the big sofa where I read an article about the Golem tale construed as a foreshadowing of the downside of our technological development.

•

I give the broken pavement a stern look as I walk past. Neil Young's "A Man Needs a Maid" drifts out from inside a baker's shop, and it occurs to me with a smile: He needs a lighter! I find a tobacconist's and buy him one with "Prague" written in curly writing on the side.

Tom is sitting outside the hotel. I feel a skip come to my step as soon as I set eyes on him! He gets to his feet to greet me. He's wearing a dark shirt with a pen poking out of the breast pocket, its golden clip gleaming in the sun. We begin to walk.

✳

Line-Maria shows up at my hotel, bearing a red leather purse, wearing red shoes with red bows and red lipstick on her full lips, eyes done up, and a sailor dress of navy blue with little white anchors around the hem and bodice. It exhibits her ivory shoulders and low-ringed décolletage. I compliment myself on my taste in women.

✳

Passing a cemetery, we decide to go in. I've always enjoyed cemeteries and churchyards—as a young girl, I lay down on Kierkegaard's grave with my hair tied up around a pencil, urging him to impregnate me with just a dash of his talent.

It's a beautifully unkept cemetery. We walk arm in arm through rustling brown leaves whose sounds accentuate that we are walking in perfect time.

*

The cemetery is vast, and the walkways are covered with fallen leaves. I remember a poem by Jacques Prévert that is titled "Les feuilles mortes" and Joseph Kosma set it to music and Johnny Mercer translated it "Autumn leaves," which was one of my favorite songs. I heard it when I was thirteen years old. The melody haunted me, brought up emotions from the well of my young soul that spoke to me of a teasing isolation that was sovereign because it was a condition of life. I don't say anything but I lift Line-Maria's hand to my lips and kiss it softly.

*

From pictures and the gravestones themselves we try to imagine the dead when they were alive. We can't understand the inscriptions, but we consider the proudly lifted or sadly lowered faces of the sculptures and wonder whether the people they commemorate are now with the angels or Jesus. One name I write down so we can look it up afterwards: It appears on the statue of a man standing erect and looking out from a small mound, and beneath him stand some smaller men, searching the sky with both admiration and trepidation.

It seems so odd that in the midst of all this verdant green there can be such great piles of withered brown leaves. The low shrubs have even been dressed with them by the taller trees, making their green tops seem as if they're wearing little brown hair clips. We peer inside the crypts and talk about who would have been grand enough to be given such a place to rest, and agree that strolling at the right pace makes the rustling leaves sound like music, and that obviously nobody ever sweeps up.

I give him the lighter at a classic Czech bar where we eat some lunch. We sit outside opposite the cemetery, but I can't find the note I wrote with the name of that proud and prominent man in the grave.

*

It was a lighter on which was embedded "Prague" and the castle on a Mont. She had noticed that my lighter was out of fluid, she always notices everything, and this small gift was invaluable, could have ignited a heap of fallen leaves, and I registered it as I only could: with silence and a lump in my throat.

✳

My grandfather once said to me that some things are poetry by their nature alone. Among other things, it was true of strawberries and streetcars, he said. Streetcars have always reminded me of the cursive of the pen, the way they never lift from the ground but glide into curves and bends. We're sitting now in a streetcar, wriggling and clattering its way along as the smells of the Vltava River waft through the windows.

✳

We cross the Charles Bridge with its two towers at either end, over Kampa Island. She takes my hand all across the bridge. I don't know if it's to protect me or herself from the tourists and traffic crossing either way. Maybe both.

✳

We walk arm-in-arm across the Charles Bridge until we come to the Dancing House, my favorite building of all in Prague—it's the one that looks most like it's alive. It really does look like it's dancing, and in Czech it bears the irresistible name Tančící dům, which to my ear could easily be the cha-cha-cha-house.

Normally I'm skeptical when it comes to boat restaurants, but the one we pass has a solemn mahogany color and is surrounded by red flowers. An aroma of plums and grilled meat assails us; we're hungry and I'm wearing a sailor dress, blue and white, and crying out for water, so we step onto the gently swaying gangway and are shown to a table. The air is cool and pleasant. I start with an Aperol Spritz, while Tom goes with Prosecco in a tall and elegant glass. The waiter is dark-haired with a very smooth face that almost looks like it was airbrushed. He comes on a bit superior, until Tom orders a bottle of Barolo—at once he's attentive, asks if we're happy with our table, and tells us to let him know if we'd prefer to sit inside. But we're fine with the cool breeze, the weather has been so hot we've both been changing clothes twice a day.

A drizzle fills the air, we hear it patter against the awning, making me think of thin-roofed holiday homes in Danish summer. Then, just as the Barolo appears with a gigantic glass, the drizzle turns to rain. The people sitting outermost move in under the cover of the awning. And within a moment it starts to pour, the kind of rain that ought to be called by some other name, for as I look at my Aperol I see the surface disturbed, not by the odd drop, but as if someone were showering it with water. I feel the rain soak my hair and start to run down my face. A violent wind picks up. The boat begins to heave. We get to our feet, not knowing quite what to do with ourselves, all is chaos, the diners squeal, plates of food crash to the deck, a piece of meat and gravy slides towards us and is halted by the toe of my shoe, an ashtray topples from a neighboring table and smashes to smithereens, the waiters dart this way and that, huddling under umbrellas that turn inside out and fill with water as if they were bowls. I try to make contact with our own, smooth-faced waiter and ask him if they have an umbrella we can borrow, but Barolo or not, all we get is a 'Sorry!' as he scuttles past with a pile of plates on a tray.

Resolutely, Tom picks up the bottle, I take his glass and wait for him. With laughter and desperation in his voice, he calls out to me—'Save yourself!'—and we hurry inside, me now calling out to him—'Save the Barolo!'—as I overtake some slower customers.

The interior is now descended upon by drenched diners. Not the tables, for we cluster around the doorway and wait. We, the deluged. Tom comes in right after me. His shirt clings to his chest and I can't make eye contact with him, his glasses are so wet. He takes them off, but everything else is wet too, so we've nothing to dry them with. There are seats enough for all of us, maybe six at one long table alone, but the dry diners ignore us, staring stiffly down at their plates. I ask a waiter what's to become of us wet people, but all he does is laugh.

'But are you going to find seats for us?' I ask.

He shakes his head in surprise.

'That would be to impose on our other customers,' he replies.

We stand and wait, wondering what they're going to do with us.

∗

My black shirt is plastered to my back, my new Boss dungarees plastered to my legs. My cardboard Vasco da Gama cigarillo box, stored in my shirt pocket, is dilapidated and wet. Even the leather belt loop on my jeans is soaked. My belt and briefs and butt, my leather sandals, are drenched. Thank god, I didn't wear socks. My hair is streaming on rivulets down my face. The lenses of my glasses run with water, and I don't have anything to wipe them with, not the handkerchief in my pocket; it and the lining are soaked. I assume from Line-Maria's stringy, streaming, long hair that she is in a similar condition. The eye shadow and dark mascara runs down her face. Her purse is dry, however; the leather is water-repellent.

*

We sip the Barolo. I shiver and try to catch the eye of some people at the half-empty tables, but they look away. I imagine the waiters might ask them to make room; we can even sit apart if need be, wet people here, dry people there. Our food will be ready soon too, and we can't eat standing up. I ask our waiter when he thinks we might be able to sit down, or if we're to sit at the bar?

'Do you have a reservation?' he asks, as if he never saw us before.

'No, we were sitting outside.'

I'm about to ask him something else, but he's already turned his back on us.

'We're leaving,' says Tom.

I give him a nod. We leave the Barolo on the bar and run out into the rain hand in hand. He's running fast now, for a moment I forget about his leg. He runs, me behind him, to the shelter of a bridge where people stand huddled.

We stay there only for a moment. 'We need to get going,' I say bravely, yet fearful of the waiters coming after us.

We run on, up the smooth, slippery steps that take us to the street above, through great puddles of rain that reach to my ankles; I can hardly open my eyes, it's raining so much. But then at last we spot a bar right by the Dancing House.

Some people are standing in the doorway smoking. We pile past them and inside. Everyone stares at us. Some laugh. I've never been so drenched in my life. I order two small beers and a taxi cab, and notice as I look down at the floor where I'm standing that I've already left a pool of rain that has run off my dress. Tom and I find the restrooms. I wring the skirt of my dress out over the sink. My cheeks are streaked with mascara. I dab at them with a paper towel. It doesn't help.

*

The beers we don't want, but it is just to order something. She tips the waitress generously. I have never witnessed her in an emergency. In my wetness, I feel useless.

"I can understand," the waitress says. "If I was out with my fifty-years father, and he got wet as this gentleman, I wouldn't know what to do."

I feel heartened. A couple of decades younger she took me for and didn't call me her grandfather! The waitress hands me a cloth napkin.

Line-Maria and I retire into the Ladies and Gents. I wipe my glasses, my face, my hair, my arms and hands, the top of my chest. My shirt and jeans are growing cold. The cloth napkin is utterly wet. I toss it in the sink. I pee. I start to shiver.

✳

When I emerge, a woman is already mopping up after us. I'm very embarrassed, but try not to think about it—even though they're all still staring at us. A group of young English-speaking guys at a corner table laugh the loudest; a broad-shouldered one wearing a cap elbows the one next to him and says, 'Lenny, now that is a wet woman!'

I go straight up to the bar and ask about the taxi. The barmaid is understanding, but tells me the line was busy and that she can't get through just yet. She says that if it was her own father she'd be concerned to get him home too. Instead of correcting her and telling her Tom isn't my father, I let it pass, thinking it might work to our advantage and ensure she keeps calling. Or maybe it's because I have such feeling for the f-word and want to allow myself to dwell on it for a while. She tells me she'll ring non-stop, and she does too; over and over I see her pick up the phone and call the number. Then Tom appears, his hair all shiny and plastered to his skull like Ken from Ken and Barbie, his shirt and trousers as if body-painted onto his frame, clearly revealing a rectangular object in his pocket, probably his packet of cheroots.

'We're going to laugh about this, once we're dry and sitting down to eat somewhere,' I say.

He nods and smiles a bit tentatively. The English-speaking guys are still laughing and staring at us. But now, thankfully, the taxi is on its way. I go outside to see how much it's raining. 'Wet woman!' the young guys call after me. 'Wet woman!' the one named Lenny calls out, and raises his beer.

'Yes, it is extremely funny!' I reply, feeling only like pouring their oversized beers all over them. They actually slap the table as they laugh.

'We'll be laughing too soon,' I say rather more cautiously to Tom as we stand in the doorway, the rain whipping in our faces. I keep running out into the street to make sure no one else grabs our ride. But now Tom smiles, my favorite smile of his.

'Laugh is what we'll do,' I say breathlessly when at last we're sitting inside the cab. I can see the pools of water already forming at our feet.

'Soon,' says Tom, and then we laugh, and maybe Tom, like me, feels lucky and adventurous and saved.

We pull up outside my apartment, I dash out, feeling like I'm on a beer run and need to be quick. I run up the stairs and let myself in, find some dry clothes I stuff into a bag and dash back down again to the car.

Shortly after, we're at Tom's hotel.

I change, pressing my wet clothes into a bag I brought; the sole of one shoe has come loose, and the heel with it—it looks like a very friendly shoe, looking at me like that, with its big, open mouth.

✳

In my room, after she has changed in the bathroom, she wrings out her soaked dress in the tub and puts it in a plastic bag. It is sad to see the sailor dress in a wet crumple in the plastic bag.

I put my drenched belt over the closet door and my black shirt on a hanger on the closet latch. I remove my watch. My wallet is wet; I remove the credit cards and the cash, stuff them in my dry pocket. The bills are soggy. My sandals I put in plastic bags which I transported the dry wingtips in. I hang my Boss dungarees on two hangers over the bathtub, using the pants clips on the coat hangers to separate the legs, Line-Maria says that it's cool how I hung my dungarees on two hangers.

✳

He's hung his trousers up so neatly on a hanger above the bathtub, separating the legs with some kind of pegs. Again, I get this feeling, being alone in a room with his things. His shirt hangs from a hanger on the wardrobe door. I stare at it while he goes to the bathroom. When he comes out, he looks at me looking at the shirt.

'Is everything okay?' he asks.

I don't know what to answer. I say something about him hanging his clothes so neatly—it strikes me as an odd thing to say, and he looks bewildered. 'Cool,' I say. 'It looks cool.'

We go down to the Marriott's restaurant. It feels so good to be dry, to sit with a glass of wine and know that food will be coming soon.

'You said we'd laugh about it,' he says when we share a chicken tikka starter. 'And you were right.'

*

After we eat, the waiter gives us gratis slivovitz in ornate little glasses which we take on the covered patio. The Japanese gentleman from the gallery opening exchanges greetings with us.

Line-Maria reads me a short piece which she has written in Danish. It is about Jan Sonnergaard, about how she tries to remember how he enters a room, and she does not have a recollection of some of the quotidian things her father did.

*

I daren't mention how well he's talking now; his movements are different too, as if the downpour has enlivened him. I can only sit and smile as he talks. The bag with my clothes and shoes in it is heavy and leaves a wet mark on the floor when we leave the table and go outside. It's stopped raining, and it feels a bit like our luck is without end. We talk about the barmaid who thought Tom was my father, and Tom tells me about the time he was working for the White House and the name Kennedy made sure he could always get a cab right away. The waiter comes with complimentary slivo. And we talk about the book Tom is writing, whose chapters are named after songs, and we agree that we must collect all the tunes that are ours and make a playlist as soon as we get home.

*

Before this moment, I have never realized something in all my seventy-four years: From the beginning, nothing at all has lasted; memory is all we have. Memory is all, and all is memory.

*

And Tom talks faster and faster now, more and more animated, and we raise our glasses of slivo and say, 'Let there be sorbet!' and 'Good morning!' and I think: Of course you understand why I love you.

He wipes his glasses dry and places them on the table for a moment, and if I look closely enough I can see that their frame has a very subtle leopard-skin effect. They remain there on the table for a second or two, before he puts them on again and looks at me.

'You should know that I'm not afraid,' he says, as if he could read my mind.

Interview Selections

Tom Kennedy is the perfect interviewee because he has so much to share with an interviewer and is so open and articulate in addressing a range of questions about his writing process, his fiction, and his life.

The subjects in this section have been selected and reorganized from a number of published interviews conducted by Duff Brenna [DB], Susan Tekulve [ST], the late Okla Elliott [OE], Roison McLean [RM], and Timmy Waldron [TW]. Because the interviews cover a range of topics and duplicate the same topics as others, the editors decided to group the selections into categories that permit combining material from more than one interview in a manner that illuminates that topic more fully.

The subjects are Tom's writing process, the novels of *The Copenhagen Quartet*, resolution in fiction, Tom's move to Copenhagen, and his role as a translator.

The complete Brenna interview appeared in *The Serving House Journal*, the Tekulve in *The Literary Review*, the Elliott in *Inside Higher Education*, the McLean in *The McNeese Review* and in *Ecotone*, and the Waldron in *The Bailer*.

The Writing Process

RM: *Your stories, essays, and novels contain rich descriptions of settings—Copenhagen, Paris, islands in the Mediterranean and Ionian Sea, New York, Helsinki, the South African bush, Amsterdam, San Diego, Stockton, San Francisco, Indianapolis, and riding on a Greyhound bus, Amtrak, or a bicycle across America, to name a few—as well as of the people and cultures of those places. Tucked between these are gems of humanity, sometimes humorous, sometimes profound, sometimes both, often phrased as rhetorical or interior-monologue questions and answers. What is it like to live inside Thomas E. Kennedy's mind, which is arguably a landscape in all of your work?*

TEK: That's a tough one. But I'll have a go at it. To live inside Thomas E. Kennedy's mind is like living on the terribly messy surface, hills, valleys, and hollows of my desk—with all its piles of unsorted scraps of notes, partly filled notebooks of various sizes and bindings (glued, perfect, stapled, or spiral), jottings of dark memory, light memory, memories of love and lust and joy and shame, pages of part-written scenes, half-manuscripts that hope to be completed, whole manuscripts that have been abandoned, weather descriptions—in short, to be pulled in a hundred directions at once, from the noble to the depraved and all that's in between and beyond and around. But once in a while, something takes overriding form, takes over the mess of my mind, takes on a voice, and suddenly, mysteriously shuffles everything relevant into place, kicks the extraneous out of sight, and the golden trumpets of what I believe are angels singing out, and I see how it might all fit together. I get an opener, or maybe it is not that opener I will go with, maybe it is something that comes later, maybe the opener I thought was an opener was only my mental throat-clearing and the best is yet to come . . .

I guess what I am trying to say is that I have a messy mind and that writing, for me at least, is a messy process. It is like what I imagine to be heart or nerve surgery: You have to do intricate, delicate things in a mess of blood and guts. So that is sort of how it is to live in the mind of Thomas E. Kennedy—maybe not that different from living in more or less any mind?

ST: *Where do your stories come from?*

TEK: Stories come from all sorts of places and are sparked off by any number of details—the look in someone's eye, an unexpected tone of voice, a glimpse through a door that closes in your face. This is one of the exciting things about writing exercises. I was in a workshop as a student once where the instructor said, "I want you all to write for the next ten minutes a scene in which there is a boy and a fish. Begin." I wrote a sentence that wouldn't stop and grew into a story that was one of my earliest published works. The image unleashed something, opened a door. On another occasion, I was at a museum of mechanical instruments listening to a lecture on the history of automated music. During the lecture we were served iced glasses of genever (this was in Utrecht), so my mind was pretty relaxed, and at one point I leaned on a street organ that was on display, and a voice started in my mind: "My name is Vincente Gasparini. I was born in sin, died in shame. I gave to life my art. My father was Arturo Gasparini, watchmaker, fitter of jewels, springs, gems, and catches into intricate mechanisms to measure the rhythmic tick of that tedious gravity which melts the faces of beautiful women." Now you might ask, where in the world did that come from? But the question is worthless. The only thing to do in such a case is pull out your notebook and pencil and start writing as long as the voice goes on. As Henry Miller said, "When the muse sings, if you don't listen, you get excommunicated."

ST: *Do you write about things you know or about things you want to know?*

TEK: The old saw is write what you know, and there is something to that of course, but what DO we know? What do we know about even those people who are closest to us? Each of us is sealed off into the envelope of our own skin, live in the cage of our skulls, and every act of communication is an act of imagination. Of blind people in the dark imagining their way toward one another.

So definitely, for me, writing is an act of discovery. It was very difficult for me to come to understand that and, until I came to understand that I was unable to write a successful fiction, was unable to activate my imagination. I think it was Updike who compared the process to driving at night: you can't see beyond your headlights, but if you keep going, keep following the light, you will get where you are going—or somewhere! Wright Morris said, "How do I know what I want to say until I've said it?"

ST: *In your "Self-editing a Fiction Manuscript" essay, in the section on linearity, you say that it is the fiction writer's job to sit and wait to catch the police-*

men of his mind asleep. "Beware the linear. Go roaming." Are you suggesting that it's okay to write a story completely on the associative level, without logical transitions?

TEK: Whenever I utter something as though it were fiat, a flood of exceptions always deluges my mind. That is why in my self-editing essay (and the talk I give, which is considerably longer), I caution against a number of things and then give a bunch of examples of exceptions that work.

Nonetheless, I think generally speaking that I do try to avoid "logic" when I am writing. I do write by association, but it is a kind of focused association process. I guess I don't see human behavior as logical. I guess I don't see human events developing logically, and since fiction is in some way a reflection of human behavior and human events, even if a highly distilled and more organized one, I try to write in a manner that arises more from my existential sense than from any cranial view.

I never (or anyway extremely rarely) think in terms of plot or in terms of causation in a fiction. I just can't work that way. To me it has to grow raggedly like the vegetation. That is why I usually don't know what a story is about until I've written it.

I guess what I mean is that I don't see myself as "masterminding" my fiction, but mostly just transmitting it. I am a tool of the fiction, so to speak. The fiction is the driving force. As a writer friend, Gladys Swan, once said, "I sometimes feel my stories come through me on their way somewhere else." Now that might sound kind of self-pleased, and I surely don't mean it that way, but there is a certain mystery to the process I think—the same kind of mystery at play every time someone opens his or her mouth and speaks.

ST: *Associative writing often leads to internalized plots, and yet so many editors seem wary of internalized stories that "aren't dramatic enough." Do you think a character's thought of an action can be as powerful as the action itself?*

TEK: The greatest human drama, in my opinion, occurs within the walls of the human skull. I find interior landscapes very dramatic. After all, what is time really? Sometimes I ask myself if the present really exists at all. It seems to me that the present is a continuous deepening of the past as we move toward the future. We stand with the history of our years at our backs, looking forward, but our brains, our minds are decades deep. This is what was so brilliant about Kurt Vonnegut's *Slaughterhouse Five* and James Joyce's *Ulysses*. The simultaneity of time.

ST: *Do you think this is a cultural issue? Are European editors more tolerant of internal landscapes?*

TEK: You are probably right that Europeans are more open to it. As my friend David Applefield, editor of the literary quarterly *Frank*, published in Paris, says, "When Americans begin to find themselves in an interior landscape when they're reading, their immediate reaction tends to be, 'Hey, what's this! We want to go to the beach and have some fun!'" But I certainly don't want to come off as some kind of effete pseudo-European. Some great American writers—and great American readers—work beautifully with the interior landscape. And I appreciate and respect the conviction of many writers and readers that the interior fictional landscape should simply be reflected in the exterior fictional landscape.

Don't get me wrong. I like a good action fiction too, but I also believe, as you suggest, that some of the most sophisticated and exciting action takes place in the distance between object and perception, including the distance between a fictional character's perception and that which he is seen to perceive.

But when you come down to it, the only really critical thing about a fiction is that it has to be interesting. Interior or exterior, the fiction has to flame our imagination or we will chuck it aside. The drama can be rich in action, but it can equally well be in the language—in fact where else can it be in a fiction?

ST: *You published your first short story at thirty-seven and your first novel at forty-four. How long had you been writing before your first publication?*

TEK: It is difficult to say precisely how long I had been writing if the question means how long I had been writing seriously. The first time I can remember the wish to write was when I was nine or ten years old and my father brought home a Remington typewriter from his office. It was technologically quite advanced in that it had a ribbon which was half-red and half-black, so you could vary the type color. I remember looking at that and thinking I could write a story with that. So I began to hunt and peck a story about a priest who was trapped in a cave awaiting his martyrdom. I wanted to explore his thoughts at this final hour of his life. I typed out a paragraph, maybe ten lines, and realized how difficult it was technically to express all that I wanted to express when I did not know how to touch type. So I flicked the switch to the red ribbon, pressed down the CAPS lock, and typed out BUT HE DID

NOT MIND BECAUSE HE KNEW HE WAS DYING FOR CHRIST! Then I wiped the sweat from my forehead and thought I would wait until I learned how to type before trying again.

When I was seventeen, I read the story "Miss Brill" by Katherine Mansfield and was so incensed by the sadness of the fate of that poor dear old lady that I decided to write a letter to the author and tell her how badly I thought she had treated her leading lady there, found that Katherine Mansfield had been dead for many years, and was intrigued by the fact that the words of a dead woman could produce such a powerful emotion in me and decided I wanted to be a writer.

So I wrote a couple of stories and, having just started college, signed up for a writing course and the professor, who was a very old-school type, impressed because I had taken four years of Latin, became a kind of advisor for me. He advised me to begin writing a journal to loosen up my writing style. "And in a couple of years," he said, "perhaps you'll have a book." All the writing I did for the next few years, which included a stint in the army, was in my journal, and that was very useful. I filled about four or five spiral notebooks with my observations, which I took with me after my discharge from the army when I started hitchhiking around the U.S. Then someone stole the bag in which the journals were stored—I often think how disappointed that poor thief must have been when he broke open the locked attaché case to find nothing but a bunch of ranting notebooks. I was disappointed and stopped writing for a while. I was on an extended leave of absence from college at the time, hitching back and forth from east to west to East Coast, living in New York and San Francisco and San Diego and Long Beach, playing Jack Kerouac and camping out in Big Sur, flirting with the Mexican Border and so forth. Finally when I was twenty-three or so, I went back to college again and took some writing courses. My teacher, Edward Hoagland, was very supportive and told me he thought I would soon be publishing. Another teacher, Irwin Stark, introduced me to his agent, who started sending out my stories, and one of the stories somehow found its way to Theodore Solataroff who sent it on to New American Library, one of whose editors asked if I would be interested in expanding it to a novel. At that same time I landed a grant from a fund at CCNY for a novel-in-progress, a couple thousand dollars, which I took with me out to Stockton, California, to live in a commune and write that novel.

I wrote the novel, but it was not very good and NAL, understandably, rejected it. In despair, I decided, in the words of Kenneth Rexroth, "that a business career would be best after all." I was by then twenty-six years old, had just fallen in love with a tall, slender, and to my mind, wonderfully exotic Norwegian woman who broke my heart by the time I was twenty-seven; whereupon I accepted an offer of a job in France.

In France, in this little country town where I lived, there was nothing at all to do in the evenings, and I had no TV and no radio and no phonograph. For about a year and a half there, I sat in my apartment in the evening listening to the unnerving winds drop down from the Alps while I read a lot of splendid books and wrote a lot of worthless pages. Then, as I mentioned earlier, I met a Danish woman, married, and moved to Copenhagen, and basked in the joys of love for about five years. But the siren song of the desire to write again began to coax me forward, and I spent the next several years trying to figure out what and how and why to write. I read a lot of books about writing during that period and finally, in 1981 or so, managed to produce my first viable short story manuscript—a story that was accepted for publication by the literary magazine *Confrontation* at Long Island University, by the editor Martin Tucker.

ST: *How important was your first publication to your development as a writer?*

TEK: Having that first story published meant a lot to me. That was twenty years after the night I read "Miss Brill," and even if I had not been working with a uniform and steady dedication to the craft, I had consistently wished to be a writer and had worked fairly seriously for a total, on and off, of probably ten years.

From the publication of that story, things began slowly to move forward. I began to get a grasp on the mysteries of craft, and within a few years of that I had published perhaps half a dozen or eight stories, and then it began to move more quickly. Then came books, more stories, more books, more stories, essays, poems, interviews, reviews, translations.

Finally I felt a kind of confidence that what I was doing was successful communication of a sort. Being published helped confirm for me that I was not just a madman scribbling on the wall of a cave. So publication in that respect was very important for me.

ST: *What is the most accurate measure of success for you?*

TEK: I hope I'll know it when I see it.

TW: *Would you explain how you go about the actual business of writing?*

TEK: The actual business of writing, for me, is a messy process. There are those who say it can be contained and inscribed on index cards of various sizes and colors and outlined and plotted and projected, but in my experience it is based on scribbles on soiled, ragged scraps of paper that come together, some of them perhaps, into a first draft. Sometimes you get lucky and hammer out a story in a few bangs. Sometimes it takes longer—very much longer. The most recent story I wrote as of this date is called "X's Xmas," and it is in its thirtieth draft now and who knows whether it will be viable, whether it will appear, whether I will come to regret it.

The novella *Getting Lucky* was a gift of sorts. I started it on quite autobiographical terms, and it continued on quite autobiographical terms. The autobiography, however, turned into a story and there are some similarities with some of the many personal essays/CNFs/stories of *Last Night My Bed a Boat of Whiskey Going Down*, although "Getting Lucky" was written afterwards and written, if I may, in a different direction from the "essays" of that collection.

TW: *What is the big regret if a story is not viable? Do you see it as a waste of time or a failure? Isn't there always something to be learned? Or is that just hokum?*

TEK: I guess I feel it as a failure to achieve what I was after—or a failure of vision; I thought something great was in some detail or other, but maybe that greatness was not in it, or maybe I failed to develop that greatness from it. What, I guess, is to be learned from such a shortcoming is that not all ideas are viable, or you can't make them viable, but you don't know unless you try. You have to try it all—or try to try it all—lest you miss something really good.

TW: *How do you decide how a story will be told?*

TEK: Purely intuitively. Or nearly purely intuitively. Sometimes I start in one person and think this feels flat and go to another person. Although many people despise writing that is in the second person (I had my personal essay I won the national magazine award for rejected because it is in the second person—not to say that prizes mean much other than that they open doors) but I think it is fun to write that way and what could be more fun than fun?

With first person I need to know the character very closely because otherwise I can confuse that character with myself. And for that reason I often choose third person because it helps me to distance myself from the persona. As soon as you say "he" did something or other, you have a free range of action (even if the action is autobiographical).

TW: *The opening paragraph of "Bonner's Women" is the most dangerous writing I have ever encountered. Every time I read it, I put the book down and go on a two-day drunk. The sadness, the happiness, the loneliness, and the joy all resonate so deeply. What is the key to writing such emotionally provocative stuff?*

[The paragraph: "What it takes on such a day, to refresh a tired heart, is an Oak Bar martini in a cocktail glass—gin, rocks, a dash of Noilly Pratt, three olives on a tiny wooden spear, and a little glass dish of quality peanuts. The uplift is instantaneous. Dry chill aross the lips and straight to the brain."]

TEK: Wow, thank you very much—I get tempted to have a martini from that paragraph, too; it was meant to be a kind of verbal monument to martinis and what they do. The thing about that story is that the reader reads the title first, then reads that paragraph and presumably thinks that each paragraph follows from the one before. And each paragraph does follow from the one before, but I did not know the title before I wrote that paragraph. I did not know what the story was about before I wrote that paragraph. But the key to it all was the Oak Bar in the Plaza Hotel, and what that bar and that hotel suggested to my subconscious mind, and I continued to riff on that—discovered that the guy was going from work to visit his mother in Jackson Heights who was senile (I discovered later), and that while he is in the Oak Bar, telephoning his mother, he spots a former mistress coming into the bar, and so on and so forth. Ideally that's how I write—from an emotionally charged sense and I go into it and discover what I can discover from that emotion or those emotions. Sometimes—ideally—I get surprised by the discovery of what lies in there. In fact, that story grew to a novel a couple of years later, *A Passion in the Desert* (Wordcraft of Oregon, 2007) from which I discovered many more things about that character and the woman he was married to. My girlfriend at the time that I was writing that novel read it in manuscript and said simply to me, "I think that woman, Jenny, is not nearly as nice as you think she is." And no one wanted to publish it. I puzzled over what that girlfriend said to me for a long time, years, then finally realized she was right.

I rewrote the novel with that in mind, and it was published and well-received critically, a finalist for the Foreword Magazine Prize when it was published.

It all reminds me, the discovery that is entailed in writing a story or a novel or an essay or whatever, of the lines from Eliot: "If you came this way,/ Taking any route, starting from anywhere,/At any time or at any season . . ." Eliot goes on in that poem to another place, but those lines evoke for me the creative process and that you just have to start, anywhere, and your language will lead you where you have to go.

DB: *Even after all your success, you've said that you still get rejections from editors. Does it bother you?*

TEK: Rejection goes with the territory, and its sting diminishes over time.

In an article I did for *Poets & Writers*, I researched the subject of rejection and found out that many writers had sent their stories out over and over, sometimes as many as seventy times. I learned that one of America's greatest short-story writers, the late Andre Dubus, had sent one of his stories out thirty-eight times before it found a home. The article on rejection gave me a better perspective on myself as a writer experiencing dozens of rejections: You realize it's not personal. You learn to be the water that wears away the stone.

DB: *Do you ever feel like you're the stone, like you're the one being worn away?*

TEK: Maybe I felt that way years ago, but not anymore.

DB: *All those years of rejection, you never thought about quitting?*

TEK: Sure, I thought about it, but the next day I'd be back at my typewriter anyway. A writer produces a story in much the same way that an oyster produces a pearl, through pain and worry and irritation (joy, too, of course), and half the time you have trouble even giving the thing away. But you can't dwell on it. Your business is to write what you can the best you can. To tell you the truth, after that initial twenty years of frustration, every time I sell a story now I feel like a kid on Christmas Eve. Five hundred bucks and I feel terrific! Sometimes I get a nice fee for coming and reading one of my stories, and to me it is like a small miracle that some college will pay me fifteen hundred dollars to read to fifty or a hundred students and faculty. I feel truly privileged even just to get that much attention and recognition for doing something I love to do.

DB: *The writing itself is its own reward?*

TEK: Writing is the reward, yes; the rest is gravy. Really, the true joy of writing, of experiencing that rush of well-being and creativity while you are in the process, feeling it happen, experiencing yourself as a tool of the craft, a medium of the story, it is spiritual feeling, a communion.

DB: *Spiritual?*

TEK: Yes, writing can be as spiritual as any religion you can name. In certain moments of creation, you are taken out of yourself and become a part of a larger world. Ideas, knowledge, scenes come into you and flow onto the paper. An hour or a day might pass and you at last awake as if from a trance, and in front of you is a pile of paper and words are on those sheets of paper that you had no idea you were going to say. It is as I said, as if you have been in communion with some force much larger than yourself.

DB: *Where does the knowledge come from? Do you believe in Jung's theory of archetypes? Is it Yeats's Anima Mundi?*

TEK: The world spirit? Maybe it is. I don't know. I only know that when it happens it is a spiritual experience. If it's a genetic connection with an archetype, or you've submerged yourself in Yeats's river of creativity encircling the world, no one can say; but I don't know any writer who hasn't experienced it.

DB: *It's like the marathoner's high, the hormones kicking in and away you go.*

TEK: Maybe so. I'm not a runner, so I don't know what that feels like.

RM: *Isaac Babel said that food for the soul comes from writing new stories. Do you agree?*

TEK: I believe that one of the highest spiritual points I can achieve is at the moment of creation, at the moment of discovery of what resides at the core of a fiction or a creative nonfiction, a piece of writing. And I might not understand that discovery with my intellect, but I do feel it, am an attendant to it, allow it to happen by clearing the path for it. And my consciousness—like the consciousness of the unnamed narrator of Knut Hamsun's *Hunger*—is continuously starving to express itself and to reach that moment of discovery. So perhaps it is a kind of food for the soul.

The Copenhagen Quartet

OE: *You've written a tetralogy,* The Copenhagen Quartet, *exploring the life of the city. Taken together, these books total well over a thousand pages. Would you discuss your process and influences during the project? How long did the composition take, what was the process of composition, and did you have the shape of the whole project before you started, or did the four novels emerge separately?*

TEK: In 1996 it abruptly occurred to me that I had been living in Copenhagen for twenty years and knew very little about the place. I decided that I wanted to really know this city. I had just acquired an apartment over the east side street lakes with six windows looking out onto Black Dam Lake—which had been the place in Copenhagen I had originally fallen in love with when, strolling its banks one sunny afternoon, I happened upon a very beautiful and very purely naked young woman, eyes closed, sunning herself in the grass. It was on those very banks that the anti-hero of Søren Kierkegaard's surprisingly modernistic 1840s novel, *Seducer's Diary*, strolled, dreaming of the object of his cynical affections who lived across the lake.

Anyway, in '96, I began exploring the city, bought books about it, its history, its sculpture, its graveyards . . . For Christmas '98, my then girlfriend gave me a guide to *The Humble Establishments of Copenhagen*—a succinct array of about a hundred old serving houses, and we decided to visit each one of them, during which I got an idea of writing a novel disguised as a guide to Copenhagen's serving houses, in which each chapter took place in a different pub. There are a total of 1,525 bars in Copenhagen, so I had plenty to choose from.

I wanted this book to include all that I had been learning about this ancient kingdom and all that I had picked up about Danish ways since the mid-'70s, and I wanted it to be a real guide to real places that people could visit, and a novel as well. The book began to take form, I discovered the voice that it needed, we began to exceed the limits of the original guidebook we were following, and I began to learn more about my counterpart, Terrence Einhorn Kerrigan, and the contemporary incarnation of the destructive goddess Kali who is pursuing him, and after about three years my novel was done, *Kerrigan's Copenhagen, A Love Story*.

Flashback to 1996, at which time, enraptured by the deep, dark noir of Danish winter, I had begun (and later completed, late in 1998), a novel about a divorced man in his mid-40s, whose soul is dark and frozen as the city. The winter of '96 was an icy one. Being noir, the novel is about the seamy side of the city, which I had also been learning something about at the time. So I had two novels completed, both about Copenhagen, one set in winter (which would come to be entitled *Bluett's Blue Hours*), one set in spring (*Kerrigan's Copenhagen, A Love Story*).

At around this time I was interviewed by an American expatriate in Paris, David Applefield, for his magazine, *Frank: A Journal of Contemporary Writing & Art*. In that interview I told about Kerrigan and Bluett and about the plan that had begun to unfold in my head to write a quartet about this city—four independent novels, each set in a different season, and each written in a different style. *Bluett* had been noir, *Kerrigan* experimental. So I would do two more—the summer and the fall books. I had boxes of notes for these books, knew vaguely that the summer book would be about a torture victim being treated in the city's Torture Rehabilitation Center, for which I have done some translation and editorial work throughout my years here. I pictured that novel as a traditional one with a social conscience. And I had some ideas about the fall book being a satire about a Danish firm with lots of characters.

The interview was published in *Frank*, and I received an email in February 2002 from a publisher in Ireland who asked to see the Kerrigan manuscript. The publisher was a man named Roger Derham who had just launched a new press called Wynkyn de Worde; he offered me a contract for *Kerrigan*, and the terms, for a small press, were pretty good. He also told me he would do launches in both Ireland and Denmark, would fly me over and put me up, and he just generally was a dream come true for me, since I have struggled all my years to find publishers willing to publish what I've written while it is still fresh and important to me. He did a beautiful job on the books—lavished care upon them, on the printing, the cover art, etc. And at some point in there, he agreed to do the noir novel as well, same terms, and agreed to go with the idea of a quartet of novels.

So *Kerrigan* was published in the autumn of 2002, *Bluett* in autumn 2003, by which time I was nearly finished with my book about the torture survivor, which, in keeping with the title style of the series, I was calling *Greene's Summer*, although when it is published in the U.S. and the U.K. by Bloomsbury in March of 2010, in a considerably revised edition, it will be titled *In the Company of Angels*.

In brief, the novel was inspired by several case stories, the horrific details of which I had to exorcise from my soul by writing in a fictional form about a torture victim in a Latin American cell, who had been there for months and lay there completely demoralized, spiritually and mentally and physically broken, on the floor of this filthy place, realizing that it was summer outside and that he would never see the beauty of that season again, and just as he decided that he would allow himself to die, two angels suddenly were there in the cell with him. They apologized to him that he had to experience such inhumanity and that they were not allowed to release him, but told him that they had secured permission to take him out of the cell for five minutes so that he could experience the beauty of summer. And although they would have to bring him back to the cell again, they assured him that at some time in the future, he would be released and that he would know the beauty of life again.

Naturally I was profoundly moved and troubled by the stories of all these torture survivors. I had tried to approach the material before by writing a short story on it in the early '90s, but I wanted to expand it into a novel. Originally I pictured it as a very short novel—something like Albert Camus' *The Stranger*. This was around the time that a small percentage of the Danish people had begun to grow xenophobic, wanting to keep their social democratic paradise to themselves. But as I was writing the book, another character appeared and began to take over the major force of the novel—this was Michela Ibsen, a Danish woman who had also survived violence—a violent marriage. And she began to assume the role of central consciousness of the book. Other characters appeared, too—the doctor who was treating the Chilean, and a younger boyfriend of Michela, and Michela's agéd parents . . . And the novel grew and was ready to be published in the autumn of 2004, by which time I already had a pretty stable vision of what the fourth book of the *Quartet* would be.

Meanwhile, Professor Greg Herriges of Harper College in Illinois had hatched a plan to make a DVD documentary about my *Quartet*. He was doing a series of such documentaries—had done one about the beat poet Pommy Vega, and another about Michael McClure, and is currently doing one about T. C. Boyle. Well, I had been visiting Harper College on an annual basis for years to give readings there, and Herriges—himself a fine novelist and film writer (check out his wonderful memoir about J.D. Salinger from Wordcraft of Oregon)—began to film my readings with the help of their masterly AV man, Tom Knoff, and the DVD was completed just about the time that *Greene's Summer* was ready for press. The DVD was released and screened, and ten clips of about two minutes apiece can be viewed on my website.

By then, I was into *Danish Fall*—originally conceived as *Breathwaite's Fall*, but I changed it to *Danish Fall*—about a dozen characters, all of whom behaved very cooperatively in satirical fashion. I love the people in that novel—even the idiots and the nasties. They feel so human to me. Now the first two volumes of *The Copenhagen Quartet* are being issued worldwide by Bloomsbury Publishers. The first volume, *In the Company of Angels*, about the torture victim, will be released in March 2010, the second volume in March 2011, hopefully to be followed by the other two and, according to Bloomsbury's announced intention, my other books as well. One can hope. The titles of all the books will be changed, by the way, each reflecting an aspect of angelic intervention and inspired by diverse sources such as Rilke and Rafael Alberti and Allen Ginsberg and the contemporary Finnish composer Rautavaara, who has composed a series of incredible symphonies about angels.

That's how *The Copenhagen Quartet* came to exist. And for the past two years I have been working at a kind of coda to *The Quartet* entitled *The Christmas Lunch at Emdrup Pond*, which I expect to have done in about another year or two. [Editor's Note: That novel was not completed.]

RM: *Although often accompanied by fear of the unknown, that decision to try again rings of the strength of the human spirit, which may explain why many readers consider new beginnings happy. Speaking of beginnings, Bloomsbury has extended your audience for* The Copenhagen Quartet *beyond Scandinavia and Ireland to the United States, Canada, Australia, and New Zealand, giving it a well-deserved new life. Bloomsbury published* In the Company of Angels *in 2010 and* Falling Sideways *in 2011. Many readers in your expanded audience look forward to the 2013 publication of the third Copenhagen novel from Bloomsbury,* Kerrigan in Copenhagen, A Love Story. *You have said you never work from an outline because it detracts from the process of discovery in the writing. That habit draws me to wonder about the initial moment of mental fertilization or spark, which after much labor results in a new novel. Please describe the beginnings of your conceptualization of the third novel. For example, did you first envision characters, dialogue, images, or ideas that begged to be developed, or a combination, or none of these? And is there a common method to how you begin thinking about a novel?*

TEK: Actually the third novel, in its Bloomsbury worldwide conception, was the first novel of *The Copenhagen Quartet*, published in Ireland in 2002; it is now a vastly revised version, and I was delighted to have the opportunity to revisit it. I didn't know at the time that there would be four novels. At that time, I had never written a novel set in Copenhagen. The three novels I had published at that point all had been set in the U.S. as had most, though not all, of my short fiction and essays. In 1996, the chain attaching my anchor to the U.S. dissolved, and I started writing about other places I had visited or lived in—South Africa, Slovenia, Chile, Helsinki, Spain, Ireland, Scotland, Switzerland, Paris, and, of course, Denmark.

At that time, I had an idea that I wanted to write a quartet of novels set in each of the seasons in Copenhagen, and to spice it up a bit I wanted each to be written in a different style, reflecting the season. So the winter book, because winter is so dark in Copenhagen, would be noir, involving jazz, violence, drunkenness, sex, and death (*Beneath the Neon Egg*). The autumn novel would be a satire about business and about the fall of an executive (*Falling Sideways*). The summer novel, because the Copenhagen summers are so bright, would be about a man and woman with a dark past seeking the light (*In the Company of Angels*). And the spring novel would be a love story, expressing my love for the city of Copenhagen, and would be experimental in style, a novel disguised as a guide book to the Copenhagen serving houses, of which there are over fifteen hundred, each chapter taking place in a different bar (*Kerrigan in Copenhagen, A Love Story*).

To return to your question, in 1998 my girlfriend at the time gave me for Christmas a guidebook to one hundred Copenhagen serving houses. She and I decided to visit each of them, and during the course of this it occurred to me that it would be fun to write a novel about the many so-called serving houses of Denmark from the point of view of a guy writing a book about the bars of Copenhagen and falling in love, despite himself, with his beautiful research associate, and incorporating in the story all manner of facts about the history, culture, literature, food, and drink of Denmark. So that was my vision, and I followed my pen to allow it to unfold of its own volition. I realized that my protagonist's name was Terrence Einhorn Kerrigan, and I more or less followed him along the streets of Copenhagen in his quest to escape his past and to evade the increasing attraction of his associate. Considering that the book was otherwise pretty well ignored by the daily press in the U.S., I am so grateful that Bloomsbury is giving Kerrigan and all the novels a chance in the U.S.—hell, worldwide.

RM: *I had the good fortune to read that book in its Irish/Scandinavian con-*

ception, of which David Applefield, editor of Frank *magazine in Paris, said, "Kennedy has elevated Copenhagen to the status of Joyce's Dublin." The book also includes numerous fascinating tidbits of Danish history as well as world-wide literary quotes. Do you have eidetic memory?*

TEK: I will always be grateful to David Applefield for that generous bit of hyperbole. I had to look up *eidetic* by the way. I do have a fair memory, or have had, but I'm really bad with names and getting worse as body and soul begin to fall asunder. I think of Billy Collins' wonderful poem, whose title escapes me, the essence of which is that the first thing you forget is the author's name, then you forget the book's title, and finally you forget that there was ever a book at all. I tend to be good at remembering bits of poems, though, and my main character in the Copenhagen serving house book, Terrence Einhorn Kerrigan, also has a facility for remembering lines of poetry and dates. He is also good at composing verse on the spot. And he remembers the years of birth and death of many prominent persons; in fact, he obsesses over placing them on a time scale as a way of trying to place his own temporal existence in world history. But it is not enough for him to know the names and dates of poets, philosophers, artists, scientists, statesmen, jazz musicians, singers, etc.—he wants to have some of their words and music inside his skull as well. He is thoroughly neurotic as well as being a drunk, but after all he lives in more or less constant regret over lost love. It was a fun book to write—the research was wet and wonderful—and, as you point out, in addition to what I hope are its narrative virtues, it is encrusted, decorated, and festooned with a great many historical, literary, geographic, artistic, musical, and other facts by dint of which Kerrigan attempts to place himself in the world and in time.

RM: *Are you as prolific a note-taker as a writer?*

TEK: I constantly take notes because what I try to recreate in my fiction is the fullness of the flow of time and existence for a character. In writing that particular book, I discovered that the more you know about the place where you happen to be at any given moment, the richer is your experience of that place and that moment. To give just one example, I learned through my research that one of my favorite serving houses in Copenhagen, The White Lamb, opened for business in 1807, the same year that the Duke of Wellington shelled Copenhagen from the British fleet out in the harbor, brutally slaying a great many Danish civilians and blowing the roof off the building in which The White Lamb occupies the half-basement. So when I sit there over my lunch of sardines on dark rye and a schooner of cold draft, my moments there are enriched by the knowledge of the fact that the Duke of Wellington, who tried to destroy The White Lamb over two hundred years ago, is now dust in his grave while the taps of The White Lamb are still wetly pouring, and the only Duke who blows off the roof these days is when the management plays a Duke Ellington CD. Twenty-five years after the Duke of Wellington's attack, the great philosopher and "father of existentialism" Søren Kierkegaard lived in an apartment just twenty meters across from The White Lamb. My time there ingesting my sardines and allowing them to swim with the beer down my gullet is further enriched by contemplating whether Kierkegaard ever climbed down the three steps into this serving house or whether I might see a shade of the master walking lopsidedly past (he is said to have had an odd gait) on the Coal Square outside the window.

One of the Danish reviewers objected to Kerrigan's frequent naming of influential historical figures and did a destructive review of the Irish edition of the novel—in fact, the only bad review it got—but this was not merely bad, it was perfidious. The essence of his review was that instead of a 450-page novel, I should have written a twenty-page essay, which would have been less tedious to read. I repaid him by borrowing his name for a child molester in my next novel.

RM: *And do you—may I ask—ever drink when you write?*

TEK: Not usually, although when I am running out of steam after two-three hours of composing, I might take a drink, which will often give me another half-hour. A second drink might give yet another half-hour, but then I'm done. I do sometimes take notes over a pint or three in various serving houses and cafés. Drink usually does not interfere with note-taking; in fact, it often enhances my facility at it by relaxing the organism and keeping the reason from stifling.

On rare days of sunlight and warmth, I might also do an exercise described in Kerrigan as "Pint of View," which entails having a pint by turn in each of the eight outdoor cafés situated around the Coal Square and registering the effect of the change of position and the numerical ingestion of pints on my own "Pint/Point of View."

By the way, I am almost always taking notes—on trains, planes, buses, in cafés, walking, etc. I have probably even taken notes while having sex—but only mental notes. I take mental notes almost continually; that is one of the curses and blessings of being a writer—a more or less constant state of consciousness with one part of the mind occupied in phrasing. But I don't think I have ever been so crass as to take actual physical notes during sex—not only would that be discourteous to the woman who is kind enough to share her body with me, but the mechanics of it would be too daunting.

RM: *Jazz and music are featured in* The Copenhagen Quartet, *particularly in the new volume,* Kerrigan in Copenhagen, A Love Story, *and in the forthcoming final volume,* Beneath the Neon Egg. *Could you talk a bit about this?*

TEK: Jazz has always had a welcoming home here in Copenhagen. Tom Kristensen, in his 1930 novel, *Havoc*, features jazz as a part of the main character's ("Jazz" Jastrau) return to "primitivism," which I touch upon in *Kerrigan in Copenhagen*. Jazz musicians, who were persecuted in the United States due to racism, were early recognized in Copenhagen as true artists. The great tenor sax men Ben Webster, Dexter Gordon, and Stan Getz spent years here. Oscar Pettiford died here. Ben Webster described Copenhagen as the only place he could go out at night without his knife. And there is a great jazz club here called Montmartre, among many others, such as the terrific Jazz Klub in the squatters' settlement in the center of Copenhagen—Christiania. Every July since 1979, top artists have met here at a Jazz Festival and hold concerts on the streets, in the cafés, in concert halls . . .

So jazz is an important part of the life of Copenhagen, as is music in general. Billy Cross, who was lead guitar for Bob Dylan, chose to settle here (he does the best version of "Blue Suede Shoes" I've ever heard, including the original by Carl Perkins). And I would no more exclude music from my Copenhagen books than I would exclude its light or the architecture or literature or history.

RM: *You also structured* Beneath the Neon Egg, *the final novel in* The Copenhagen Quartet, *in imitation of John Coltrane's four-part* A Love Supreme. *Do you also imitate the sounds of the music?*

TEK: I try to describe the music in prose, but I don't think that prose can really imitate jazz—or really any music. Poetry can come near, but not prose, I don't think, even though Kerouac tried. What I did with the Coltrane symphony was to structure *Beneath the Neon Egg* in four parts like *A Love Supreme,* and I named each part after the four parts of Trane's great work: "Acknowledgment," "Resolution," "Pursuance," and "Psalm." And I tried to reflect the spirit of that powerful symphony and to touch upon some of its themes—Coltrane approaches pure vibration in his music, and I tried to imitate that with symbolism. At the end of the fourth part, for example, there is complete disintegration in the music, but I couldn't do that in language, in prose, so I tried to do it with symbols. For instance, the book takes place in winter, and as a street lake outside the main character's apartment begins to melt, he comes to terms with the ungodly elements with which he has been dealing. It is, after all, a noir novel with all that's included in that genre—jazz, violence, alcohol, and sex—all those fun things.

The music of Miles Davis also plays a central part in *Beneath the Neon Egg* and focuses on a fusion symphony that Palle Mikkelborg, a Dane, wrote for him in 1989, two years before Miles died. Mikkelborg is a phenomenal musician and a phenomenal human being. The symphony he wrote for Davis, called *Aura*, has an agreeable bombast to it, which seems to me to personify the Copenhagen winter. At times when Miles plays his trumpet in that Mikkelborg symphony, I can close my eyes and picture a great beast slouching across the frozen lake—again, the ungodly which battles the godly.

Actually, every chapter in the book derives its title from a song or piece of music—from "No, Woman, No Cry" to "Night in Tunisia" to Buddy Holly's "It's So Easy to Fall in Love," which has a particular ironic twist in the novel, to Arab on Radar's noise rock, "A Rough Day at the Orifice."

RM: *So you don't emulate the rhythm and sound of the music, in the same sense that Matthew Arnold emulated the rhythm of waves in his poem "Dover Beach," which I notice you mention in your Copenhagen novels.*

TEK: No, I try to describe the music and use symbols and images to emulate it. But Coltrane, Davis, Mikkelborg, and my love for this music all cooperated with my writing of it, as Rautavaara's incredible Finnish symphonies about angels did in *Kerrigan*.

RM: *Both* Kerrigan in Copenhagen *and* Beneath the Neon Egg *have been considerably revised since their first publication by Wynkyn de Worde, a now-defunct Irish press, in 2002 and 2005. Why and how did you revise these two novels in* The Quartet?

TEK: I wrote the original versions of *Kerrigan* and *Neon Egg* fifteen and sixteen years ago, and I would be a very static individual if I did not grow as an artist in all those years. So, although I was happy with the earlier *Quartet*, I was enormously happy to have a second chance with Bloomsbury and not just in Ireland and Denmark but worldwide. I didn't change the first two novels (which in the original *Quartet* were the third and fourth) all that much, because I was in my stride with them, on a roll with them, and I did not have to change that much on the redux. But I changed considerably the original first two novels in the *Quartet*, which became the third and fourth novels in the Bloomsbury incarnation. I retained the basic structure, but the backstory changed considerably. I am as grateful to Bloomsbury for giving me this chance to redo the four novels as I was to Roger Derham—an Irish physician, writer, and explorer who decided he wanted to be a publisher—for the chance he gave me back in 2001 when he read the first two books and said that he would take the chance and publish the whole *Quartet*. That is the kind of gesture of confidence that gives a writer the courage to undertake a project like this.

RM: *Some of your protagonists can be perceived as extremists. For example, the protagonist in* Kerrigan in Copenhagen *decides to write a guidebook to Copenhagen's drinking establishments, of which there are 1,525. Kerrigan's plan is to visit and imbibe at each one—an extreme goal.*

TEK: Kerrigan is a man who was betrayed by his young wife, almost unforgivably so, and he more or less vows never to love a woman again, but he is in love with Copenhagen and tries to clothe himself in her language, her history, her architecture, her light—and her serving houses, which is a fancy word for a bar. He takes a contract to write the Danish book in a series of books titled *The Great Bars of the Western World* (which of course is a play on *The Great Books of the Western World*). His volume will focus on the best hundred bars in Copenhagen, a project he embraces with gusto because, as Raphael Holinshed said in 1577, "Whisky: It abandoneth melancholy, it relisheth the heart, it lighteneth the mind, it quickeneth the spirit" and for Kerrigan, it also keepeth the reason from stifling. So he has been extremely betrayed and responds extremely.

RM: *Most of your protagonists are male, yet your female characters are just as much a part of your writing as your male characters. Do you find inspiration for your female characters from merging characteristics of various women you have known, from your "dream woman," or from a combination of these?*

TEK: From a combination of them, but what surprises me is that when I write from the point of view of a woman—most notably Michela Ibsen in *In the Company of Angels*, the first Bloomsbury *Copenhagen* novel—I tend to become that woman. Even when I start from observing a woman or women I know, at some point, if it is a successful characterization, I become that woman. It is an eerie process. I became Michela. I became a woman for that role. It was strange and liberating as well. And some of my own experience was interpreted into her character. Actually, the book started from the character of Nardo, and I thought he would be the main character, but as soon as Michela appeared, she became the primary consciousness of the book.

Someone asked me once whether women have ever complained about that character, that I got her wrong. No women have ever complained about Michela, although a lot of women complained about Voss, her boyfriend, because they despised him. The only person who ever vocalized compassion for Voss was an inmate in a writing group I visited in a maximum security prison, and he said, "I understand Voss. He's honest but insecure." I was moved by that. Obviously Voss came out of me, too, and I didn't much like him either, so I was grateful for that inmate's understanding.

Same with the green-eyed research associate in *Kerrigan in Copenhagen*—I discovered things about my attitude toward women from the fifties and sixties. How unfair, how unthinking those attitudes were. What a bad deal women got in the fifties and sixties and even later.

RM: *If you had to choose one theme from* Kerrigan in Copenhagen *that you yearn to be a key word in your writing legacy, what would it be, and why? And for* Neon Egg?

TEK: Well, who knows if I will even have a writing legacy? It is so easy to have your work forgotten quickly after you die. Maybe it lives on in the minds of a few people—some image, some sentence, some character that a few people remember. I think with *Kerrigan* the important thing is that the more you know (and I know that this conflicts with what I said earlier), the more you know about any given place, the more present you become when you're there, the more alive you become.

I also knew a singer, Asger Rosenberg, whom I heard sing at The White Lamb many times; he had a terrific voice and knew so many songs and the whole formal introductions to them. Asger is dead now, but he gave me such pleasure. I think he's mentioned in all four of the *Copenhagen* books I've written, and he knew that, too, and always said a warm hello to me. The awareness of all that enriches every moment I sit in there and write and sip beer and maybe eat a sardine. The more you know about a place, the more your life is enriched. I hope readers get that idea from the novel—both in general, about the places they themselves live, but also about Copenhagen, which after all has a thousand-year-old history. And I also hope that reading the book will give people pleasure, too—and make them think and feel their place in history as well.

The theme of *Beneath the Neon Egg* probably harks back to the way I felt when I was fifteen and first began intensely reading fiction. Almost immediately I understood that by reading a book I could enter into the mind of another human being. And I realized something else—how basically alone I was—but I gradually began to understand that everyone is equally alone and that reading can make you feel less alone. So it is a book about the ultimate solitude of all the characters and how they try to transcend that loneliness—some try to do it via extreme sexual behavior, which relates to your earlier question about extremist characters.

RM: *In one novel of* The Copenhagen Quartet, *you note that Robert Coover wrote, "It is important to begin when everything is over." Of course, everything won't be over after the fourth book is published in 2014, but after the massive effort to write, sell, and market the books—with the writing starting in late 1996, their first publication in 2002-2005, their publication in a new conception and revised editions for a worldwide audience by Bloomsbury in 2010-2014, and the reading tours to help market them—the almost twenty years of your life devoted to* The Quartet *will be over.*

Resolution in Fiction

RM: *I have heard you speak about resolution in fiction. Would you share your theories about that?*

TEK: I don't know that I have an actual theory about resolution in fiction, but I do have a sense of resolution that has to be fulfilled for me to walk away satisfied—there might still be questions and resonances in my mind or heart, but the way I see it, the music can't just stop. It doesn't have to stop with a flourish or with too pat a figure, but it somehow has to be "resolved" for me to feel that the piece is complete—even if the completion is only meant to give a sense of life's lack of completion.

I suppose that the resolution is the end of the ending in a sense, the denouement (the disentanglement or unknotting, as opposed to the tying of a ribbon and bow around it all), but the unknotting needn't, perhaps shouldn't, be so explicit, although it can be (e.g., Joyce's "The Dead" is explicitly and exquisitely if complexly resolved). Usually what you remember—or what I remember—about a fiction is not the ending so much as an overall impression, a complication, a revelation of character, but sometimes you (I) remember the ending, the closure, the unknotting that reveals the heart of the knot and the art of the knot and the strands of the art—and sometimes you remember it because it is, to my mind, flawed. Some writers just can't end a book; Joseph Heller was one—the endings of, e.g., *Catch 22* and *Something Happened* were completely off, as though he said to himself, in the former case, "I'll make this a zany kind of happy ending," and in the latter case, "I'll make this a very sad, tragic ending where he kills the boy by trying to protect and love him," but both were over-determined and not credible, though we (I) forgive Heller that because the entire fictional experience was otherwise so rich. (Who says that flawed art can't be good?)

Joyce was a master of resolution, of endings, even when he was being "scrupulously mean" as in *Dubliners*, though the richness of the resolution in "The Dead" is symphonic: you (I) finish reading that story just feeling stunned in every way—it is so full of sorrow and beauty; it is like dying a beautiful death, like the moment after a magnificent orgasm, the little death.

The ending of *Ulysses* was, of course, celebratory—celebrating human life in all its contradictions and leading to a single affirmative of the urge to love and to procreate. I would say that the word "Yes" or the phrase "Yes I will, Yes," is the resolution of that novel, whereas the final forty-five dense, single-spaced, unpunctuated pages are the ending, though this ending has an introduction, middle, and end, too, although these are not neatly shaped.

The resolution and ending of *A Portrait of the Artist as a Young Man*, too, was, for all its destructive intent, affirmative and thoroughly right and satisfying—and the destructiveness was creative of a way to live on, a new beginning, if you will. The resolution of, say, Kesey's *Cuckoo's Nest* (there is no system to my examples here—I just mention what comes into my mind), for all the novel's flaws, was also good and inevitable and sorrowful and as affirmative as the story of Christ, of which it was a reinterpretation (sometimes badly so).

The greatest of all endings, in my opinion, if I may include a play in this, is that of Sophocles' incredibly powerful *Oedipus Rex*—ironic and tragic all at once. Count no man happy until he is dead. And that play, by the way, is a reminder of the fact that there is no progress in art—only a variety of evolving styles.

RM: *A related topic you debated on a writer's panel concerned happy endings, which some authors consider taboo. In light of the clear suggestion of a happy ending in your extremely well-reviewed* In the Company of Angels, *what advice would you give aspiring writers on endings, happy or otherwise?*

TEK: Let me go back to Sophocles and quote his ending to *Oedipus*. The last words of a character in the play are Kreon's, in response to Oedipus' plea that his children not be taken from him; Kreon says, "Think no longer that you are in command here, but rather think how, when you were, you served your own destruction." And then the chorus comes in with one final song, which starts, "Men of Thebes: Look upon Oedipus . . ." and concludes, ". . . let none presume on his good fortune until he find life, at his death, a memory without pain."

Who truthfully can find at his or her death a memory, without pain, of life? Maybe when we're young we think we will, but like Oedipus, we all serve our destruction, even when we do our utmost to be virtuous and to avoid doing that. As Philip Larkin puts it, "They fuck you up, your mom and dad. / They may not mean to, but they do." And we are all both parent and offspring, guilty and blameless, but ultimately we fuck up and fuck them up or fuck it up. But we try—we do try, most of us.

So that is my introduction to responding to your question about "happy endings." Is the ending of my novel *In the Company of Angels* really happy? Can a broken, tortured man and a battered woman find happiness with one another? As Hemingway put it at the end of *The Sun Also Rises*, when Lady Brett says to Jake Barnes, "Oh Jake, we could have had such a damned good time together," Jake responds, "Yes. Isn't it pretty to think so?"

If the ending of my novel *In the Company of Angels* is in a sense happy, it is not because Bernardo and Michela have found happiness, have found a happy-ever-after ending, but only because they are willing to try to love again—they are trying again. Bernardo has suffered great pain and great loss, as has Michela, but they see beauty in one another and hope, and they want to try again—and perhaps wanting to try again is the best anyone can ever do. As Beckett says, "Try again. Fail again. Try to fail better." I don't know if that is a happy ending. Maybe it is more of a beginning, a new beginning, than an ending—where everyone has tried, is trying. Even callow, self-involved, young Voss Andersen begins to see the possibility of a new beginning in which he might try to understand.

Moving to Copenhagen

OE: *What caused you to first move to Europe, what has caused you to stay there, and how do you think it has affected your writing? I'm thinking of Gore Vidal as another writer who has spent most of his career living abroad and much of that career critiquing American history and politics. How has the perspective of your expatriate experience altered your writing as an American author?*

TEK: My reasons for moving to Europe were multi-faceted: First of all, ever since I was fifteen and began reading seriously, I was very taken by European authors—Dostoyevsky, Camus, Gide, Huxley, Turgenev, Conrad, and, of course, Joyce, to name a few. And Joyce identified for me the place in my heart that had already fled—the experiences he describes in *A Portrait of the Artist as a Young Man*, although taking place in Dublin, were so like my own experiences as a Roman Catholic Irish-American youth in Queens that I might as well have been in Dublin and preparing to break away and move into European exile already at seventeen. When I visited Joyce's grave in Zurich (see Web Del Sol's *The Literary Explorer*—"Limmat Run Past Joyce and Nora") I was keenly aware that I was visiting the grave of my spiritual/aesthetic father—"Old father, old artificer, stand me now and ever in good stead."

And when I finally did move to Europe in 1974, it was very much with the spirit in my heart of Joyce's great declarations from that book: "I will not serve that in which I no longer believe, whether it call itself my home, my fatherland, or my church; and I will try to express myself in some mode of life or art as freely as I can and as wholly as I can, using for my defense the only arms I allow myself to use—silence, exile, and cunning."

My secondary motivation was that New York City, where I lived in the early '70s, was a bloody violent place. In '71 I had a Norwegian girlfriend who lived on East 2nd Street between Avenues B and C, whose neighbor had fired a rifle through her door because the dripping of her faucet was disturbing him. When I saw the bullet holes in the door, I thought, Jesus, let me out of this madhouse . . . And along with that, one year later, I was sent to Copenhagen to participate in an international conference, and it was love at first sight.

My third motivation was that I had gone completely stale at home in New

York. I had done my thumbing around the country in the '60s, bounced back and forth between New York, southern California, and San Francisco half a dozen times or more and traveled through most of the rest of the country by bus and thumb, looking for Jack Kerouac, unaware that he was back in Queens, living with his mother, right across town from my own mother. Also, at the age of twenty-nine, I considered myself a failed writer—even if I did have a big-name agent, a recommendation to New American Library by Theodore Solotaroff, and a three-year grant from CUNY's Goodman Fund for a novel-in-progress. But nobody wanted to publish anything I wrote.

Then I had the good fortune of being invited by my company to relocate to France. From there I was offered a job in Copenhagen, where I moved in '76. I continued to try to write, and although my stories continued to be set in America, I think that being in Europe enabled me to see America through the lens of this new society. Finally, in 1981, precisely twenty years after I had decided I wanted to be a writer, I sold a story. And I knew while I was writing that story that it was going to sell. I knew that I had finally found the place where my stories were. The story was "The Sins of Generals," and it was published in *Confrontation* magazine, out of Long Island University.

ST: *Why do you live in Denmark?*

TEK: I fell in love with Denmark the first time I visited here in 1972. Later that year after the bullet holes, I visited Copenhagen, and my first night there I was sampling the good Danish beer and got a little tipsy and lost my way. In the wee hours of the morning I was wandering through these empty cobblestoned streets, hearing my footfalls echo off the ancient stone walls, and suddenly I stopped and thought, I'm lost, have no idea where I am, and I am completely relaxed. Had it been New York—had it been, say, Central Park, where I also once lost my way at night—I would have been decidedly uncalm.

Shortly after that I fell in love with a Danish woman. By then I was living in France. I was offered a job in Copenhagen. She and I married, had two fine kids, Daniel, who is now nineteen, and Isabel, who is about to turn eighteen. [Editor's Note: This interview was published in 1999.] Sadly, my wife and I decided to part ways after twenty-two years, but I am staying in Denmark. It is my home now, even if the U.S. is also my home. I live now in an apartment on the street lakes just at the edge of central Copenhagen. I have six windows looking down on Black Dam Lake, and this is the area of

Copenhagen I first fell in love with. It was an amazing coincidence, or whatever you want to call it, that when the time came for me to have to find an apartment of my own I went out and this place was vacant, the first place I looked at, the apartment of my dreams. I love to look down at the water rippling in the summer wind, a dance with specks of light, and in winter when it freezes, I love to walk across in the blue late afternoon to have a drink at the café on the other side. I like the Danish people and the Danish way of life. The taxes are high, but no one is poor, no one goes without medical care or education. And people don't hassle each other. It is very much a "live and let live world," as long as you don't swing your arms too wide and wildly.

ST: *Do you think of yourself as an expatriate writer?*

TEK: Not really, but others seem to. I believe that we carry our world with us, although I would not deny that my way of thinking and my way of writing have been affected by the experience of living in another culture. It was useful for me to leave the States and look back at it through the lens of life in Northern Europe. I learned something about my behavior and attitudes simply by noting how out of place I felt for a time, until I had learned to fit in here. As a New Yorker, I had a bit of a chip on my shoulder; ask a New Yorker a question and he is likely to take a fighting stance, feel threatened. Ask a Dane, and he is likely to smile, flattered that you would ask, even that you would challenge his position. Of course, generalizations are mostly bunk, but there's something to it.

An expatriate writer? For years, my stories were set in New York. And there were some practical difficulties in that because when you've been away for ten, fifteen, twenty years, things do change. If you set a story in the skating rink at Rockefeller Center, and then have the people eat in the restaurant there, you might inadvertently give it the name it had in the '70s, which is not the same as the name it has in the '90s. But these are minor details. In the course of time, I do find myself comfortable setting stories in other places as well. I have set stories now in Copenhagen, Madrid, on Cyprus, in South Africa. The last novel I completed is set in Copenhagen. Still, probably most of my stuff is either set in the U.S. or, in the case of the surrealistic stuff, is set nowhere in particular.

Translation

OE: *You have done translation in the past. Would you discuss the process of translation, the joys and obstacles of it?*

TEK: Actually I find myself doing more translation now than I ever did before. The way I got into it was that when I first moved to Denmark, after I had some of the rudiments of the language but did not quite have a functional ability with it, I would translate things into English for my own sake, to try to get a sense of the English equivalent of something I'd heard or read in Danish. This taught me as much about English as it did about Danish, made English clichés take on a new delight, gave me a more immediate sense of the power of English, but, also, eventually, made me more humble about my own language. English is the lingua franca of Europe. Even the French speak English now. But it is so easy for a native English-speaker to think that English is more important than other languages—an intolerable arrogance.

I started translating to try to grasp more deeply what I only weakly understood in Danish, twisting the syntax until it could fit into my head. I had discovered years before that I had a fairly good ability to translate from French into English—this might sound odd, but my ability to translate from French was better than my ability to speak or understand French. I was just good at eliminating my lack of comprehension by putting it into English. I did the same, at the start, with Danish. And in the beginning I translated somewhat impatiently—trying to get to what I seemed to see as the English that was waiting behind the Danish. This was an arrogant approach and at one point it got me into trouble when I became too energetic in transforming the Danish to English. Then one day I was speaking with an American woman I know, Stacey Knecht, who translated a couple of novels by Marcel Möring from the Dutch and is clearly very good at it. I asked her what makes a good translator, and she said, "You have to put yourself second." Which is exactly what I, as a writer myself, was not doing as a translator. So now when I translate I try to remember that advice—although to some extent you have to bring your writer's intuition with you, so you put yourself second but you also let your intuition share the driver's seat. And having two drivers of one vehicle can be tricky.

Anyway, the whole process also had the effect of strengthening my grasp of the language, and slowly I began to think in Danish and to enjoy speaking it, and, when I got to that point, I began to feel very much more at home in Denmark, when I could go to a party, say, where no one was speaking English and I felt at ease (despite my accent which still gives me away instantly).

But then I found that I also began to enjoy translating from Danish to English—mostly poems, the occasional short story. And most Danish writers want their stuff to be translated into English. It vastly increases the potential audience.

When I translate, I select what seems interesting to me—at present I am particularly interested in a few poets. I have a grant from the Arts Council to translate a poetry collection by Henrik Nordbrandt, who is an amazing poet—some of my translations of his poems are scheduled to appear in *American Poetry Review* and *Agni* and *The Literary Review*, and *The New Yorker* has also expressed interest but so far no *New Yorker* cigars.

Among others, I have also translated quite a few poems by Pia Tafdrup, also a highly celebrated poet especially in northern Europe—and have done a bunch from the new collection of a young talented poet named Martin Glaz Serup, whose work I like a lot. Samples of all these were included in the special Danish issue of *The Literary Review* which I guest edited in Spring 2008. And I am currently most deeply involved in translating the poetry of Dan Turèll, an amazing cult poet here who died in '93 at the age of forty-seven. I have had two grants from the Danish Arts Council to translate his work and it has so far appeared in *New Letters* and *Absinthe: New European Writing* and *Perigee*, and I am about to record the translations as a CD with musical background of an amazing Danish composer named Halfdan E.

The other book I have just finished is by Thomas Larsen, a biography in interviews of Inge Genefke—the Danish physician who was the prime mover in the establishment in Copenhagen of the Rehabilitation Center for Torture Victims and the International Rehabilitation Council for Torture Victims, both of which have inspired the creation of other such centers throughout the world, resulting in treatment being offered to hundreds of thousands of torture victims. The book is entitled *The Meeting with Evil: Inge Genefke's Fight Against Torture.* For more than thirty years, Inge Genefke has been fighting against torture and struggling to ensure that treatment is available for its victims and to make known the fact that torture exists and is being used in the world. Which, unfortunately, is no longer any surprise to Americans. Or fortunately.

The literary journal *New Letters*, out of University of Missouri–Kansas City, published a series of articles carved out of that translation—the first of them, in the Fall 2007 issue, is about the dreaded Villa Grimaldi, a torture center founded by Augusto Pinochet in Chile. I also did an interview with Inge Genefke—and her husband, Bent Sørensen, a surgeon who joined her in her fight about twenty years ago—that came out in the online magazine *Exploring Globalization*, published by Fairleigh Dickinson University. Inge Genefke has also been nominated repeatedly for the Nobel Peace Prize. Odd to think she never got it, but Kissinger did.

Inge Genefke's work was a direct inspiration to the Spanish director Isabel Coixet with her very powerful film *The Secret Life of Words*, about a torture victim, starring Tim Robbins and in which Inge Genefke herself is played by Julie Christie. Julie Christie, in fact, has written a blurb for my translation of the book about Inge Genefke, as has Tim Robbins and Isabel Coixet. And U.S. Congressman Tom Lantos—who was himself a survivor of the holocaust—has written a foreword for the book's American edition.

Time with Tom: Friends' Memories

WE INVITED TOM'S FRIENDS to contribute memories of special times that typify their relationships and offer examples of what it's been like to spend a evening or many years in Tom's company. Some of these contributors were classmates in his MFA program, some teaching colleagues when he was a faculty member, some fellow participants at conferences and residencies, and some editors of magazines that published his work. Today they live throughout the United States and in cities throughout the world. Wherever they are and however they knew Tom, they share examples of his wit and enthusiasm and his commitment to writing, theirs as much as his own.

Tom Kennedy at a writers' conference in Vienna

Susan Tekulve
A Window

I FIRST MET TOM KENNEDY when I badly needed a window. It was in 1999, and I'd taken my first salaried job as the Assistant Director of the Writing Center at Converse College, a four-year liberal arts college in Spartanburg, South Carolina. My office was a gutted-out supply closet sectioned off from the consulting room of the Writing Center by a makeshift wall and a door, roomy enough to hold a slender desk, a chair, a computer, and me. On the other side of the office was another door, an emergency exit that I kept locked so I wouldn't sound off the fire alarm by bumping into it as I squeezed by to reach the chair behind my desk. There were no overhead lights or windows or air vents in that office, but in February of my first year in it I bought a desk lamp and wall calendar called "Windows," which featured famous paintings of windows. I hung it on the blank wall to the left of my desk, above the desk lamp, so I could gaze upon a different vista every month.

My favorite month on the calendar was graced with the "Red Room." Matisse's masterpiece, the painting features a blond woman leaning over a table, its cloth swirling with cobalt blue flourishes, bright yellow lemons, two tan loaves of country bread. To the left of the table, a window opens out to a view of a serene Parisian monastery garden flowering with hazy white trees and yellow flowers flickering across the grass. It is said that Matisse painted the room blue first. Then, dissatisfied, he repainted it scarlet so the bright swirls of colors would invite viewers to contemplate the joys of the fecund table, and the contemplative garden. He painted each element of the room—the table, the chair, the window—with distinctly different brush strokes so the surface of the original painting is much more complicated than it first appears, pulsating with cross-rhythms.

Despite having to work out of a gutted-out supply closet, my days weren't empty or joyless. I had everything I was supposed to have by the age of thirty-two, at least on the surface: I was married, and had a five-year-old child. I had a salary and health benefits. Beyond that, I had the faith that I was becoming a writer. I'd already published three short stories and a slew of book reviews. I woke every morning at 5 a.m. to clock in two hours of writing before I began my "day life" as a mother and as the Assistant Director of the Writing Center. In between consulting sessions with students struggling with semi-colons, I taught writing classes and helped the Director of Creative Writing run the program's visiting writers series. That year, we'd created an esteemed writer-in-residence position that would allow us to bring a nationally-recognized writer to campus to live and teach an undergraduate fiction class for the entire month of January. The first esteemed visiting writer would be an American writer who lived in Copenhagen, Thomas E. Kennedy. He would arrive the following year, in January 2000.

I recall the Director of Creative Writing floating Tom's first novel, *Crossing Borders*, across my desk. "Have you read his work?" he asked. I opened the book, read the first page, and closed it. The prose was muscular and controlled, but not too controlled. The narrative voice was so distinct I heard it inside my ear canal. This was the writing of someone at the height of his powers and, as I learned later, it was fiction that cost him more than years to hone. Like the Matisse on my wall, Tom's writing was all bright swirls of color, and his novel was an invitation to contemplate a pulsating portrait of a man living in such existential pain that he burns down his "perfectly acceptable" life with hopes of re-inventing himself, and securing a more meaningful existence. I slipped the book into my satchel so I could take it home, and savor it—without having to stop every half-hour to consult with a student over her semi-colons.

The next day, a Saturday, I read Tom's book in one sitting on the heart-pine window seat in the master bedroom of my 1924 bungalow, across the room from the writing desk where I sat every morning at 5 a.m. Perhaps, on some level, I connected with Tom's anti-hero because I, too, had been feeling the pitfalls of a staid and secure life. During my dutiful 5 a.m. writing sessions, I'd been writing stories as airless as my supply-closet office at work. Perhaps I intuited what Tom already knew: Stories are not born of stillness; writers cannot work in isolation. We work alone, but we need the community of other writers. I had writer friends from graduate school, but we lived scattered across the U.S., writing our first books, working our first jobs. We no longer swapped book titles, or told stories on bar stools, or engaged in lingering conversations over cheap meals served with even cheaper wine. This silence and isolation from other writers had begun to dull my current attempts at writing.

I decided that I owed Tom a "thank you" for writing his book that spoke to me so directly. Then I had the idea that I'd like to hear his voice in my head a little longer. With the permission of the Creative Writing Director, I sleuthed out Tom's email from his application for the esteemed writer position with the college. In my thank you note, I outlined all I liked about his book, and asked if he'd ever allow me to interview him. His reply came immediately. "Why, yes," he wrote. "I'd be happy to give you an interview. When can we start?"

We agreed to begin the interview in May, after the spring term ended, but Tom offered to answer any "preliminary" questions before then. I shot off a basic question, "Why do you live in Copenhagen?" and he replied the next day with a two-page answer about how he came to live in Copenhagen. He also mentioned that he'd searched the storage space in his apartment building to gather documents that had been written about him, or by him. He asked for my street address so he could put them in the mail to me. About two weeks later, I received a fat package from Copenhagen that smelled of good must, like old paper and the ghost of cigarette smoke. It contained original copies of reviews of his books and other author interviews he'd given, as well as first-edition copies of his other published books—*A Weather of the Eye*, *The Book of Angels*, *Unreal City*, and *Drive Dive Dance & Fight*.

That was in March. As I prepared for our May interview, reading Tom's other published books and all the attendant reviews and interviews, I found myself shooting off two or three questions that came to me while reading his work. His replies always came the next day, and though his answers usually addressed the craft aspects of his work they were woven so seamlessly with anecdotes about his life that the two were as one. The interview developed organically, like a lingering conversation. For three months, I sent him two-three questions every few days, and he replied with voluptuous answers that were wise, funny, spontaneous, real. Slowly, as our dialogue unfolded that spring, I sometimes quoted him to my students. "We must be alert to the things happening in our hearts," I'd say. "This is the core of fiction." And I believed what I was repeating. As I began awakening to the things within my heart, and in the world around me, my fiction began to feel a little less airless.

By the time our May starting date arrived, I had a transcription of over sixty pages of an interview that needed to be shaped, and carved down into a publishable length. By the time *The Literary Review* accepted the revised, thirty-page interview for its Summer 2000 issue, I'd already met Tom in person. I recall picking him up at the local airport on a January Sunday, and trying to connect the physical human being with the large, effusive voice that had loomed in my head for almost a year. I recall locating an unassuming man in a long black coat, leaning against a wall near the gate where his flight had disembarked, quietly watching the other passengers file by, a wry smile on his face as he patiently waited to be identified by me. His luggage had been lost in Rome, and the campus apartment where he would live for January wasn't ready. He wasn't jet lagged, but he was hungry. These were the days of the old blue laws, when no restaurants served on Sundays anywhere in South Carolina, but I'd been to the grocery the day before. I had some cold cuts at home, I offered. Would he like to come to my house for some lunch?

I brought Tom home with me to eat sandwiches. My husband and I made a tray out of fresh deli meats, ham and roast beef, and we sliced a loaf of sourdough. We set out some smoked salmon with lemon and capers, a block of cheddar cheese with a sleeve of Ritz crackers. Dessert was a cluster of red grapes. As Tom tucked in to this humble fare, he confided that he was relieved and surprised that I'd brought him—a stranger—into my home for a meal. In Denmark, he said, all meal invitations, even those for family and friends, take weeks to organize; they involve flourished invitations sent out weeks in advance to a selective guest list. It takes days to prepare the several ritualized courses of food.

At the time, I was surprised that Tom thought himself a stranger in my home. Looking back, that's what makes the interview he gave me all the more remarkable. He didn't actually know me on that January day twenty years ago, but he'd given me so much of his time, his wisdom, and confidence that I no longer thought of him as a stranger. We did eventually become friends, and my husband and I have met up with him every few years in places as far flung as South Carolina, Rome, Kansas City, and Seattle. I believe he still counts me as a friend even though he's produced twenty more years of accomplishments, which include four story collections, two essay collections, two books of translations, six anthologies, and twelve novels, including *The Copenhagen Quartet*, four independent novels set in the Danish capital, and published by Bloomsbury. Despite his astonishing body of work and the much-deserved acclaim he's received since I first met him, this interview remains for me the document that forged our friendship. It affords a glimpse into the kind of human being, writer, teacher, mentor, and friend Tom Kennedy is.

Susan Tekulve
Survivors

ONE EARLY SEPTEMBER, a writer friend who taught English at a small college an hour south from the Carolina mill town where I live called me up and asked if I would help her rescue some books. My friend had found these books in a local thrift store, boxes of Penguin paperbacks stacked from floor to ceiling. Someone had tried to donate them to the nearby county correctional facility, but the prison had a strict policy against allowing paperbacks in its library. Apparently, this prison would only allow its prisoners to read hardbound editions. When the prison wouldn't take the paperbacks, somebody else had dumped them off at the thrift store. My friend was browsing this shop when she stumbled upon the store's owner dragging the boxes of books out the back door. Unable to sell the books, the owner was preparing to burn them in a steel drum in her parking lot.

"How many are there?" I asked over the phone.

"I don't know," my friend said. "A lot. Maybe 5,000? We've got them in a house on campus now. My students took a few, but we've got to move them all by tomorrow."

"What'll happen to the ones you can't give away?" I asked.

"We give them back to the store so that they can account for them, something about taxes," she said. "They're going to burn whatever we give back."

She paused, letting me reel from the image of book burning—not for political reasons or censorship, but because nobody wanted them. "There are some good titles left. Why don't you come down and take some?"

The next morning was a Friday. I set out for Clinton, South Carolina, in my black '89 Toyota Corolla, with my son's empty safety seat strapped in the back. All summer, Carolina heat had sucked the air conditioning fluid from my car, and I hadn't yet replaced it. As I drove the country road south, hot September wind swept through the car's open windows. I passed lone horses grazing sun-bleached pastures, ancient oaks bowing beneath a whole summer's weight of kudzu. Unseen cicadas churned inside the trees and roadside ditches, their trills thickening the blue morning air.

Driving through the deep greens and blues of late summer, I felt sweaty and urgent. I dreaded the thought of my friend having to give those books back to a thrift store owner bent on burning them because they would not sell as well as her second-hand treasures, such as aluminum Christmas trees, or sets of salt and pepper shakers shaped like friendly Italian chefs. I felt guilty too, greedy for the good titles that might be taken away by the students who'd gone to the campus house filled with books ahead of me. Certain those students were carrying off all the titles that could be mine, I stepped harder on the gas pedal, ignoring the hot gritty air that tore through my hair, the sparse and insignificant speed limit signs, those little white crosses that elegize car crash victims on country roadsides.

I arrived at the college campus and found the white Victorian house where my friend said the books would be. Its lawn and front door were camouflaged by an enormous oriental magnolia whose leaves spooned blooms the size and color of bone china teacups. I tried the door. It was locked, so I walked around back. Pushing open the screen door, I entered the dining room and found the books—classic, modern, and contemporary—stacked on every surface of the room, towering up to the crown molding that flared just beneath the twelve-foot ceiling. I identified titles by Kundera, V.S. Naipaul, and Neruda in the stacks along the dining room table. Over the fireplace mantel, I spied volumes one and two of the collected short stories of Somerset Maugham, Dennis Covington's *Salvation on Sand Mountain,* and Carol Shield's *The Stone Diaries.* Copies of Oliver Goldsmith's *The Vicar of Wakefield* and *The Lais of Marie De France* leaned into each other along the window seat below an elegant stained-glass panel.

The room smelled wonderfully of books that spilled into the hallway and up the back stairs to the second floor, but the house was nearly empty of people. Only a couple of students browsed the tables and chairs stacked with books, slipping one or two beneath their arms to take back to their dorm rooms. My friend came into the dining room, and we stood admiring the books, contemplating the bureaucratic whim that nearly destroyed them, the fortunate turn of fate that allowed her to shepherd them all to this temporary safe house.

I picked up the Kundera, Naipaul, and Neruda titles and walked over to the fireplace, filling my other arm with my selections from the mantel. I wasn't sure if I would be reading Oliver Goldsmith or the *The Lais of Marie De France* any time soon, but I collected those too. They were classics, I reasoned. There might come a day when I would regret not having them in my library.

"Are you sure it's okay for me to take all of these?" I asked. This was a small, ceremonial question. We both knew that I'd already claimed these books. We both knew that I'd be taking them home.

"Of course," she said.

"Well, I *could* take a few more back with me, maybe give some away to my students. Do you think that would be okay?"

"Take as many as you want. I've already taken as many as will fit in my apartment. I've got to have them all out of here by this afternoon. We have to give up the space for some student life function."

A plan formed. I would take the remaining books in the house, as many as my Corolla would hold, and bring them up to the college where I taught and worked as director of The Writing Center. The following Monday I would announce to the entire campus that there were free books in The Writing Center, that people need only visit to pick them up. This would allow me to place the surviving books in the hands of people more cash-poor and book-hungry than even I was at this time. It also would remove the stain for those students who were referred to The Writing Center after they'd already failed their writing assignments. These students could come to the center *before* they failed at writing, without sanction, to find a book they might read for pleasure.

I began stuffing books into my car, piling them in the front and back as high as I could, without completely obstructing my rear vision, filling the empty child safety seat. Next I put them in the trunk, nestling them around my spare tire. By the time I finished, I'd packed over two thousand books into my car, so many that my back bumper sagged.

I arrived home in mid-afternoon and unloaded the books into the dining room of my own house, a three-bedroom bungalow, stacking them above and below my dining room table, all along the heart-pine window seat. I'd been in such a hurry to rescue the books that I'd stopped sorting through the titles and simply loaded them all into my car; I needed to sort through them all again that weekend, decide which ones I would keep, which ones I would give away. I began putting the books I wanted to keep for myself in the front office of the house, leaving the rest on the dining room floor, beneath the table. All weekend, I shuffled and decided. The pile on my office floor grew as the piles in my dining room shrank.

At some point on Sunday afternoon, I invited over my neighbor, a retired librarian who hailed from a tiny town outside Mobile, Alabama. This town no longer existed, and she spent her days of retirement collecting photographs and documents of people who once lived there, recreating this Dixie ghost town with her memory and research. I told her about the prison library that wouldn't take the paperbacks, the thrift store owner who'd wanted to burn them. I confessed my inability to part with so many of the rescued books, even though I had no place to put them. My neighbor shook her head, her face impassive. I don't believe she was unmoved, just unsurprised. In her early eighties, she'd already survived three husbands, a child, and her entire hometown. She was used to the relentless tidal rhythm of loss and recovery.

"You're not being greedy for keeping them," she said. "Or, if you are being greedy, you're doing exactly as I would if I were in your place."

She took home a copy of *The Stone Diaries*. I took roughly fifteen hundred books up to the college on Monday morning, leaving the other five hundred in my home office. Throughout the day, students and colleagues descended upon The Writing Center, carrying off the books so swiftly that by the time I left at five p.m. there was only a tiny pile left behind. That night, I began double-shelving my own five hundred titles on my already-brimming shelves. I took my time, opening one to read its first line, putting it down to read the back cover of another. Soon the piles of books toppled, scattering into heaps. I nested among them, feeling luxurious, and deeply satisfied.

This was my first year working at the college, when I was still new to my duties and prone to taking my professional life home with me. In January of that year, I hosted our first visiting writer-in-residence for the college, Thomas E. Kennedy. A fiction writer from New York City, Tom had lived the last two decades of his life in Copenhagen, writing fiction and working for the Danish Medical Association. It never occurred to me that it was unusual to invite an internationally-acclaimed author into my house for a ham sandwich after I picked him up from the airport. I'd read all of Tom's books before he arrived, and I admired his work tremendously. I knew his writing, and therefore I knew *him*, or so I believed. It never occurred to me that we would *not* become friends. After I'd plied Tom with both a ham and a roast beef sandwich, I took him to see my collection of five hundred Penguin paperbacks, recounting the saga of how my friend and I rescued them from despotic prison bureaucrats and a fire.

Tom did become a good friend, and he has remained so for fourteen years. About a month ago, he sent a note, recalling my stash of rescued books that I showed off to him on the day we first met. He was writing to ask my permission to tell the story of "the book rescue" in an essay he was writing, but, in Tom-like fashion, he also encouraged me to write my own essay on this subject. In his essay, Tom writes that I stuck a fat Penguin Classic into his hand, saying, "Look. Pablo Neruda!" Only now, after reading his version of what happened, has it occurred to me that Tom did not want this book that I so heartily offered, mainly because he had even less bookshelf space in his Copenhagen apartment than I had in my tiny American bungalow. But when he saw that the book was by Neruda, he couldn't resist. An avid Neruda fan, he'd recently made a pilgrimage to the poet's home, Isla Negra, which now serves as an archive holding every imaginable relic of Neruda's personal and literary life. Tom hadn't seen the book I was trying to give him in the Neruda archives at Isla Negra. He'd never even known it existed. A memoir Neruda had been editing when he died in 1973, the book recounts his childhood, his travels, his flight from the Chilean police, his exile and life as a poet. In his essay, Tom writes that he kept the Neruda memoir I gave him, jotting down a single line from this book about the torture and death of a Santiago poet in 1920, Jose Domingo Gomez Rojas. Tom saved this line about the tortured and murdered poet on a scrap of paper. He tried to locate the poetry of Rojas, but couldn't find an English translation.

Around the time he discovered the poet Rojas in the Neruda memoir, Tom's job with the Danish Medical Association required him to translate into English the first psychiatric treatment manual for torture survivors, a Danish publication used by the Torture Rehabilitation Center in Copenhagen. The work required him to read graphic case studies about torture victims. He said these "tales of torment inflicted on human beings by other human beings" made him feel damaged to the point of needing to unburden himself in some way. He wrote a short story about a fictional Latin American torture survivor, a poet bearing a strong resemblance to the Santiago poet, Rojas. Then he wrote a second story on this subject. But the character and the story still weren't done with him yet. In 2002, he began a novel that opens with an image of a Chilean poet named Bernardo Greene. Outcast and hopelessly damaged by torture inflicted by his own government, he sits in a street-side café in Copenhagen on a chill June day. "How much of a survivor, in fact, survives?" Bernardo muses. "How much must remain of a survivor for him also to be called a man?"

Tom's book, *In the Company of Angels*, is a wise, beautiful novel that is now enjoying publication in Europe and the U.S. It's a contemporary work that I already count as great literature, and it blessedly continues to survive in this ever-changing publishing climate. As I sit here on this end-of-summer day, listening to the cicadas churn as loudly as they did the morning I trekked south to rescue those books from burning, I contemplate all the great print books that are rapidly disappearing from our lives, and I feel damaged. It seems that there is an almost mystical thread that connects the survival of a man with the survival of the printed word. Surely the torturing of a human being is a much more savage crime than book burning, but the bureaucratic impulse that nearly led to the burning of those five thousand books is the same impulse that allows despotic leaders to deny, and often hide, even greater crimes that dehumanize us as individuals and as a culture. The destruction of human flesh, and the destruction of the flesh made word by books, are both acts of savagery.

Good writers are part archivists, part guardian angels. They safeguard us by recalling and imagining stories about people, baring truths that the faint-hearted turn away from, and that the purely evil try to hide. Great writing also evolves from the reading of great books, as Tom's novel evolved from reading Neruda's memoir and from re-imagining the tragic figure of the lesser-known poet, Rojas. So now that I've been nudged gently into writing about this subject, I return to the questions asked by the torture survivor who haunts the pages of a book that arose in the mind of a fiction writer as he read a great poet's book that survived bureaucratic whim and fire. There are those who would say that literature will survive, but in a different form, and I heartily applaud the writers, editors, and publishers who are transitioning gracefully into other forms of publication so that literature will endure. I am in awe of librarians who continue to create free literacy programs for every member of our communities, despite the continuous cuts to their yearly budgets. Still, I wonder. If the printed book disappears from our daily lives, if we can't hold a book in our hands and savor it page by page, how much of ourselves will survive, and how much of ourselves will remain wholly human?

H. L. Hix
This Tom

There's a passage in Thomas E. Kennedy's essay "Life in Another Language" in which he is not so much explaining differences between his acquired Danish and his native English as *relishing* them. He observes that Danish can be quirky, as in the common exclamation upon receiving a gift, "*Hold da kæft, er du rigtig klog?*" meaning "Shut your mouth, are you really stupid?" Danish can be very direct, he notes, as in the word for a bra, *brystholder*. Wrapping up the passage, he adds that "Danish can also be circumspect. To be in '*vældig godt*' humor (very good humor) or to have 'a couple under the vest' is to be pretty drunk."

I have seen Tom Kennedy often with a tumbler of Hennessey in his hand, or with a pint of pilsner on the table in front of him, but I have never seen him with a couple under his vest. Because I know Tom through the low-residency MFA program at Fairleigh Dickinson University, I am certain that a fair number of others have seen of Tom just what I have seen, and that they, thinking of Tom, see in their minds a Tom very like the one I see in my mind.

This Tom is seated on the bench beside the main entrance to the spartan Park Avenue dorm on the FDU campus, with the aforementioned tumbler in one hand and a cigarillo in the other. This Tom is talking, and whoever is seated next to him is laughing.

This Tom is at the lectern in Hartman during an MFA residency, reading his essay "I Am Joe's Prostate" to the community. He has to pause often for the gales of laughter. Because we the audience are seated at those circular plywood tables, this Tom can't see what is in my line of sight, the face of the person across the table from me, and thus facing me rather than Tom. This individual (nameless here to protect the innocent, but a person possessed of a prostate) is wincing at every description, getting queasy until I think he's going to have to leave the room. Until then, I had thought "turning green" was only metaphorical.

This Tom is in Hartman again, but this time for a generative workshop led by another faculty member. We've all been given a prompt, and five minutes to jot something down in response to it. The rest of us are managing a sentence fragment or a clunky paragraph, and this time I'm actually getting nothing written because I'm mesmerized, watching Tom move that Mont Blanc of his across line after line of his note pad, filling the page, writing as fast and fluently as if he were taking dictation from God.

As maybe he was. After all, there's another passage in Tom's work, this one at the very end of *Beneath the Neon Egg*, that (never mind it's a fictional description of the book's protagonist, Patrick Bluett) I've always taken as a sly self-description by Tom, a little window onto his frame of mind when he writes. Coltrane's tenor, the passage says, "loosens the fist of his mind so it can move with the urgency of the notes to escape form, to find the source of cohesion, vibration." This Tom, the Tom who, because there is an ocean between me and Denmark, I only get to laugh with and listen to in my head, keeps company with Coltrane, on the far side of form.

Steve Davenport
Tom's Bar, Where Everybody Knows Your Name

MY TOM KENNEDY BAR STORY starts on MySpace fifteen years ago. My first collection of poems, *Uncontainable Noise*, had been published in Columbus, Ohio, by a small, non-academic press. I didn't know what to do for it, so I went online to see what others did and soon found two young guys I knew, Kyle Minor and Okla Elliott, Ohio State MFA students who had taken an interest in my poems when the collection first came out. As I made the occasional lonely post, I watched them move about and make connections, promote things and people they liked. Two of those people were writers I had never heard of, Duff Brenna and Thomas E. Kennedy. A couple of names. There were probably other names, but those stood out because Kyle and Okla kept mentioning them together. They were names to me only. I should read something by them, I told myself, and then didn't.

Jump forward a year. Okla Elliott asks me to submit "Murder on Gasoline Lake," an essay of mine first published in *The Black Warrior Review* around the time of my first MySpace efforts, to a New American Press chapbook contest that he is helping run. He promises me that all entries will be read by the judge with the writer's name blocked. I enter the contest and forget about it. A few months later I am about to pull out of my garage for a drive to Southern Illinois University Edwardsville, my undergrad alma mater, for a reading with, yes, Kyle Minor, when my phone buzzes. Since all writers' lives are scripted like movies, the caller is Okla, who tells me my essay has won the contest. It takes me a few seconds to remember what he is talking about. Who was the judge, I ask. Duff Brenna, he says. That name, I think, from MySpace. The one that sounds like he played ball for the Detroit Tigers in the 1950s. I should thank him, I say to myself and maybe out loud, and read something of his. So Okla gives me his email address and soon I order *The Holy Book of the Beard* and hot damn that's a novel. So is *The Book of Mamie*, which I read next while exchanging emails with this great American writer, one who liked my writing before we became friends. And because sometimes you can't make up things that happen because they just do, Duff introduces me via email to that other MySpace name, Thomas E. Kennedy, another equally friendly guy, Tom, whose *Kerrigan in Copenhagen A Love Story* I quickly read and fall in love with. By the end of the novel, last chapter, I believe Gideon's take on Kerrigan: "'You got fuckin' talent,' he says. 'You deserve an Oscar, an Emmy, a Tony, and a Golden Palm.'" But I believe even more Kerrigan, and love him for it, when he replies, "I feel dirty," to which Gideon says, as I would have, "Yeah but that's when it's best." And right there in the next paragraph, in a book full of writers' names, a library full of things and people to read, whose name pops off the page? Duff Brenna. One great writer naming another, who happens to be a friend. And in my in-box? Two great American writers who are now my friends.

There was no turning back. I was living in a movie made for writers, a world I planned to keep riding through the universe. What happens next follows the movie script but could use some help from a fact-checker. The next year, I get a request from Walter Cummins at *The Literary Review* to contribute poems (twenty to twenty-five pages) to their upcoming chapbook issue. Never mind that I had never heard of Walter or *The Literary Review*. They had never heard of me either until Tom Kennedy showed up with a couple of copies of *Uncontainable Noise* for the poetry editors, David Daniel and Renée Ashley, and told Walter about my murder essay. Never mind that I said I had enough poems to fill twenty to twenty-five pages when I didn't and wasn't sure I would. I was at that time just starting on the curtal sonnets that would define my second collection, *Overpass*. What I really wanted was to get my fiction, pieces from my *Black Guy Bald Guy* series, in front of people and purposely waited until it was too late for anyone at *The Literary Review* to remind me I was supposed to be submitting poetry only. The curtal sonnets I sent did well enough that word came back to me that Renée loved them. As I got to know Renée through funny, late-night emails, she told me she was getting a new dog. Black and nearly bald, she said. So she named him Steve. And who's the angel who set all of this chapbook-building and dog-naming in motion, the guy who led me to a bar where everyone is getting to know my name? Tom Kennedy, of course. And the bar? Tom's Bar.

When I set out to ask writer friends to record some of my poems for a project I was calling "Soundtrack for My Funeral" as an in-joke about a stroke I'd suffered and survived a few years earlier, I approached friends at *The Literary Review*: Renée Ashley, Kathleen Graber, Walter Cummins, and, yes, Tom Kennedy, who recorded two of mine. One of the poems, "Last Night My Bed a Boat of Whiskey Going Down," led to an email I couldn't have imagined I'd ever open my in-box to, one in which Tom asks me if he can use the title as the title of a book of his. Imagine you'd written a sonnet with the title "Midsummer Night's Dream Yodel Sonnet" or "Beloved Bomb Sonnet" and your friend Shakespeare or Toni Morrison writes to ask if they can use it for the title of something of theirs. Even if you knew from then on search engines would blow gaskets trying to find your poem, you would say yes. You would say Yes, Please. Because of the title of that poem and because Tom Kennedy is an angel and he runs a bar where everyone knows everyone's name, he talked up my titles and poems to Bob Stewart, then editor of *New Letters*, who suggested I send some poems. I did and Bob published three of them. One of them, "Dear Last Nerve," Tom liked so much he sent me the very Tom-like email blast: "You are the freakin' Poet Laureate of my life." What could be better than that and even more Tom-like? I'll tell you: the story he either told me in person over drinks when I drove up to Harper College to hear him read or in an email I now can't find. (Where's the fact-checker when you need one?) Tom admitted being a little drunk when he entered a bookstore he knew in Copenhagen, cornered the owner about this great American poet he knew, and either recited or read him "Last Night My Bed a Boat of Whiskey Going Down." The owner's response? According to Tom, he shrugged, wasn't impressed. I laughed and laughed at how Tom-like that was. Even if everyone knows your name at Tom's Bar, which is an international, mobile bar by the way, they don't all have to love you, but they all, if Tom has his way, have to do you the courtesy of hearing you.

The history of American literature is the history of friendships, of connections, of what I've come to call "literary citizenship." Tom Kennedy and the generous bar he led me to, Tom's Bar, where everyone knows everyone's names because of Tom, taught me that.

Steve Davenport, Okla Elliot, John Griswold, Duff Brenna

T Nicole Cirone
Dart Night and the Miracle of the Three Bullseyes

IT IS TOO WARM IN THE LIBRARY, and too calm, and instead of your usual red wine, you accept a glass of vodka, straight up. You never drink vodka, let alone straight up, but it seems to be that sort of night, midway through the Winter Residency at Wroxton College. You've just come in from the Italian Gardens, where some of the cool kids are hanging out and smoking pot, brought back from London by one of the coolest cool kids—a writer from Brooklyn with gorgeous hair and a writerly aura. You were never one for smoking, so when Dr. Tom found you outside, standing awkwardly in the cold among the cool kids, and not smoking, and asked you if you would like to move inside, to the library, where people were drinking and reading Tarot cards, you said yes without hesitation. Tom thought it would be more your thing. And it was, for a while. But now, the crowd is dispersing, it is too warm, and you are getting sleepy; it is still early, and there's lots of vodka, so you both decide to leave the library and take a walk.

You run into another professor and a classmate of yours who are going to the student lounge in the basement to play darts, so, although you have never really, actually played darts, you are now willing to do pretty much anything other than smoke outside in the middle of January or sit in a too-warm library and read Tarot cards, so you accept their challenge.

You aren't sure exactly how the scoring works, but you do know that a bullseye is the best score you can get. The other team—J and D—start. You and Tom are hanging back and drinking your vodka. You share stories from your Catholic school upbringings. "Leave room for the Holy Spirit!" you joke as you both reach back to balance your tumblers on the narrow ledge behind you. You commiserate over the fart smell pervasive to all-boys' schools—which he remembers from his high school days, and which you are accosted with daily as an English teacher at a Catholic boys' prep school. Tom teaches you the Danish word for fart, "*prut,*" and you vow to put that on your next vocabulary test as a bonus question. You almost forget about the dart game, but your opponents are cheering, and you wonder if you're supposed to be doing something. You also wonder if there is a Patron Saint of Dart Players that you can pray to for intercession because you'll need some kind of miracle to come close to hitting the board.

Neither of you play darts, you confide to one another, but you don't let on to your opponents; and, trying to figure out how this all works, you watch them hit the board and write their scores on the little chalkboard. A few rounds into the game, you still don't have any points, and your opponents are throwing the darts for what seems like so long you don't know if you will ever have another turn, but it's not like you really care. You feel warm and happy, and you and Tom are engaging in the most excellent sort of friendly trash talk about your opponents. The lively mood is magnified by the good-natured banter and the vodka and the fact that you are playing darts in the basement of what used to be an Augustinian monastery and a famously grand manor house before it became a college.

And then suddenly, something, well, not so good, happens with the other team's throw, and it's finally your team's turn. Out of respect for your teacher, and also because you aren't really sure yet what to do, you let Tom play first for your team. He hits the board, somewhere along the bottom, and your opponents slap hands and laugh.

"NOTHING," smirks J.

"Why nothing?" you ask. "He hit the board. We should get something!"

He tries to explain the scoring to you, but it still doesn't make any sense, and you point the injustice out to him.

"That's not how it works," he shrugs, and louder and with greater pleasure than the first time, he proclaims, "NOTHING!"

You resign yourselves to the fact that it is a stupid game. You make up funny cheers and laugh at yourselves. Tom is playing it cool, with a dart in one hand and a half-finished glass of straight vodka in the other, and now a group of undergrads has gathered to watch. Spurred on by the crowd of kids and wanting to show your opponents with their "NOTHING!" that you mean business, you confidently grab the dart from Tom's hand and step in front of the dartboard. You hesitate, for just a moment, before the circles and numbers that mean nothing to you. And then, the dart leaves your hand and whizzes through the air, landing directly in the center of the board. A BULLSEYE. No one, not even you, can believe this. Your opponents are shocked.

The undergrads laugh and chalk it up to beginner's luck. Then, in ensuing turns, you throw two more bullseyes. Three bullseyes! It is nothing short of a miracle, and now that you have stunned the entire crowd, anything could happen. And it does: you and Tom win the dart game. "NOTHING!" you laugh as you cheer together, clink half-filled vodka glasses and marvel at the Miracle of the Three Bullseyes.

Even J, ever-ready with his snarky, "NOTHING!" is speechless. Now you and Tom are the ultimate cool kids—the Dart Night Champions, not just of the game but of the miraculous *three-bullseye game*. You could be in a Hall of Fame at the college. Maybe they will hang a plaque in your honor, right there in the student lounge. There are so many possibilities running through your head as J snaps, "NOTHING!" and everyone laughs because you are all writers and you love irony, especially tonight, which from now on will be known as Dart Night, when you and Dr. Tom have become legends.

And as you are high on miracles and possibilities and a good amount of vodka, there is nothing more to do than celebrate with the wonderful, hot pizza the undergrads have ordered and left, momentarily, on the pool table. You feel only slightly guilty when you, Tom, and your Dart Night opponents sneak off to the library with the entire pizza and a glowing sense of victory.

Gladys Swan
Four Decades

Dear Tom,

I had just about finished a long letter to you several weeks ago, but the computer ate it, and I'm having to start it over. Difficult for me, but this morning I went to a computer expert, and some of my problems have been resolved. And I try to catch my many mistakes by having the reader in the computer read to me.

But it's slow work. I think you know about such things. I do want to tell you that you have been much in my thoughts as I have gotten Walter's accounts of what you have been going through and its impact on your life. You have my concern and empathy. That you managed to complete a novel with only the use of a forefinger is a feat beyond belief. Congratulations on its publication.

What I particularly want to tell you is how much your friendship has meant to me over the years, ever since you came into the Vermont program and worked with me. It was a great pleasure having a part in your efforts there. I think my main function was to cheer you on. Your talent was obvious and it was clear that you were willing to work hard to get results.

I think that anyone who had a connection with the MFA Program in the '80s, before it got so big, was given a gift that went beyond workshops and critiques and enhanced the very good things in the program itself. There was a kind camaraderie among faculty and students that I greatly appreciated. I think of the many nights we gathered after the readings, frequently in Gordon's room for drinks and conversations and jokes. Being in an atmosphere in which we had a common purpose and an interest in literature and a dedication to writing gave us a sense of the value of what we were doing. Perhaps it made us less lonely.

I also enjoyed those excursions to town for a breakfast of "eponymous" Raymond's pancakes or a good seafood dinner. But the high point for me was the Danish Breakfast you created with such wonderful bread, cheese, and herring. I had never before begun the day with schnapps, an uplifting experience, which I would be glad to repeat at a moment's notice. I think it gave a certain oomph to the workshops afterwards.

After you got your degree, I was delighted to follow your career, to read your first published fiction through your creation of a significant world of significant human experience in the bars of Copenhagen or the wrestling with angel or the anguish of *Greene's Summer*. Your fiction alone would have established your reputation. But in the process you became a Man of Letters with your reviews, interviews, translations, and essays. I think your essay on verisimilitude is one of the best essays I have read on an aspect of fiction. You have certainly earned the recognition you have received culminating in an award. None higher in your adopted country. Along with all this, you have been a supporter of my work, in fact, a mainstay.

It was a fine thing for me to have your review of *Carnival* in *The Sewanee Review*, an honor to be included in your dissertation and in "Two Books for Tomorrow's Readers." I think you may have been the first to understand what my work has really been about, to see its dedication to the imagination as a way of knowing. Your valuing of my work has continued over the years, with your many nominations of my stories for the Pushcart Prizes. And your comments on the story I wrote following upon "The Snow Queen" were what finally convinced Bob Shepard to publish it.

And your invitation to have your class of teachers read and respond to my work was more significant to me than you might have guessed. I was very anxious about being in the midst of that group. Theirs was a different culture after all, I was afraid they wouldn't have much interest or liking for those stories you gave them to read. What surprised and delighted me was that the stories apparently met some of their own concerns and experiences. That was a gift.

I visited you three times in Copenhagen. Your family gave me a fine welcome. I had paintings by Daniel and Isabel on my bedroom door. I believe you took me out to lunch and I got to know something of the Danish sandwich. I believe you introduced me to eel, to a wonderful discovery.

You also took me to the Writers' Union, where I met Benny Anderson, whose work I have enjoyed. I still have one of my favorite quotes from him.

We did have some fine encounters at the AWP, in Geneva, Oberdiesbach. You and Daniel visited me here once. And then there was that fabulous 70th birthday party cum literary festival that marks one of the special events of my life. It was such fun. So great to have half a dozen people there that I really care for. Such diversity of talent, and we got to show our stuff around town. You showed your video, I remember.

Finally, what has been such a gift to me is the creation of Serving House Books. I can hardly put words to what I owe to Walter and you for its existence. It has given me an opportunity to publish my books and have them in print. An opportunity I doubt would otherwise have existed.

And so, dear Tom, this letter comes to you with love, admiration, and gratitude.

And as Benny Anderson put it, "Life's not the worst thing we've got. And the coffee's getting hot."

Christina Warren

I miss Tom. He was a tremendously kind and generous person. When I found my name and paragraph in his latest novel(s), I smiled—a lot. I may never accomplish anything in my life, but by golly, I have a mention in a Tom E. Kennedy novel. I love the mysterious way he moves between fiction and non-fiction—leaving me wondering if these books are autobiographical or not.

Linda Lappin

I FIRST MET TOM KENNEDY in Castle Well, the Netherlands, where I attended his fiction class at the *Ploughshares* workshop over twenty years ago. We met exactly three times after that, always in workshop settings. I have never spent more than an hour with him—for a coffee or aperitif in the company of other writers. Mostly our contact has taken place through emails, and yet Tom has had an enormous impact on my writing career. Aside from his insightful advice, savvy editing suggestions, world-opening reading recommendations, and generous sharing of opportunities and contacts, for which I am indebted to him, Tom Kennedy also passed along to me a piece of philosophy that continues to rattle about in my mind like a pebble in my shoe. Just a phrase dropped at the end of a class, addressed to a student who had asked a question—what exactly I can't remember—but Tom's answer was: "The writing is its own reward." I didn't know it then, but he was quoting Henry Miller, a writer whom in some ways he resembles. Like a koan, this little phrase seems easy to interpret—you'll find a hundred blogs on the subject, but really getting it and accepting it is quite a different matter, as its meaning constantly shifts. Sometimes when writing feels like a punishment, an addiction, or a curse, I ask myself—well, where would I be without it, and an abyss yawns. Through writing, we knit out of our own substance a suit to wear in the days when we escape the abyss as Thomas E. Kennedy has done with masterly intent.

David Applefield
Interviewing Tom

The late David Applefield, an American expatriate in Paris, with a wife and children, was a novelist who edited the significant international literary magazine *Frank*. In addition to publishing Tom Kennedy's work and collaborating on many editorial projects, they shared the experiences of life as an expat, meeting at writers' gathering in European cities.

This selection is excerpted from *Frank 18* – September 2001, "A Literary Conference Call with David Applefield [*Frank*], Duff Brenna, and Thomas E. Kennedy."

Frank: Tom, how have readers surprised you?

Kennedy: For me intuition is essential. I don't want to have an intellectual understanding of a story I am writing, if ever, until long after it is done. I need *not* to have. And surprisingly, after groping through the dark of the characters' actions to find the story, a fairly clear kind of "meaning" often proves to be there anyway, constructed by my unconscious, or whatever. If I understood the thing from the start, I would never write the story because if my writing doesn't yield a discovery to me, it is pretty worthless from my point of view as a writer. I write to understand, to discover what is there. Not to explain what I already know. Sometimes after a public reading, the audience will ask questions and it amazes me how smoothly the essence of a story is grasped by at least one of them—an essence which to me was inseparable from all the story's elements (voice, character, plot, language, movement, process), and which somebody suddenly sums up in a sentence. If I had grasped these instant summaries in advance, the "cliché gong" might have sounded in my head and killed the story for me before it was born . . .

Frank: Tom, you're an avid writing teacher. How do you teach aspiring fiction writers to trust what comes naturally while also insisting on a strict attention to craft?

Kennedy: For me, the hardest thing to teach, but one of the things that has occasionally seemed to work, is to advise the person struggling with a story to take a walk with its main character or with its voice. To imagine the narrative persona strolling through a known or imagined landscape and seeing that landscape through the persona's sensibility and allowing language to crystallize around the thread of that movement. As often as not, I find my character or my voice will lead me to the heart of my fiction and reveal what the story is seeking.

Frank: Don't you often have your writing students shine flashlights into the dark corners of their childhood to see what really lurks within? I remember once in Amsterdam you completely freaked out a young writer by having her go down into the cellar of her house when she was five.

Kennedy: Yes, I do a "basement" exercise which I contributed to Pam Painter's book *What If*—which seems to have been useful to a number of workshop participants. The object is to find an unknown door by traveling through remembered sensations into the basement of your childhood home, by remembering the smell of your father, the sound of your mother's voice, etc. Once you find the door, you open it and start to write. It is supposed to convey you from deep remembrance into an instant outflow of expression. Afterwards, those in the workshop who wish to are invited to read what they have written . . .

Frank: Tom, at the end of the first chapter of *Neon Egg*, your protagonist, Bluett, thinks about what he's done wrong in his family life. Does the act of writing, especially at this stage of your life, force you to contemplate how you have conducted your personal affairs?

Kennedy: There is no doubt that my aesthetic development is informed by my existential experience. One learns and grows from one's personal failures as well as from the occasional enlightenment or even triumph of emotion with which one is blessed. Having children greatly enhanced my capacity to experience existence, I think, and to experience love, and having been married for nearly a quarter century was a tremendous experience for me. So, yes, I do contemplate my personal affairs constantly—as one reviewer said of one my characters "constantly assessing." I want to know what has happened to me in my life, and to do that I have to think about it from as many angles as I can, and that experience is certainly closely related to one dimension of the progress of my writing. Other dimensions would include those of language growth and experience, philosophical expansion, historical perspective, immersion in the hated elements, etc.

Frank: As readers we connect to the lives and pain of the characters we spend time with, but we are obscured from what the writer endures. Tell us about your "weight of living." What have you been living, psychically, while writing *Beneath the Neon Egg*?

Kennedy: *Beneath the Neon Egg* started with my divorce and two images of Copenhagen—the frozen street lake beneath the window of my apartment and an animated neon sign on a brick wall on the other side of the lake. The sign depicts a neon chicken that goes through a series of movements resulting in its laying a big neon egg that I saw that winter again and again reflected in the black frozen ice of Black Dam Lake. The egg would glow there on the wall for a moment, then go out, and the chicken would reappear to go through the motion of laying the egg again. This neon sign has been there for many years—a dairy ad—and is a kind of emblem of Copenhagen. It became an emblem for me of the winter of my discontent—those frozen months following my divorce. In that state of mind, I somehow conceived a character named Bluett ("Blue" for short). Bluett is an Irish name pronounced "Blew It," but that association, believe it or not, managed to evade me while I wrote the book. Bluett, it turned out was a freelance translator who, in order to survive financially had to translate five pages a day every day. Bluett, too, is divorced and alone and wandering the frozen streets of winter, seeing that neon egg, and I followed him in my mind's eye to the end of the journey of a winter. In the background I've placed the music of John Coltrane's magnificent jazz symphony, *A Love Supreme*—the four parts of the novel are written parallel to that symphony, one feature of which is the disintegration of musical notes into pure vibration preliminary to the creation of a new reality—the pure love of God, the supreme love.

So Bluett takes a journey through his isolation and physical longing to the beginning of an understanding of the divine connectedness of the human race. What the character experiences is pure fiction, but the emotional course beneath the fiction paralleled my own emotional life at that time. I suspect that most or many novels do that for their writers and hopefully also offer themselves to be translated into the reader's emotional reality as well.

The new novel I have just finished [never published], *Waiting for the Barbarians,* begins in a spiritual sense from the other side of that discontent. It is subtitled *A Love Story,* and that is what it is—a story of a man's love of life and all that life can offer, even if his consciousness is defined by great pain. The starting image for me to write this was a true story of a mother who killed her children, husband, and siblings in cold blood with a pistol. I met the only child to survive the bloodbath, he had hidden away beneath a bed, listening to the mother searching to get him too. Paradoxically, the novel was a pure joy to write because there is room in it for everything I care about —history, literature, music, physical joy, the intense pleasures of surrendering to the unimpeachable desire to live and be happy in spite of all.

A writer produces a story much the same way that an oyster produces a pearl—around some grain of irritant.

Roger Derham
Wandering after Kerrigan

We had so many good days (and nights!) wandering after Kerrigan, you and I, and I am forever the better for it. We will all meet again in the "Fifth Season". "Go n-éirí an bóthar leat Tomás" (May the road rise to meet you, Tom).

Thomas E. Kennedy has died and I am.... we all are poorer for his passing.

Thomas was an author who anchored our young publishing company 20 years ago with the four great novels that we midwifed into the world; a former important contributor to the work of and employee of the Danish Medical Association; a father; a lover; a teacher; a friend and most of all a Copenhagener.

Farewell Tom. We will meet again in the Fifth Season.

Azly Rahman
Yes, indeed, Tom, it is going to be published. By Penguin Random House. THANK YOU!

"Azly's creative thesis is a fitting project for my final thesis as the second reader before I retire at the end of June 2017. It is quite simply superb—and publishable."—Tom Kennedy

I STILL HAVE THE WORDS *"This is quite simply superb—and publishable!"* in Tom Kennedy's handwriting, etched on my MFA in NonFiction thesis. Tom was my second reader, with Walter Cummins as my advisor. I consider both my "gurus" to use the Sanskrit term as a spiritual teacher who helped me out as a writer. From "Gu" to "Ru" from Darkness to Light. Yes, these are the Socrates and Plato of the cave of my MFA program at Madison where I surrendered my mind, body, and soul to be turned into what I told my first teacher, Minna Proctor, a "gangsta writer"!

And here I am reading Tom Kennedy's words of inspiration, as I submitted the synopsis of my memoir to my publisher in Singapore who's taking care of the Southeast-Asia and India regions of the English Language World Series for the newly restructured global Penguin-Random House.

My dream came true. I wanted to be in the same house, under the same roof with major writers who have been with Penguin—contemporary ones such as Toni Morrison, Salman Rushdie, Don DeLillo, and those in the past such as Hemingway. Yes, that logo of the penguin and orange label was preserved.

Thank you, Tom, and I will always remember your words which I reread, as I await my memoir *Grandma's Gangsta Chicken Curry and Stories of My Hippie Sixties* in its final copyedit stage, and as I continue to work on my novel *The Great Ganja War: Book 1* to be submitted to Penguin, again. That will be based on my second MFA thesis in Fiction, from FDU too!

I want to honor Tom by sharing what he wrote that inspired me to continue working on the manuscript for my first memoir, and my ninth book to date:

It is spellbinding reading the way Mr. Rahman works the "patois" of jar-

gon hip and Malay, Islamic, Chinese, Indian, bling-bling hip hop, sixties and seventies American and British rock and roll, and original Malay and other magical realism and international ghost-lore (the personifications therein are certainly magic realism), a trace of style from Mr. Rahman's inherited and adopted languages—now poetic, now lyrical, now down-to-earth, now religio-ethical, historical, sociological, and economic post-colonial academic considerations—and renders it responsive to his subject matter. It is an integral part of his subject matter.

I think of Junot Dìaz, without the footnotes, except that it is about Malay rather than Dominican, told in Mr. Rahman's patois rather than English and Spanish patois; of Gordon Weaver's Foto Joe Yamaguchi in The Eight Corners of the World, except about Malay and the U.S. and the U.K. rather than about Japan and the U.S. with a Japanese-English patois; and a tincture of Alain de Botton's creative nonfiction books.

This is contemporary, a Muslim view of the world married to an American and British colonial and post-colonial view (not so post in the case of the U.S.), sorted out intelligently so that the humanistic, ethical values, through the dramatic, lyrical prose stand clear. It has the value of irony, but especially of humanism and ethics.

As to verisimilitude, there is a bouquet of smells of "petrol-diesel-stinky-river-rotten-egg smell of the town of Johor Bahru." As to magical realism cum everyday experience, there is a parrot that tells, by picking up cards, "the exact date one would die." As to narrative drive, the narrator vividly comes to life!

Chapter by chapter, Mr. Rahman tells in extremely well-written language, composed of the patois of high and low, of Malay and British and American, of Bollywood and American movies, and U.S. and U.K. and Jamaican and world rock and roll: From "Grandma's Gangsta Chicken Curry," where the five brothers gleefully select a chicken from the barnyard for the Grandpa to bleed to death in Muslim and Hebrew fashion; to the "Screamings and Slaughterings" of the Chinese minority on May 13, 1969 (which is prepared by sleight-of-hand of two Islamic jihadists); to the "Appeasing Pain" of religion which causes the pain in the first place, of the Sharia Law, of the beatings in religious schools, and ritual circumcision of twelve-year-old boys told by the fear and flesh of the narrator; to the "Dead Village Talking," killed by various drugs, especially "gangsta" pot from southern Thailand, while the narrator was saved by his love of words and of books and of rock and roll; to the "Fourteen Nights They Died," where we see the ironic and literal clash of cultures of a fourteen-year-old Taliban (moving through the world in white robes as though the world was filthy) and Sharia Law and a school musical talent contest and how *a bogus Buddha seen on a roof, rubbing his stomach and speaking low-pidgin Malay, creates havoc in the girl's dormitory; to the "Men Loving Men," which in comic-realistic terms speaks of the Colgate-brand snickering and unethical abandon of "men loving boys," with boys who could not "see the gates of Paradise in another man's eyes," but the "indescribable beauty in a woman's"; to "Grandpa's Kite," where the narrator makes, following his grandpa's skill, what he doesn't see as a colonial Union Jack, but the irony of the chapter that tells it is post-colonial; to the "Closing," which turns into a beautiful poem, summarizing the seven earlier chapters.*

I can only say, Bravo, Mr. Rahman! This will be published because it is important and professional, exhibiting the compassion, respect and care for human beings caught up in a religious, socio-economic, colonial/post-colonial storm, in well-composed, beautifully-written language.

I wish you well, Tom.
My guru.
My inspiration to continue writing stories you think important.
Publishable.
Because they are important, as you said!

Warm wishes,
Azly Rahman

Lisa del Rosso
Tom Kennedy Sings On

One boozy summer's night late,
at an outdoor table,
Tom Kennedy found out I was a singer, so
he asked me what most do:
"Sing something for me."
I never do this but
wanted to oblige, because of the drink
or the asking, or because Tom, at that point, to me,
was a legend and came with legendary stories,
so I did not want to disappoint.

All I could think of was Mozart,
the brat genius
So I leaned in and in my best Cherubino
sang a bit of "Voi Che Sapete" from
Figaro, into Tom's ear
though I am not a mezzo
not an opera singer
don't care for opera
But I do love Mozart.

And Tom smiled and sighed
and said, "That was wonderful I
wish I could do that, too."
His face, lit up with admiration and wonder,
made me happy.

Then he told me a story
about being in a pub—
with David Daniel, I think?
About being in a pub the worse
for wear and he told
the proprietor he was going to sing

the entire score of "Oklahoma,"
this part delighted me
the first musical I was ever in.
And Tom Kennedy did sing
the entire score of "Oklahoma"
at the top of his lungs, he said,
and only when he began to sing
the entire score of "Oklahoma"
for a second time
at the top of his lungs
did the proprietor blow his
stack and throw him the hell out.

And I don't know which I liked
best—
the expression on Tom Kennedy's face
after I sang for him
Or
the image of Tom Kennedy
singing the score of "Oklahoma"
for a second time
at the top of his lungs
right before he's thrown
the hell out of the pub.

Magic

David Daniel, Tom,
me and Vodka once spent
a long night together
in Tom's room
during a residency
I remember laughter
and
basking in the warm glow
of Tom's stories til dawn.
When we finally left
Tom's
reeling out into the light
punch drunk
we both knew
we had been given
an ephemeral gift
by a conjuror.

Mark Cox
Tom Kennedy Tribute

TOM, AS I THINK ABOUT YOU TODAY, I can't help but hear you very clearly in my head. It is all about voice, whether it be the narrators of your unique, intelligent, and ballsy prose, or the tenors of our conversations. I remember you as a vital force. Loquacious, animated, and infectious—a world-class raconteur—your energy could take over and enliven any gathering. At parties during graduate school you were a popular fount of arcane knowledge and trivia. The intimate details of the sex life of the blue whale comes to mind! I believe you regaled us with those particular factoids during one of the famous Danish Breakfasts you instituted—breakfasts that sent us all into our morning workshops smelling like herring, and entirely too full of aquavit, but with a deep sense of friendship. And indeed, you are the kind of steadfast friend one always wants in their corner when they need help the most. Witness your dedication to Gordon Weaver's work; without you, Gordon's tour de force novel *The Eight Corners of the World* would be out of print. Tom, you are a stand-up guy and are fondly remembered by myriad friends and readers. I feel fortunate to have known you and will always be grateful for your belief in *Sorrow Bread*, and my work generally.

Susann Cokal
Lucky Coincidence

Many of us read for the pleasure of meeting a new friend, someone whose life they're sharing in a deep and significant way. So I was very lucky when *The New York Times Book Review* asked me to review *Kerrigan in Copenhagen*, which I did while I was on a (coincidental) family visit to Denmark and could fact-check the serving house offerings myself. It would have been inappropriate to go up to tavern patrons and ask, "Are you Tom Kennedy?" but of course I imagined that I saw you a dozen times. And in reading the book, I did get to know a remarkable character, someone who leapt off the page. I thought about Kerrigan long after I closed the cover.

Getting that review was even luckier than I realized at first, because you and I really did become friends off the page. You wrote me a nice note afterward, and then we exchanged books, figured out that you live around the corner from the building where my mum grew up, and compared notes on migraines and head injuries and Kierkegaard. We even chatted in depth about the antique family silver I was polishing in order to trace the hallmarks and see where my grandparents' friends had bought their wedding gifts. We debated the merits of the sack dress and argued over the date ABBA released "Dancing Queen." And I told you about the murder of my uncle, who shared a name with one of your friends. Things sometimes got kind of dark, but that's life.

You have that gift of making family out of strangers.

Naturally, I hit you up for a contribution to the magazine I was editing, *Broad Street*. You gave me *"Prix Fixe,"* which is one of my favorite essays ever: a wistful, philosophical, and uplifting account of your Christmas dinner in a Copenhagen restaurant—"an orphan in his late sixties," as you wrote, surprised to be seated next to two beautiful women and chatting with them over mustard herring and sorbet. As you work through the menu, you achieve both *hygge* (coziness) and good *astri* (stars) during an evening you expected to be lonely.

In the editing process, what we talked most about—other than the delicious Danish food—was a general difference between male and female memoirists and their relationships to their own bodies. In short, I suggested that your readers would like to know how you saw yourself, especially since you described the two women so painstakingly.

You agreed, and you did it with just the right, precise details, offering a sort of *prix fixe* of that aging orphan:

So you have showered and shaved, splashed your jowls with Acqua di Giò, donned your three-button, olive-green Italian corduroy suit, a crisply laundered shirt, your MOMA blue-and-beige silk necktie, and your beaming, polished wingtips. In honor of the evening, you have even worn your father's gold wristwatch, which your sometimes-girlfriend fitted with an alligator band a Christmas ago. You thought to slip some notepaper into your inner breast pocket and clip your Montblanc there, too, to busy yourself taking notes about the food if you feel called upon to hide your face at some point.

. . .[Y]ou maintain what you hope is a pleasant half-smile behind your bushy, freshly waxed mustache and point your face around, hoping you don't look too much like a lonely old guy.

That night proved that you are never lonely for long. You and the women (one mother, one daughter) have a lovely conversation and even move to a different spot for an after-dinner drink. You exchange addresses and promise to write. You end the essay wondering if that will really happen . . .

It didn't. That Juleaften was your only contact with the women—until the *next* Juleaften, when you went to the same restaurant, and there they were. That second meeting came too late for the essay, but it's a testimony to the *hygge* you create. When they made their plans that night, they must have wondered if they would see the dapper writer in the olive-green Italian suit, the MOMA tie, the freshly waxed mustache, the charming dinner conversation . . . So there were good *astri* over another orphaned night in Copenhagen.

I hope that someday the good stars will shine over you and me, too, because I would really like to share a drink and a talk about all the weird coincidences that make up a friendship and a life.

Jayne Thompson
Photo Album

HERE IS ONE OF TOM SITTING in the foyer of a Copenhagen red-light-district hotel, hat in hand, waiting to take me out for the day. I tell him about the man staying in the room next to me, how I have to tiptoe to my room and silently slip the key in the lock and try to open the door before the man hears and invites me into his room—AGAIN!

Here is one of Tom buying me a hotdog that I "must have" at a stand in the park. Tom is right about the chili and onions.

Here is one of Tom sitting at an outdoor restaurant telling me that he will publish the book I am working on with incarcerated men at a prison in Pennsylvania. The canal waters run gently beside us as Tom changes the lives of twenty men and one woman with one sentence.

This one is of me on the train from Copenhagen to Greifswald, Germany, where I am teaching for two months. Tom's *Last Night My Bed a Boat of Whiskey Going Down* is on my lap, and I am openly weeping because I didn't know that a writer could be this good, this honest—I didn't know that a man could be this good, this honest. And I am weeping because I know him.

Here is one of Tom standing between iron doors in that no man's land of the prison waiting area—the space that separates us from the free world and a group of twenty men who may never cross that threshold to the world of freedom again.

Here is one of Tom taking the seat of honor in the prison classroom I have come to love. The men gaze at him with naked admiration and amazement. For months they have uttered phrases like "I bet he won't come," "Something will happen, and he won't be able to come in the prison," "I don't want to hope and have it not happen," and "Jayne, are you sure nothing will get in the way of his getting in? You better check that paperwork again!"

Here is one of Tom signing copies of *In the Company of Angels*, books that he purchased and shipped so that the men could read his novel before his visit. When R.C. approaches him, he says that he will write a story from the point of view of the watch strapped to Tom's wrist, "And then, as your watch, I'll be traveling with you to all the cities of the world you travel to, and I'll see all the places," R.C. says. Tom's eyes mist as he looks into the slim, older man's gentle face.

Here is one of Tom sitting in my car at the end of the night and nearly the end of his visit. His face, his hat, the smell of him so close in the car. I think of kissing him, as I imagine most women do. I don't know what to do with my emotion. It bubbles over. I have no way to express my gratitude for all Tom has done for me, my writers at the prison, and the hundreds of people who will read the book. I say, "Thank you. Thank you. Thank you."

If you look closely at this next one, you will see Tom. His spirit is in the room when James, one of the incarcerated writers says as he holds the anthology Tom promised to—and did—publish, "Now I know who I am."

In this one, I imagine that Tom holds my hand as I deliver copies of the prison anthology to children in a juvenile detention center. A teen boy with beautiful dreadlocks asks me if I know his father who is incarcerated at a prison where I teach—and I do. Another boy tells me that his sister died in childbirth a few days before. She was fifteen. I squeeze Tom's imaginary hand. I need him for this visit.

In this last one, Tom has on that wool cap that looks so absurdly good on him. He is wearing a tweed jacket, and he visits as I open the pages of *Kerrigan in Copenhagen*. The pages are as smooth as his freshly-shaved cheeks. He turns the page to the really good part, and I smile.

Phyllis Barber

HIS EYES LIT UP when he talked about the Danish Breakfast. That was his tradition, and he was always the "sponsor" of these breakfasts: fish, breads, sauces, a true memory of Denmark. He invited his literary friends to this event and went grocery shopping to include all of the traditional items on the menu. His pleasure was always a great joy to those of us who were lucky enough to attend.

Tom would light up every residency with his mischievous smile, the sense that something would be happening any minute, and his affection for Gladys Swan and Gordon Weaver. The memory of Tom is always a nostalgic memory of the residencies at Vermont College of Fine Arts and the part he played in making them something to remember.

René Steinke
Things I've Learned from my Friend, Tom

First of all, I am late for Mass.

Second, the best exercise is swimming.

Copenhagen is either a labyrinth or a map of serving houses. Copenhagen is the world.

It's better to write more or less all the time, when you're awake.

We should think about angels more.

If you pick the right restaurant on West Broadway on a sunny April day in Manhattan, and if you sit at the correct angle to the door, the actress Catherine Keener will come to your table and ask, "Are you who I think you are?"

In Copenhagen in the winter, there are only a couple of hours of daylight.

Sometimes the perfect words visit you in your dreams.

In Heathrow Airport, there is a bar with wooden tables and pictures of sheep in green hills on the walls, where waiting even hours for your flight doesn't feel like waiting.

This is how to speak to a toddler with respect. This is how to listen.

Katherine Mansfield.

Medical words, PSA, "micturate" can be very funny, even lyrical, when repeated at the right intervals.

This is how to choose the most beautiful and lucky pen.

"You might think that you see where this is going, but it's probably not what you think."

Licorice is best when it's bitter and salted.

"Friday, Bluett follows desire, abandons his work, escapes to the wild."

Coltrane: *Thought waves—heat waves—all vibrations* . . .

This is the way to give a proper Danish cheer.

Sylvia Petter

Tom was good enough to give me words for my collection, *Back Burning* (2007): "In simple, direct and compelling language, the stories reward the reader with a variety of distinct and memorable experiences: from the complexities of love (and unfaithfulness) to those of history and the way it treats, mistreats and selects its victims, building its ironies on the accidents of race, nationality, personality, place, and parentage. With its broad geographical span and array of venues, this book would make a fine companion for a journey. Not only does it entertain; it makes you think, it makes you feel, it makes you appreciate the humanity of its many characters."

I attended several of the workshops he led in Geneva and learnt a lot from him. When I organised the 13th International Conference on the Short Story in English in 2014, I was pleased to be able to have Tom on board.

I am the proud owner of several of his works including *The Copenhagen Quartet, Realism & Other Illusions: Essays on the Craft of Fiction* (2002), *In the Company of Angels* (2010), *Unreal City* (1996), *Drive Dive Dance & Fight* (1997), and his two latest, *My Life With Women,* Vol. 1 and 2, which I was able to get through Shakespeare and Company, Vienna.

Tom was an important connection on my writing journey and I am grateful for the knowledge and support he gave me, in person, and through his writing.

Michael Neff

I fondly recall your contributions to *Writers on the Job* and our interactions on it. The column received lots of attention and everyone benefited from your smarts, insights, and devotion. I recall too the one time we met at AWP and had a great time. I felt very much at ease with you. I miss those days.

Susan Tiberghien
With a Smile and a Bottle of Cognac
Remembering Thomas E. Kennedy

TOM, I SEE YOU at the door, with a smile and a bottle of cognac.

It could be back in 1998 when you arrived for our first Geneva Writers Conference. We welcomed over 150 writers from around the world to a weekend on the shores of Lake Geneva with the Alps and Mont Blanc in the distance.

We built bridges to twenty different countries, bridges of understanding and peace. You were an early pillar to our conferences, you in Copenhagen, along with Wallis Wilde-Menozzi in Parma. So we continued, every two years. We were together for seven conferences.

How many students listened and learned from you? At each conference you taught a new course in writing fiction. Here are a few of your titles: "Letting It Happen," "Crafting the Illusions of Fiction," "Getting Spontaneous." They point to what makes a good novelist.

All the time you kept writing your own books. I remember listening to pages from *The Copenhagen Quartet* at the Saturday evening readings by our faculty. "A love affair begins this story—a love affair with a city." (*Kerrigan's Copenhagen*, 2002)

Tom, you gave of yourself to the Geneva Writers Group. We missed you in June 2018 when we celebrated our 25th Anniversary. We honored all our instructors. You were remembered.

At the door, with a smile and a bottle of cognac.

Sudeep Sen
Poetics of Solitude, Songs of Silence
for Tom Kennedy

"I FIND IT WHOLESOME to be alone the greater part of the time. To be in company, even with the best, is soon wearisome and dissipating. I love to be alone. I never found the companion that was so companionable as solitude," wrote Henry David Thoreau in *Walden*. Solitude is something most creative writers and artists crave for, and yet when it is forced on to you—how does one cope?

As a poet and literary writer, and as a person who works from home (unless I am travelling on work), 'self-isolation' is nothing new, abnormal, or unusual. Over the last three decades, I have spent most of my working hours happily and voluntarily self-isolated and quarantined, cocooned in the world of ideas, surrounded by books and literary artifacts in my office-study. The only ostensible ambient sounds—rustling florets of *neem* leaves outside, assured metronomic ticking of an antique clock, soothing sounds of running water from a clay Zen water-fountain, familiar scratch of graphite point at the end of my sharpened pencil, and the seamless score created by the soft tap-touch of my fingers on the laptop keyboard.

I have never needed external causes to internalize and live life solitary and indoor. Wherever I am, I'm always at once at 'home' and in the 'world.' Perhaps this ease of simultaneity comes from a sense of rootedness. Like a large banyan tree with tertiary trunks and branches resembling fused stalactites and stalagmites—the veins and arteries of ideas flowing omni-directionally at all times. And yet in this isolation and solitude, there is an inherent yogic sense of centredness, where being with oneself is both wholesome and multitudinous. It is a precious zone for philosophical and creative thinking, a space for silence and "stillness" (as Pico Iyer says) that allows an inner voice to be heard.

The idea of 'white' space has always been important to me, both in my art and living. In an increasingly noise-polluted world, it is a space of calm, silence, and solitude. Khalil Gibran has said: "You talk when you cease to be at peace with your thoughts; And when you can no longer dwell in the solitude of your heart you live in your lips, and sound is a diversion and a pastime. And in much of your talking, thinking is half-murdered. For thought is a bird of space, that in a cage of words may indeed unfold its wings but cannot fly."

In white we have the entire spectrum of colour and beyond, beyond infrared and ultraviolet. In poetry, art, or photography presented on a flat surface—what is left out of the frame is equally important to what is inked-in as words and images. Without the silence of the white space—the work's overall entirety would never be balanced. The visible and the invisible act as a *yin-yang* with a calibrated fulcrum providing the mood and texture to tonality's subtle equilibrium.

This theme often finds expression in my writing, as in my poem, 'Silence', from my book *Fractals*:

SILENCE

Silence has its own
    subtle colour.
Between each breath

pause, heat simmers
    latent saliva —
tongue-entwined lisp.

Here and there,
    errant clouds wait,
yearning for rain.

Desire melting
    even silence to words —
word's colour bleed

incarnadine, as your lips
    whisper softly
the secrets of your silence.

Your fine *chikan* blouse —
    white, sheer,
and almost transparent —

cannot hide the quiet
    of your heart-beat
on your wheat-olive skin.

The milk-white flower
    adorning your hair,
sheds a solitary petal,

just one. In that petal
    silence blooms colour —
white, transparent white —

    pure white silence.

I have grown up, worked and lived for many years at a stretch, in some of the busiest cities of the world—Delhi, New York, London, and Dhaka. In India's capital city of 26 million and a country that hosts 1.6 billion people—I have got so used to the cacophony and external sounds that I can instinctively tune them out, at will. Whether I am in a packed train, or in a café, or walking on a crowded street, I can—if I choose to—just detach completely and go into my own zone of blur, which within seconds turns to a calming silence. Through years of untutored regimen, this process has become second nature, like any meditative practice.

Albert Camus, in *The Myth of Sisyphus and Other Essays* wrote, "In order to understand the world, one has to turn away from it on occasion." At one level, as a poet, one can often feel out-of-sync with the pedestrian conduct of the world at large. Being alone and confined is often a refuge from banality. Whichever way one looks at it, I must confess to being more than a little amused (even though I understand it), to see the world enter the phase of 'social distancing' 'self-isolation'—an idea that some of us have known as a lived reality for a very long time. So one carries on with the day as usual, the week, the month, the rest of the year, and more—without any fuss, distress, or alarm.

Throughout history, writers have sung paeans in favour of isolation and solitude. Aldous Huxley: "The more powerful and original a mind, the more it will incline towards the religion of solitude." Albert Einstein: "I live in that solitude which is painful in youth, but delicious in the years of maturity." John Milton in *Paradise Lost*: "Solitude sometimes is best society." Thomas Mann: "Solitude gives birth to the original in us, to beauty unfamiliar and perilous—to poetry." For me, ultimately everything begins and ends with the poetics of solitude—poetry is omniscient, poetry is life, poetry in its widest sense is a way of living. The unipolar focus on what one is engaged in, both centripetal and centrifugal, is the key—a well-made, well-worn, universal key that is robust and resilient enough to open up any vista you can imagine.

Greg Herriges
The Evening of "The Great Master," and Other Treasured Moments with Thomas E. Kennedy

I'D RECEIVED THIS PALE GREEN BROCHURE from Emerson College in my mailbox in the Liberal Arts Office of William Rainey Harper College, where I was an English professor. It advertised Emerson's Summer Fiction Writing Seminar to be held at their European Campus, a 13th Century Castle in the Village of Well in the Netherlands, known as Kasteel Well. It was 1995, and I had done some publishing—novels, stories, articles, and so this wasn't remarkable in any way, but I held on to the pamphlet, studied the photos, the names, James Carroll, Askold Melnyczuck, Alexandra Marshall, and a fellow named Thomas E. Kennedy. I had my hands full on the Cultural Arts Committee, helping to choose the next writers to bring in for the fall semester. I had a wife, a son, a suburban home to take care of, and a new novel that I was working on. All this, and my mother was now in a nursing home.

But the Dean thought it was a good idea for me to attend—I needed some writing time, and Kasteel Well seemed the perfect environment. So now I will take you with me as I fly off to Brussels, drive my rented red Fiat to Well, the Netherlands, and there I was one night attending a dinner in the castle with twenty-three other writers and faculty members—some of us novelists, some of us short story artists. We were in "Sophie's Room," named after the daughter of the former owners, a nineteen-year-old-girl who met with an early demise. Her portrait was prominently displayed on one of the walls. Gathered around the table we were encouraged to read aloud samples of our work.

On this particular night, Kennedy, a man I had yet to formally meet, stood up to read one of his works, "The Great Master." I listened attentively, nursing a Brand Beer, and soon became impressed and entranced, not just with the mixed allegorical absurdity and humor of the plot line, but by the quality of Kennedy's writing, and his reading voice. "The Great Master" left us with an intimate awareness of a major human dilemma—the unrelenting nature of desire, of appetite. It was quite a story, and set the bar high as to the expected caliber of our output.

There were eight of us in the novelist section, and all the rest were in one of three short story writer groups. I fell in socially with the younger writers, and being the early-bird riser that I was, jumped in my Fiat every morning to drive to the BP petrol station and come back with coffee for a few newfound colleagues. The breakfast room (actually a former dungeon) didn't open until 8:00 a.m. Always at this time I would call my wife from an antiquated payphone to check on the condition of my mother. Then it was time for my morning's writing.

I knocked off at around noon one day and hiked uptown to get some money from an ATM. It was a mild, late August day, and the local primary school was already reopened for the fall semester. I encountered a parade of blond children on tiny bicycles, some of them ringing the bells on their handlebars, and all of them exclaiming "Hallo" to me, one-by-one. It was like an official welcome, and it delighted me, as I was lonely and had this overwhelming feeling of having been temporarily transplanted, away from the people I loved.

At the bank I inserted my card in the machine and all this colorful Dutch money came out, not really that much unlike larger versions of Monopoly money. It didn't look real; that's why I never felt guilty spending it. Out on the street I spied a restaurant up ahead, and I tossed around the idea of going in there for a solo lunch, but the mental picture of me sitting alone at a table in a land I knew little about redoubled my loneliness, so I decided to return to the castle and get back to work on my novel.

The sun was high in the sky and the heat of the day rose as I walked along the fence on the flat land of a horse farm, where I watched a young woman feed an apple to a pony. Further up the road I saw the figure of a man, carrying in each hand those semi-transparent white plastic bags, the sort they give you at Walgreens. As I gained on him I recognized that here was Thomas E. Kennedy himself, and there was clearly a six-pack of Heineken in one of the bags. I called out from behind him, "Sure could use a cold beer on a hot day like today."

He turned around, stopped, waiting for me to catch up. "Are you from the castle?" he asked, and I said "yes," that I was. "Would you like to come back to my room so we can have a beer?"

And so we walked along the road together and began chatting right away. I told him how much I had enjoyed his reading the other night, and he was very appreciative. Up in his room—a circular one, because it was in a turret—he opened two frosty bottles of Heineken and we sat and drank and whiled away the afternoon, talking about fiction, our latest projects, and writers we admired, and those we both knew or had known. He lived in Copenhagen, he said. I lived near Chicago, I said, taught in a college. He was an ambassador for a Danish medical society and traveled the world for them, though he was born and raised in Queens. The afternoon came and went pleasantly, and I never got back to writing that day—I dare say there was little left of that six-pack—but I felt I had made a new friend. He showed me around the castle, the flights of stairs and the many entrances, and then each of us went off to wash-up for dinner.

After dinner there was another reading in Sophie's Room, this one by me, reading my story, "The Worst Suspicions of Stanley Glickner," and afterward many of us went out on the wooden bridge that crossed two concentric moats. The stars were piercingly bright as they only can be far from city lights, and I met up with some of the young folks, and Tom and I each had a cocktail. And so it went on like this, evening after evening, until one Saturday when everyone went off sightseeing.

As per my habit, I phoned my wife early in the morning (it would have been two in the afternoon in Chicago), but there was no answer. Perhaps she was out with my son, perhaps a movie, shopping.

I drove three of my young colleagues to Cologne that morning, and we visited the Dom Cathedral, and I bought them all lunch at a German restaurant. I marveled at the city, which after World War II had been rebuilt so that it surrounded the only un-bombed, intact structure, the Dom itself.

On the way home on the Autobahn, cars full of soccer fans, singing their teams' victory songs, displayed national flags, flapping furiously in the wind (it was, after all, the Autobahn). By the time we returned to the castle, I retired to my room, fairly beaten by all the walking I'd done that day.

I was awakened by repeated knocking at my door. I sat up in bed, in the dark, confused and fresh from sleep.

"Greg? Greg, it's Tom. I have a phone call for you in my room. It's your wife. She needs to talk to you."

Tom had the only direct-line phone in the entire castle—not counting the payphone. I told him I'd be right with him as I threw on my clothes, an ominous suspicion growing in my mind. My wife didn't just phone me overseas to chat. This was not going to be good.

And of course it wasn't. Tom and I spoke during the hike to his turret. "I think it has something to do with your mother," he said. "I hope everything is all right. I'll leave you alone and you can feel free to stay as long as you want."

I said that there was no need for that.

That was the night my mom died. The doctors had predicted that she had another six months, but the doctors were wrong. My wife was very kind and spoke gently and gave me the details, and then we had to make a decision as to whether I should continue my course at Well, or come home immediately. There were arrangements to be made, relatives from out of town to inform. I should stay, she decided. There was a hollow sensation in my stomach when I hung up, for now I was officially an orphan. A parent is a tough loss (no need to explain that), though I had not been thoroughly unprepared for this development. I thought for a moment about my mother's life, all the interior photographic scenes that flash across the memory. Tom had some kind words for me—though I don't now remember what exactly they were, but he did, very kindly, see me back to my room. I couldn't sleep for the rest of the night.

That two-week stay in the Netherlands began a twenty-six-year friendship between Tom and me—and it's not just a friendship. We have worked together at readings, teaching my English Lit classes (sometimes in person, sometimes by overseas telephone conference calls), making a DVD documentary about his life's work, making another film short about his novel, *In the Company of Angels*. I filmed Tom giving a salute to Hemingway on the back porch steps of Hemingway's home. He, in turn, helped edit my collection of short stories. My son, who has known Tom since he was a little boy, has come to think of him as an uncle, has even presented him as a guest reader at his high school's Writers Week.

But indulge me for a moment while I try to sketch a few more indelible moments with Tom. He has visited me and my family here in the States no fewer than twelve times, maybe more. Typically I will pick him up at Chicago's O'Hare International Airport, drive him to our home in Deerfield, Illinois, and then he, my wife Carmen, and I will head out to an elaborate dinner. The next morning I will drive him to Harper College in Palatine, Illinois, where he will give either a noontime or evening reading, and appear for a book signing. Then I'll whisk him off to our vacation home in Lake Geneva, Wisconsin, for more elaborate meals and finally a reading at a lovely upscale wine and champagne bar called Pop More Corks, where he has developed a following among the locals.

One February morning I was driving Tom to Harper College in my spiffy new red convertible. Tom and I always talk of jazz, and on this commute I slipped in a CD of John Klemmer's *Waterfalls*. Klemmer is a first-rate saxophonist, and the opening solo is played through a device called an Echoplex, which causes all the notes to trickle into each succeeding note, creating an aural waterfall—hence the title. Tom listened while we drove under snow-covered tree limbs through a forest in a suburb called Riverwoods.

When the solo was over, he popped the CD out and said, "Greg, that's the most beautiful sax solo I've ever heard."

I promptly returned the disc to its gem case and handed it to him. "It's yours," I said. He protested, said I was too generous, but I insisted. Of course, little did I know that disc was out-of-print, and it took me a year to find a replacement—though I never told Tom that. What paid off for me was his later, written description of lying in bed at night, listening to Klemmer, while watching the Hale-Bopp Comet over the lake outside his apartment window. We emailed one another on a nearly daily basis by then, and just that image of his enjoyment (he is a true jazz aficionado) gave me great joy.

To top off that wintery-drive-in-my-new-convertible anecdote, a year or so later he included the moment in an essay he had written. I was alerted about its publication by a friend, so I went to Barnes & Noble to buy a copy of the journal. By Tom's account, we weren't driving through the woods in February. In his version it was a summer evening, and we had the top down as we zoomed along Chicago's Lower Wacker Drive, blasting Klemmer on the car's stereo. When I later emailed him about the discrepancies, his response was, "It's Creative Nonfiction, Greg"—a remark that always sparked laughter when I recounted it for my fiction writing students.

During Tom's last visit to Lake Geneva in early September some seven or eight years ago, he had brought me a bottle of Remi Martin Cognac and fine cigars. It was a sunny afternoon as we sat on my backyard patio, facing the woods, the leaves of the trees all summer-faded, temperature in the mid-seventies, and we lit those cigars, and we poured one another glasses of cognac and talked for two-and-half hours straight—one of the best conversations we've ever had—caught up in the moment, spurred on by the fine Remi, the cigars, the lovely day, the quickly approaching autumn. Then he went off to the guest room to take a nap, and soon I went to my bedroom and slept soundly until dinner time. When we woke up, neither of us could remember what we had talked about, but you can bet it had something to do with fiction and fiction writing, teaching, fabulous food and liquor, jazz, classic cars, politics, and current as well as past loves. As I say, the particulars are lost to the ages, but it was a great talk.

The last time I was with Tom was in his beloved city of Copenhagen, some six and a half years ago. My wife and I had flown in so that I could interview him for *The South Carolina Review*. He was our host and tour guide, introducing us not just to famous architecture and legendary streets, avenues, and museums, but to artists and writers as well, talented people with whom he had forged bonds over the years. He was in his element, and he allowed us to share his great enthusiasm for all that was Danish.

I've recently gone through the Kennedy section of my bookshelves, through volumes he regularly gifted me with—*A Weather of the Eye, Crossing Borders, Unreal City, Drive Dive Dance & Fight, A Passion in the Desert*, the individual novels of *The Copenhagen Quartet*, and many more. I am very grateful for the enjoyment they have given me, for all the writerly lessons they have taught through example. No, Tom is not simply my friend, my good friend; he has been a mentor, a brother in arms, a confidant, an example of a fine and rare human being. I owe him so much, so very much.

Greg Herriges and Tom Kennedy

Kerstin Lieff
The Unforgettable Thomas Kennedy

WROXTON, JANUARY 2010

I HAD MET TOM KENNEDY the summer before in Madison. It was a chance encounter. I was on my way to my dorm room, when I got stopped short in my tracks. A stranger was sitting on a bench at the entrance, a man who, I thought in that moment, could be Ernest Hemingway's twin. Cigar hanging from his mouth, a book in his lap, a glass of bourbon glinting in the sunlight. My imagination could be filling in the blanks, because I'm not exactly sure about any of this, but what I know caught me off guard—actually quite contrary to that Hemingway image—was the beaming smile on his face. We made eye contact and I felt, more than saw, a genuine curiosity in him. That look was like he knew me already, and he proceeded to say my name. Only he pronounced it in Swedish, the way only my mother ever did—like this: Tchersteen—and then he bade me to sit with him a while. I'm not sure what we talked about, but I left that encounter feeling excited for my future. I had come to Fairleigh Dickinson University with all kinds of stories swirling inside me that I wanted to learn how to tell, stories about war and prison camps, dysfunction, what it was like being the child of immigrants in America, about brain tumors, paranoia and insanity, about racism. Somehow, I left that meeting knowing I could do this—write about it all.

Fast forward to Wroxton, six months later. My first time there and the first time in over twenty years that England was hit with snow—two feet, if I remember correctly. Nothing worked. Trains stopped running. Salt needed to be imported from Scotland, and, until it arrived, all the major roads were closed. Traffic was at a standstill. The castle where we all stayed ran out of heating oil and the delivery truck could not make it up the driveway's incline to the castle. Without heating oil, there was no heat. Without heat, the best the staff could offer was extra blankets for our beds, and, of course, the pub at the end of our lane. The pub, with a roaring fireplace so tall you could step inside it and not hit your head, even standing on tippy-toes—in the summertime, of course. The pub that served pub food, excellent beer, wine that was palatable, and I'm sure bourbon. This is where I remember Tom best. Teaching his class here, where it was warm, staying well into the night, laughing, cracking jokes, and what I remember him best for, his uncanny ability to pull stories out of you, asking in all sincerity, "So, tell me about . . ." and when your story came to a lull, he'd ask more, or he'd fill in the details ("Didn't those apartments have really high ceilings?").

Remembering Tom, one of those evenings stands out more than the rest, where, like memory can do, his smiling face hangs like a mist over the scene. A few of us late stragglers were walking home from the pub, and that "gentle incline" to the castle seemed incredibly impossible to navigate. For every step we took forward, it seemed we slid two feet back. The drive, the lawn, whatever surface we attempted, there was the sense we were on a backwards rolling sidewalk. We slipped and fell and giggled like children as the snow continued to fall. And every bit of it made it all that much funnier. And there was Tom, laughing, in the midst of it all.

How we managed to finally get home and into our beds is something I have only my imagination to rely on. Did we pull each other along? Crawl on all fours, clawing at the snow? I do remember the next day we asked the management for sleds. They had none. We asked for trashcan lids, they had none. We finally made do with plastic trash bags that we climbed inside and proceeded to slide down the hill in back, playing in the snow all afternoon. And somehow, in my memory, Tom's impish grin continues to hang over even this scene.

It was Tom's easy-going, eager enthusiasm for his students' work—and he was equally engaged by everyone's stories—that gave me the courage to believe I could write. Tom's stories and his uncanny ability to read them, and his poetry, in such a way that allowed you to see into his soul. His wonderful writing. And his brilliant ability to help me believe in myself. I consider myself a writer now. I have many more stories to tell, and I write. I know, though, I could never have gotten here without the humble encouragement of this man, my mentor, Tom Kennedy.

Renée Ashley

Dearest Tom,

I want to share with you my experience of your reading, one particular evening, at FDU.

The room, of course, is bubbling with conversation (it's evening, someone's turned the air conditioners up to high) and two small clusters of MFA students are leaning against the walls, just talking, shoulders or backs pressed against the chestnut panels (chestnut from an era predating the parasitic blight); others, the ones who have settled down already, are chatting over the round tables spread around the room for the residency, and there's still a small flurry of voices in the hallway. It's more than likely, as well, that early birds have commandeered the two plush settees at the back of the room, one either side of the door (cushioned seats, comfortable distance, the less desirable one to the right by a window smack next to the a/c, the other, more desirable one, in shadow to the left). The electric chandeliers are turned down a bit to quash the glare. Perhaps, one or two students are still in the bathrooms, hoping to scramble back at exactly the last minute. Welcome to Hartman Lounge. Walter Cummins tells us it was once the billiards room, with its rich walls and moldings. There's also a fireplace into which you could stuff more than one body with ease. It is the loveliest room in the Mansion.

All conversation stops when Walter stands, though there's a jostling of chairs as the last-minute-bathroom-trip students come dashing, breathlessly, in and find seats, whether a single chair, or atop the long rectangular tables on the north side of the room. You're introduced by Walter Cummins and when you lay your papers down on the lectern, beneath the small readers' light attached to one side, you announce you're going to read from your essay, "I Am Joe's Prostate."

There's a small sputter of laughter from some of us (those of us old enough to remember *Reader's Digest*'s series, of the '50s, the "I Am Joe's [talking] [organ]" stories, and, perhaps, there's a sharp intake of breath from a couple of the older students, likely from the Midwest, who never dreamed they'd be served postprandial prostate. The others, the young ones, relatively speaking, likely have only the denotatative understanding of the title (which, I'm guessing, they imagine is some sort of cartoony and good-for-your-soul bastardization of something archetypal or disciple-ish, like *Veggie Tales*, the cartoon series in which Larry the Cucumber and his friends, Bob the Tomato, Archibald Asparagus, and Mr. Lunt, a decorative gourd with a Spanish accent though he grew up in New Jersey—behave in very human ways).

You, as the poised and congenial reader that you are, focus on the eight-and–a-half-by-eleven sheets beneath the light, and I'm certain that you're tracing the words there and recalling the rhythms and sonics before you begin to read.

When I listen to you read, I inevitably grow another set of eyes, a sort of magical pair, fixed beside the blue ones, and I see two things at once—(1) the rich scenes you render so palpably and musically, and (2) the sight of you actually reading at the lectern. Evidently, I grow, too, a second pair of ears: I hear your reading voice, but also the voices of the people you've portrayed.

You begin: "It is 1994. You are fifty years old." Suddenly, everyone in the room is fifty years old! (For some of us, that was good news; for others, unimaginable.) Then, almost immediately, we hear your wife tell you, "You piss like an old man." And there is, of course, more laughter in the room. (Very intimate, yes, but again, for those not from the coasts, close to naughty.) In good time, then, you find yourself in a doctor's office, you've already entered the examination room, where you've been told that you might like to get undressed and jump up on the table and assume, on hands and knees, the cow/cat asana, a somewhat vulnerable position if there's a zealot behind you. Then "[w]ithout prelude or warning, [the doctor] shoves his finger up your kazoo." This time there are some nervous "*ewww*"s in the audience. But what I hear most clearly is something else—a sound coming from behind me to the right. I look and a couple of guys are shifting around uncomfortably in their seats. Their discomfort makes me laugh. (I got my sense of humor from my mother.)

It's odd . . . I'm not so much experiencing my third and fourth eyes and ears, this time, but half of my attention is behind me, though I'm looking at you and listening with pleasure. In a page or two, you learn the word *micturate*, a word you claim as your own and are forever happy to have added to your vocabulary. And, me, mine, too.

And soon, and I admit it, I find this very funny, too, but in all likelihood even my own laughter is beginning to be a nervous-for-you cry/laugh: you read: ". . . he is inserting a wand the thickness of three or four pencils into your Private Johnson . . ." and before the "n" of Johnson can resonate in the room, I swear there is a swooning behind me. Almost all the men, young and otherwise, it seems to me, are getting a bit more twitchy now; when I turn around several of the guys have absented the tables for, I can only assume, the carpeting, a more private and buttock-and-bunghole-friendly environment, and a less observationally-exposed spot. But my friend, let's call him A (because his name begins with an A), is still sitting atop one of the empty, round tables, but now he's clenching the table edges and he's the color of mucus. I believe he's either going to sprint to the garbage bin at the back of the room to vomit or he's going to run out the door and we'll never see him again. But he does neither. (He's a sweet, polite man, maybe late thirties? I suck big time at ages, so just assume he's at least a heaping cupful or two younger than we are, and far too polite to run screaming from the room during a faculty reading.) But his hands, clamped onto the table's edge, really, seriously clenched (the way a child holds onto the roller coaster safety bar when he rides alone for the first time and he's sure his parents are trying to kill him). A's leaning a bit forward and looking toward the floor, in a seeming hopping-off position, and he's swinging his legs. I don't think he could let go if he wanted to. I double-check his proximity to the waste bin and decide he can make it in a pinch.

Soon, back in the essay, you're dressed and at patient's side of the doctor's desk. He's given you two options for the treatment of your condition, though you have not been told what that condition might be: "Surgical or pharmaceutical." You opt for the pharmaceutical. The doctor wants you to reconsider: "Don't dismiss the surgical possibility . . . ," he says. And you reply: "I think I should prefer the pharmaceutical." I know that tone of voice! But the doctor goes on to explain, anyway. "*Pre-cision*," he says. "With surgical precision, we can take the thinnest slice or two, thin as the thinnest salami slices, thinner."

I hear the thinnest sound behind me, it's one of those sounds emitted from a human who clearly doesn't even know he's doing it. It's a high-pitched *eeeeeeee*, the sound a bat might make, if its vocalizations were projected within my hearing range . . . When I turn around, A has become the color of dark cherries and I'm afraid he's going explode. The sound, as though he were an inflated balloon released and flying around the room. I have to ask if he's ok, and he bobs his head more loosely than I might have imagined. So, he's good. Sort of.

But very quickly, my mind leaves A clutching in his misery. All four of my eyes and ears are latched onto you and the scene you read—though it is speculative, it is excruciatingly vivid, so sensual . . . so awful. In the Epilogue, you determine, if it comes to it, your "own future plan of treatment" is suicide. You'll go to Black Dam Lake, a place you love, bring along your favorite foods, rent a boat, eat, and "watch the beautiful swans float past like beautiful, white question marks," until you are sated with delectables. Then you'll take out the high-caliber pistol, put it in your mouth, point it up towards the cranial cavity, and pull the trigger.

I will never, in this lifetime, unsee that scene. It's burned into my own brain.

In your closure there is relief, but not erasure: "Thus, after two years, twenty blood tests, thirty-four biopsies, the last three of which were surgical, and two weeks of micturating fire, you are sent out into the world, onto the sunny pavement to find your way in a world of health."

Everyone in the room, of course, is relieved; now the moans I hear are less visceral, and more sympathetic. My friend, A, is still a little peaked, and it's easy to see he's utterly exhausted. I am still in two places: Black Dam Lake and Hartman Hall, the room that used be the billiards room.

That reading, Tom, was as masterly as the writing. Not a pained look, not a whine or a wince, not a tear for yourself or your experience. Brilliant. In writing it, you'd put the living-it onto the page, and then were able to see it from the outside. Once it existed outside of you, outside of your body and mind, your focus was on the words you wrote, the phrases, clauses, the sentences, and paragraphs rather than on the long and more-than-hellish story of your experience. I can't think of a better sharing of both process and mastery from anyone, ever. I was lucky to be there. Not a person, not even the hardasses, was left unmoved, Tom; I'm certain of it.

I don't know, really, whether you were aware of A, but I had to share; it still makes me laugh. But you were the writer at the head of the room who turned agonizing experience into a brilliant piece of writing that perfectly rode the cusp between horror and humor. A brilliant presentation by a deeply loved friend, colleague, and writer.

Much love and infinite kissiefooples,* Tom,
Renée

* Tom knows what these are!

Robert Stewart
THE GREAT DRYING OFF
OF THE WOMEN
(*Poetry Day 2006, Denmark*)

—*for Thomas E. Kennedy*

We got soaked Copenhagen way,
at the Frederiksberg Garden, a Sunday,
scads of Scandinavian poets
with frikadellers for snacks
and a snag in their trouser backs
from the vodka, I think, Stoli,
equally wet; we shouted
among the water courses,
trumpeted in groves and glades,
in the innocent camaraderie
of perhaps a thousand—no
exaggeration—Danish moms and babes
in strollers loosely tarped
so the tots could see verse
carolers standing like herons—no,
they were herons, beaking
the low clouds of August, and one,
reciting squeakily near the "pacifier tree"
where all those kids in strollers
will someday hang up their binkies
with a note like this from a little Alex:
Here are almost all my pacifiers (His opening
syntax the model of order).
I only keep my night pacifier (now, disorder)
for a little while yet. Loving regards.
The little Lear, standing-for
and standing-against, in no-
regret acknowledgment of love,
had strung up all—or mostly all—

his sucking and mumbling devices.
What a man. Out Copenhagen way,
Frederiksberg, our words ran
sonorous and dense as water
rushing off walls and the backs of swans.
Men and women equally, including me,
in my gray, billed cap and wool, poetry-day
blanket crawled to our posts
like crawdaddies to recite our lines.
For a short while, I was miserable
(a predictable syntax) in the rain
and then deliriously happy
with Kennedy at my side, screaming,
"What is it most you want me not to say?"
and off a ways, Neils and Lotte,
Lennox and Gorm, Erik and Marianne
shouting their lines; even the base
of the statue of Frederik VI
had something to say
of his sad childhood and tough life.
Our purple, poetry-day umbrellas,
buoyant as beer caps, bobbed in the green.
What could I do with my curling
pages and sodden underwear but speak
well for the people of our time?
Let the 18th century fend for itself.
"I think I can still name my friends dead
of mortar fire," I yelled
out toward Helsingor Strait,
"half a world and full century away."
Oh, you birds, remember that.
Your dazzle in the gray sky
did not empty us. A rivulet of poets
began to move toward the dry
and ancient lobby of a theater
near the *have*—whose name no
longer rises on the bread crumbs
of my brain, though puddles
had all those hungry ducks—

into the bar and audience area,
where the women smelled like waterfalls
and were drying their hair
with paper towels and squeezing
their hems, and kicking off
their sneakers and baring their feet;
birds in the gilded ceiling
or peeking through stained glass
circled them, fanning their bodies
with sunlight. I remember
there was Kennedy, Lisa, Lene,
and Alice, too, with friends from the bar,
and having traveled
(with Lisa) the farthest for this
simple test of adulthood—
to come in out of the rain—I decreed
in a way to be heard at the footlights
that time has come for the drying off
of the women. And the women,
being Danish and American, mostly,
and altogether fit and generous forgave
me immediately, as I knew they would,
which might even have redeemed
the poor, sad life of Frederik the VI—
but why mention him after all this time,
with his autocratic tendencies?
Tom was poet of the day and gave
away his prize to charity.
We had our beets and sausages
for dinner later,
and a featherbed for sleep,
as did the Danish moms and babies
for whom a little rain
is a little lyric; and the rain
that soaked us, men and women, alike,
out Copenhagen way,
revealed how close we come
at times to each other's
bodies, the earthly goodness

of our skin, and someone
needed just then
to speak up
about it.

Tynia Thomassie

For Tom.

How do you thank someone for showing you how to craft when you are not currently crafting?

How do you express gratitude to a word conjurer and life capturer who is paused in words, still capturing it all, surrendering to it,

All in one-way ingestion.

I've lost patience with words. They don't do it for me anymore. They've been so misused and artlessly hijacked . . . I feel in good company with great characters: Iago, Hamlet, Tynia, and Tom, wordless. With Act V's in progress all around us, all over the Globe, silence somehow feels fuller and truer than getting it down . . . so I'm taking my hat off to silence, laying my phrases down. And I'm gonna pull up a spirit-chair and sit next to you.

I hope, Tom, as we wordlessly sit together, you there, me here savoring some cognac, breathing in quiet jazz, in a dark corner, near a crackling fire, sharing a cool vibe and an unforced smile.

Let's just Be.

Love you.
Tynia Thomassie

Dave Poe
Drinks Beside Water

TOM AND I MET in 1992 at Kasteel Well, the Netherlands, at a writer's conference where he was an instructor. On a free Saturday afternoon, Tom, myself, and Mike Lee, a writer from Cape Cod, sat on a big wooden porch at a place called Nellie's. She served us beer after beer as we talked and joked. At one point, Nellie said, "I love the sound of you guys laughing." We were looking out at the River Maas about a hundred yards away. With that began a pact with Tom. Whenever possible, he and I would get together and have drinks beside water. That's included his nearby Nyhavn, the Seine, the Atlantic, and the English Channel. As I now look out the window at a steady rain, I raise my glass of wine to you, Tom. And to Nellie.

Danish Literary Friends

THOMAS E. KENNEDY is well known in Danish literary culture, receiving awards for his contributions. He has devoted much of his attention to Danish writers and poets and the world of books and bookstores. He is regarded for his efforts to bring recognition to many of these authors through his translations, placing English versions in magazines throughout the world. They are among his closest friends, as is clear from their contributions in this section.

In keeping with Tom's bilingual interests, two of the pieces are presented in both the original Danish and in an English translation—Lee Morvin's talk given when Tom won the Dan Turèll Award and Pia Tafdrup's explanation of Tom's contribution to her reputation as a poet.

Lars Movin
Tale til Thomas E. Kennedy i anledning af overrækkelsen af Dan Turèll Medaljen, Vangede Bibliotek, 19. marts 2016:

Det er altid sundt for en kultur, et samfund, et folk, at blive set udefra, gennem fremmede briller. Det kan være smigrende, og måske også en lille smule angstprovokerende. Men altid interessant og i bedste fald indsigtsgivende. Og i Danmark—og specielt i København—er vi så heldige at have sådan et udefrakommende blik vandrende lyslevende rundt iblandt os i form af en amerikansk forfatter, som har gjort det til et halvt livsprojekt at filtrere den danske virkelighed gennem sin fiktion. Et udefrakommende blik. Jeg siger med vilje ikke et *fremmed* blik. For den person, jeg har i tankerne, lever ikke ligefrem op til klichéen om den amerikanske turist, der hopper af krydstogtsbåden ved Langelinie, snuser rundt i byen et par timer og derefter føler, at han har *gjort* Danmark. Nej, den person, jeg har i tankerne, har slået sig ned i vores land, og han har indtil videre brugt fyrre år af sit liv på at gøre observationer fra denne særlige afkrog af den globale virkelighed, som vi kalder den danske. Faktisk har han været her så længe, at han næsten er begyndt at tænke som en dansker. Tag bare hovedkarakteren i hans roman *Beneath the Neon Egg* (2014). Bluett hedder denne hovedkarakter, Patrick Bluett—og så kan man jo tænke på alt muligt, både *blue* og *we blew it*, som de siger i filmen *Easy Rider*—og så han minder i øvrigt i påfaldende grad om bogens ophavsmand: Denne Bluett er amerikansk forfatter, han er bosat i Danmark, han tjener sit levebrød som oversætter, og han er vild med at drive rundt i Københavns indre by og brokvartererne, vild med barer, bodegaer og værtshuse, vild med jazz, vild med danske kvinder—så vild, at han endda har været gift med én og har fået halvdanske børn. Men nu er ægteskabet forbi, og Bluett er lige så blå som sit navn. I sin nyvundne ensomhed leder han efter nye kvindelige bekendtskaber, møder forskellige, heriblandt én der ikke er så tosset endda. Men så viser det sig, at hun bor i Albertslund. I *fucking* Albertslund! Bluett *har* altså været i Albertslund, og dér skal han fandeme ikke ud igen. Så hellere ensomheden og flere hvileløse vandringer gennem den blå nat, altid ledsaget af en sejlivet optimisme og et indre lydspor af jazz. Og alt sammen skildret med en blanding af melankoli og humor, livskundskab og sproglig præcision. Men først og fremmest med empati og et knivskarpt blik på den danske virkelighed. Et blik, man kun kan have, hvis man på én gang er meget stedkendt og lige tilpas fremmed til at omfatte hele sceneriet med samme type kærlighed som antropologen, der iagttager det eksotiske.

Det er selvfølgelig Thomas E. Kennedy, jeg taler om. Forfatter og oversætter. Og gennem en årrække en trofast og kongenial formidler af Dan Turèll ud i det amerikanske sprog—og i øvrigt også af mange andre danske digtere—men først og fremmest Dan Turèll, tør jeg vist godt sige.

Og Dan Turèll dukker da også op indtil flere gange i historien om Patrick Bluett. Overordnet kan man sige, at bogen er fyldt med blåtonede beskrivelser af et noir-København, der kan vække mindelser om stemningen i Dan Turèlls kriminalromaner. Men helt konkret er det Dan Turèlls digt "Charlie Parker i Istedgade", der fungerer som en blå tråd gennem bogen. Og undervejs dukker også andre af Dan Turèlls digte op. Et sted fremgår det endda, at protagonistens yndlingsdigt—selv om han er amerikaner—rent faktisk er Turèlls "Gennem Byen Sidste Gang". Ja, han overvejer endda at gå hen på Café Guldregn og drikke en genstand som en hyldest til den afdøde digter. Det bliver nu ikke til noget, men da han senere i bogen, på endnu en nattevandring, dropper ind på værtshuset Femmeren i Classensgade, kommer han ved et tilfælde til at sidde i baren ved siden af en ung mand, der viser sig at være Halfdan E. Og netop denne Halfdan E har indspillet hele to album med Dan Turèll, betror bartenderen Patrick Bluett, efter at den unge mand er gået. Dét er noget, der gør indtryk. To album med Dan Turèll!

Siden har bogens forfatter—Thomas Kennedy—selv indspillet et album med Halfdan E. Det er en cd med titlen *An Introduction: Dan Turèll + Halfdan E Meets Thomas E. Kennedy* (2013), hvor Thomas Kennedy gør det umulige: Han har sammensat et udvalg af materialet fra de to album, som Halfdan E lavede sammen med Dan Turèll, *Pas På Pengene!* (1993) og *Glad i Åbningstiden* (1996), oversat teksterne og indtalt dem på engelsk til Halfdan E's tracks. Og det fungerer! Hvis I ikke kender cd'en, kan jeg stærkt anbefale, at I får fat i den.

Den roman, jeg talte om før, *Beneath the Neon Egg*, er en del af Thomas Kennedys store værk, den såkaldte *Copenhagen Quartet*—fire uafhængige og temmelig forskellige, men ikke desto mindre beslægtede romaner, der alle sammen udspiller sig med København som kulisse. Alene den kvartet burde have gjort Thomas Kennedy verdensberømt i Danmark. Det kommer forhåbentlig nu, hvor det lille forlag Rod&Co omsider har fået øje på bøgerne og er begyndt at udsende dem i dansk oversættelse. Det første bind, der har fået den danske titel *I selskab med engle*, er netop udkommet. Og de øvrige følger forhåbentlig snarest.

Har den danske forlagsverden været sløv i optrækket, har Thomas Kennedy til gengæld for længst høstet anerkendelse for sit forfatterskab, og ikke mindst Københavner-Kvartetten, i det store udland. For nogle år siden tegnede han kontrakt med det hæderkronede forlag Bloomsbury, som siden har stået for udgivelsen af hans bøger i England og U.S.A. Og i den forbindelse traf Thomas Kennedy den lidt usædvanlige disposition, at han underkastede alle fire bind i Københavner-Kvartetten gennemgribende revision og forsynede dem med nye titler. De fire bøger, der oprindelig udkom på et lille irsk forlag i årene 2002 til 2005, foreligger altså nu i spritnye versioner dateret til perioden 2010 til 2014. Titlerne er: *In the Company of Angels, Falling Sideways, Kerrigan in Copenhagen* og *Beneath the Neon Egg*. Og i øvrigt er der også referencer til Dan Turèll i de øvrige tre bind, men det vil jeg lade være op til jer læsere selv at opdage!

Thomas Kennedy er født i 1944 og opvokset i bydelen Queens, New Yorks svar på Vangede. Der er adskilligt, vi kunne sige om hans ungdom, men lad det være nok med at slå fast, at han allerede som teenager fostrede drømmen om at blive forfatter, men at han lige skulle have noget at skrive om først. Der gik altså nogle år, og så, efter en begivenhedsrig og berejst ungdom, ville skæbnens træf det, at han i 1976 havnede i Danmark, hvor han lige siden har boet og arbejdet—blandt andet som en meget flittig oversætter.

I starten af 1980'erne fik han sine første tekster trykt, i 1988 udkom den første bog, og siden er det blevet til mere end 30 udgivelser—alt i alt et imponerende og meget varieret forfatterskab, som i sig selv kunne begrunde en tildeling af Dan Turèll Medaljen.

Men så er der altså lige den lille ekstra og i denne sammenhæng nok så væsentlige omstændighed, at Thomas Kennedy på et tidspunkt opdagede Dan Turèll og tabte sit hjerte hen over alle kulturelle og sproglige barrierer. Til at begynde med var kærligheden af privat og kollegial karakter, men på et tidspunkt begyndte han at oversætte Dan Turèlls tekster til amerikansk, og siden har han turneret med oversættelserne i U.S.A.—og vistnok også flere andre steder—og fået publiceret en del af dem i fine litterære tidsskrifter. Sideløbende har han så fornøjet sig med at indspille den føromtalte cd med Halfdan E. Og i 2010 fik han også i en dansk kontekst udgivet et enkelt af de oversatte digte, nemlig "Gennem Byen Sidste Gang" ("Last Walk Through The City"), i en smuk og eksklusiv publikation med illustrationer af vores Medalje-kunstner Barry Wilmont.

Det seneste projekt fra Thomas Kennedys hånd er en oversættelse af selveste *Vangede Billeder*, hvoraf de første 24 sider i løbet af dette forår vil blive publiceret i det velanskrevne amerikanske tidsskrift *New Letters*. Og hvem ved, hvad der så kan ske!

Men lad os nu skrue tiden 40 år tilbage: I efteråret 1976—samme år som Thomas Kennedy bosatte sig i Danmark—satte den 30 år gamle Dan Turèll ud på en pilgrimsrejse til New York. Det var første gang, han var i U.S.A., men i en vis forstand havde han allerede i mange år forinden levet i sit eget indre Amerika. Han havde trukket vejret gennem jazz og rock, ladet sig inspirere af beatforfatterne og identificeret sig med de kuldslåede eksistenser, som i kriminalromaner af Dashiell Hammett eller Raymond Chandler driver rundt i den store amerikanske nat.

Da Dan Turèll få år efter New York-opholdet—i 1979—skulle skrive forord til et udvalg af sine americana-tekster fra 70'erne, *Amerikanske Ansigter*, erklærede han blankt: "Jeg *er* amerikaner-dansker. Og en meget stor del af min generation og de fleste af mine venner er amerikaner-danskere". Og så satte han trumf på ved at jokke godt og grundigt på 70'ernes U.S.A.-forskrækkede ligtorne: "Danmark er i forhold til U.S.A. som musen i forhold til elefanten eller Nørre Snede i forhold til København. Danmark er den 53. stat i det amerikanske flag (. . .). Det er U.S.A. der definerer vor Kulturkreds, det er U.SA. der definerer os, kulturelt som økonomisk".

Og så. til slut i en mere poetisk form: "Jeppe Aakjær sang måske om farfars jord, men Jack Kerouac sang om mit baghoved og hvad der skete i det."

Det var som sagt i 1979. Tilbage til New York i 1976. Under sit ophold i The Big Apple skulle Dan Turèll selvfølgelig se alt dét, han allerede kendte og havde skrevet om, og møde alle sine helte. Men så gik det hverken værre eller bedre, end at han også mødte en landsmand—eller en landsdame—nemlig Suzanne Brøgger. De delte kærligheden til dét, man kalder Det Andet Amerika, og Brøgger ville vide, hvorfor Dan Turèll med hans glødende engagement i og identifikation med alt det amerikanske ikke flyttede til U.S.A., lod sine tekster oversætte, *blev* amerikaner. Hvortil Dan Turèll svarede, at i U.S.A. var der så mange som ham—i Danmark var der kun én.

Det er på sin vis rigtigt. Og så alligevel ikke. For med Thomas Kennedys oversættelser af Dan Turèlls digte—og nu også en del af *Vangede Billeder*—har vi fået bevis for, at Dan Turèll undervurderede sig selv. Thomas Kennedy har—som Chili Turèll så smukt har formuleret det—givet Dan Turèll en amerikansk stemme. Og modtagelsen af hans tekster *over there* vidner om sandheden i den gamle antagelse: At det er det mest lokale, der er det mest globale.

Kære Thomas! Hvis vi har undervurderet dig som forfatter hér i vores lille andedam, så undskylder vi mange gange og håber, at vi med overrækkelsen af årets Dan Turèll Medalje—denne gang oven i købet i sølv—altså sølv som i Sølvstjernerne — kan rette en lille smule op på fadæsen. Du har om nogen fortjent at blive hædret. Selvfølgelig ikke mindst for din utrættelige indsats med at fungere som selvbestaltet ambassadør for Dan Turèll (og mange andre danske digtere) i det amerikanske. Men i høj grad også for dit forfatterskab, der under alle omstændigheder er imponerende og prisværdigt, men som set hér fra denne 51. stat i det amerikanske flag er ekstra interessant, fordi du belyser den virkelighed, vi troede, at vi kendte til bevidstløshed, fra nye og overraskende vinkler.

For os mennesker er der ikke noget bedre end at blive set. Du ser os, Thomas—tak for det. Og TILLYKKE!

—*Lars Movin, marts 2016*

Lars Movin
Speaking to Thomas E. Kennedy at the ceremony of the Dan Turèll Medal, Vangede Library, March 19, 2016

IT'S ALWAYS HEALTHY for a culture, a society, a people, to be seen from the outside, through a stranger's eyes. It can be flattering, and maybe also a little bit anxiety-provoking, but always interesting and, at its best, insightful. And in Denmark—and especially in Copenhagen—we are fortunate to have such a stranger among us in the form of an American writer who has made it a half-a-life project to present Danish reality through his fiction. An outside look. I'm deliberately not saying a foreign look. For the person I have in mind doesn't exactly live up to the cliché about the American tourist who hops off the cruise boat at Langelinie, sniffs around town for a few hours, and then feels like he "gets" Denmark. No, the person I have in mind has settled in our country, and has, so far, spent forty years of his life making observations from this particular corner of the global reality, which we call the Danish one. In fact, he's been here so long that he's almost starting to think like a Dane. Just take the main character in his novel *Beneath the Neon Egg* (2014), Patrick Bluett—and then you can think of everything, both blue and we blew it, as they say in the film *Easy Rider*—who is so strikingly like the author. This fictional Bluett is an American writer who lives in Denmark, and earns his livelihood as a translator. He loves to drive around Copenhagen's inner city and the bridge districts; he loves bars, bodegas, and pubs, loves jazz, loves Danish women—so much so that he has been married to one and has had half-Danish children. But the marriage is over now, and Bluett is as blue as his name. In his newfound solitude, he seeks out new female company and manages to meet a variety of women, one of whom doesn't seem too crazy. But it turns out she lives in Albertslund. In fucking Albertslund! Bluett's been to Albertslund, and he's not going back. So he recaptures his solitude, and takes restless walks through the blue night, always accompanied by a tough-life optimism and an inner soundtrack of jazz—and each walk is depicted with a mixture of melancholy and humor, life knowledge and linguistic precision, but, above all, with empathy and a razor-sharp perspective on Danish life. The kind of perspective you can have only if you are at once both very well known and alien, and come to the project with the love of an anthropologist for his finds.

It is, of course, Thomas E. Kennedy that I am talking about: author and translator, and a faithful and congenial translator of Dan Turèll, as well as many other Danish poets, into English—but, the work of Dan Turèll, I am certain, most importantly.

And Dan Turèll will show up several times in the story of Patrick Bluett. The book is filled with blue-tinted descriptions of a noir Copenhagen that evoke the mood of Turèll's crime novels. But specifically, it is with Dan Turèll's poem "Charlie Parker in Istedgade" that his poems are quoted as well. The protagonist's favorite poem—even though he's American—is actually Turèll's "Through the City Last Time." In one scene Bluett contemplates going to the Café Guldregn and drinking a toast to the late poet. It doesn't happen, but, later in the book, on another night walk, he drops into the Pub Femmeren in Classensgade, where, by chance, he sits at the bar next to a young man who, he later finds out from the bartender, is Halfdan E, a man who has recorded two albums with Dan Turèll. Two albums with Dan Turèll!

Since then, the book's author—Thomas Kennedy—has himself recorded an album with Halfdan E, entitled *An Introduction: Dan Turèll + Halfdan E Meets Thomas E. Kennedy* (2013). In it, Kennedy has put together a selection from the two albums that Halfdan E made with Dan Turèll, *Pas På The Money!* (1993) and *Happy in the Year* (1996), and has translated the poems, and recorded them in English for Halfdan E's tracks. If you don't know the CD, I highly recommend it.

The novel I spoke of before, *Beneath the Neon Egg*, is part of Thomas Kennedy's great work, *The Copenhagen Quartet*—four independent and varied-but-related novels, all of which play out with Copenhagen as the backdrop. That *Quartet* alone should have made Thomas Kennedy famous in Denmark. Hopefully, he will become more widely known now that the small publishing house Rod&Co has finally spotted the books and started to publish them in Danish translation. The first volume, *In the Company of Angels*, has just been published. The others should follow soon.

Despite the Danish publishing world having been slow to acknowledge his greatness, Thomas Kennedy's work has been lauded abroad, including, of course, *The Copenhagen Quartet*. A few years ago he signed a contract with the illustrious publisher Bloomsbury, which has since been publishing his books in the U.K. and U.S.A. Kennedy thoroughly revised all four volumes of *The Copenhagen Quartet*, including their titles. The four books, originally published by a small Irish publisher (2002-2005), are now available in new editions (2010-2014). The titles are: *In the Company of Angels, Falling Side-*

ways, Kerrigan in Copenhagen and *Beneath the Neon Egg*. Kennedy references Dan Turèll in the other three volumes as well.

Thomas Kennedy was born in 1944 and raised in the borough of Queens, New York's answer to Vangede. There is much we could say about his youth, but let me focus on the fact that, even as a teenager, he was fostering the dream of becoming a writer—but felt he needed more life under his belt first. After a few years, after an eventful and itinerant youth, his travels ended in Denmark, in 1976, where he has lived and worked as a writer and translator ever since.

In the early 1980s he had his first pieces published, and in 1988 his first book. Since then he's had more than thirty publications—an impressive and diverse body of work, which in itself could justify the award of the Dan Turèll Medal.

It's momentous that Thomas Kennedy discovered Dan Turèll and translated his work into English, and has toured widely with those translations, including to the United States, and has published some of those poems in fine literary journals. He recorded the aforementioned CD with Halfdan E, and, in 2010, published a volume of the translated poems, including "Through the City Last Time" ("Last Walk Through The City"), in a beautiful and exclusive edition with illustrations by our Medal artist Barry Wilmont.

Thomas Kennedy's latest project is a translation of *The Vangede Images* themselves, the first twenty-four pages of which will be published in the American literary journal *New Letters* this spring.

But let's turn the clock back forty years to the autumn of 1976—the same year that Thomas Kennedy settled in Denmark and the thirty-year-old Dan Turèll made his pilgrimage to New York. It was the first time he'd been in the United States, but in a sense he had already lived in his own inner America for many years. He had breathed jazz and rock, taken inspiration from the beat writers, and identified himself with the brooding, shadowy lives that, in crime novels by Dashiell Hammett or Raymond Chandler, drift around in the great American night.

When Dan Turèll was writing forewords to a selection of his 1970s Americana texts, *American Faces,* he was blunt: "I am an American Dane. And a very large part of my generation and most of my friends are American-Danes." And he said, sadly, as well, that "Denmark is compared to the U.S.A. as the mouse is compared to the elephant, or Nørre Snede compared to Copenhagen. Denmark is the 53rd state on the American flag (. . .). It is the United States that defines our Cultural Circle, it is the United States that defines us economically." And then in a more poetic form, he's said: "Jeppe Aakjær may have sung about grandpa's land, but Jack Kerouac sang about my mind and what happened there."

During his stay in the Big Apple, Dan Turèll would of course see the things he'd read about and meet some of his heroes. He also met a compatriot—or a country lady—namely Suzanne Brøgger. They shared a love of America, and Brøgger wanted to know why, with his ardent commitment to and identification with everything American, he did not move to the United States, let his work be translated, and become an American? Dan replied that in the United States there were many like him—but in Denmark there was only him.

That, in a way, is true. And then not. Because with Thomas Kennedy's translations of Dan Turèll's poems—now part of *Vangede Billeder*—we have proof that Dan Turèll underestimated himself. Thomas Kennedy—as Chili Turèll has beautifully formulated it—has given Dan Turèll an American voice. And the reception of his work there testifies to the truth of the old saying: It is the local that is global.

Dear Thomas! If we have underestimated you as a writer in our little duck pond, we apologise many times and hope that with the ceremony of this year's Dan Turèll Medal—this time even silver—everything's silver as in the Silver Stars—we can put right, a bit, our blunder. You, if anyone, deserve to be honored, not least for your tireless efforts in serving as a self-made ambassador for Dan Turèll (and many other Danish poets) in America, but also for your own writing, which is impressive and commendable. You've illuminated what we thought we knew of ourselves, from new and surprising angles.

For humans, there's nothing better than being seen. You see us, Thomas. Thanks for that. And CONGRATULATIONS!

—*Lars Movin, March 2016*

Pia Tafdrup
HÅBET BÆRER OS

Her ses Tom og jeg optræde sammen i Paludans Bogcafé i juni 2008

Februar 2021

Kære Tom

Det er fantastisk at have dig i Danmark. Her kan du udfolde dig som forfatter, få dine bøger udgivet i U.S.A., hvor du ustandselig har rejst rundt og præsenteret dem. Et kæmpe forfatterskab har du bygget op i de mange år, jeg har kendt dig, men du har tilmed oversat. Mig og flere andre. Hvor er vi ikke bare heldige, men også privilegerede.

Du var min første oversætter til engelsk. Det var dig, som introducerede mig på det sprog, jeg nu er mest oversat til. De fleste danske forfattere, der udkommer i udlandet, er især oversat til tysk. Det gælder ikke mig. Jeg er sikker på, at din indsats for mit forfatterskab i tidsskrifter og antologier slog døre op for de bøger, der siden er udkommet i England.

Jeg debuterede i 1981, og bare få år efter kontaktede du mig vedrørende *VERSE*, issue three, *Osiris* 23 og siden *Frank Magazine* No. 6/7. Du sendte grundig information om, hvilke eksperimenterende berømtheder, der i tidens løb havde været trykt i Frank, det fransk-amerikanske tidsskrift i Paris: Italo Calvino, Allan Ginsberg, William Burroughs, Charles Bukowski og mange andre. Du skrev, fordi redaktøren David Applefield, der dengang var studerende på Sorbonne, ville have en nordisk sektion i sit tidsskrift, der blev læst af 2000 europæiske og amerikanske læsere. Her syntes du, at jeg burde indgå, og jeg kan ikke sige dig, hvor svimlende det føltes, at du også havde lyst til at oversætte mig til dette lille, men meget fine tidsskrift. Dengang var du gift med Monique, der er dansk, og du oversatte sammen med hende.

Digtene blev sendt til Paris af dig. Den 26. oktober 1986 skrev du til mig, fordi du var blevet ringet op af David Applefield, der gerne ville have mig med i nummeret med de nordiske digtere. Du havde regnet med, at han havde antaget to eller tre digte, men det blev blot til "The Last Soft Membrane" fra *Den inderste zone* (1983), skrev du i 1987, da nummeret udkom. Det var helt fint for mig. Jeg var lykkelig for at få endnu et digt publiceret på engelsk, men du og Monique begyndte nu at sende nogle af jeres mange oversættelser til andre tidsskrifter i U.S.A. Det var dit indtryk, at det var et godt tidspunkt for oversættelser. I ville holde mig informeret om positiv feedback, når den kom (!), skrev du. Den slags varmer og løfter og giver håb om en fremtid. At du involverede dig i mine digte, og virkelig syntes om dem, gjorde mig glad.

Mine digte er skrevet på dansk, de er tænkt primært til et dansk publikum, men at det lader sig gøre at oversætte dem så godt, at de bliver trykt og læst i andre lande, det er overvældende. Du lukkede op for den store verden for mig, og du gjorde det af eget initiativ, fordi du holder af poesi og finder det vigtigt, at den når ud. Det betyder meget, at nogen brænder så inderligt for ens digte. Det betød vildt meget for mig, at du påtog dig at bringe mine digte i de mange tidsskrifter og antologier med alle de brevvekslinger, det krævede. Du og Monique fortsatte med at oversætte, I oversatte fra *Springflod* (1985), og jeg kommenterede som altid. Vi udvekslede breve og talte ofte i telefon dengang. Vi var meget enige om, hvordan digtene kunne grupperes, og jeg lyttede til dig, når du valgte, hvor de enkelte digte skulle sendes hen.

I kastede jer ikke mindst over *Hvid feber* (1986). I håbede at oversætte den hele og finde et amerikansk forlag. Ikke nogen let sag! Du skrev til mig i et af dine lange og grundige breve i april 1987, at "*WHITE FEVER* which possible could have a chance in the New York houses, even though—as you probably know—to publish a book of poetry in New York or Boston, you practically have to be a candidate for the Nobel Prize and even then they worry about losing money". Omkring et halvt år senere sendte du et håndskrevet brev, hvor du skriver "The 40-page collection of translations, mainly from *Hvid Feber*, was submitted to the ASF competition and is still awaiting judgement (I don´t expect anything there, but one can always hope)."

Håb bar os begge gennem mange år og har givet os et sublimt venskab. En hel bog blev det ikke til, men mange digte til et væld af tidsskrifter og antologier i U.S.A.. Fra Hvid feber var dine favoritter digtene "Alligevel", "Drømmen om en den læsende", "Dit ansigt" og "Lystens terror". Jeg var vildt imponeret over, hvad du og Monique fik oversat og placeret både i undergrundstidsskrifter og etablerede steder. Jeg begyndte at bruge disse digte til oplæsninger i England og U.S.A.

Dine breve. var fulde af navne på nye tidsskrifter, der skulle forsøges: *Paintbrush: a Journal of Poetry, Translation and Letters, Prism International* i Canada og *The Spirit That Moves Us* ("terrible name, but a good, nicely made journal", sagde du). Forunderligt meget lykkedes, og disse tidsskrifter blev sendt over Atlanten til mig i Rudme på Fyn, hvor jeg boede dengang med drømme om også at rejse ud i den store, vide verden. Det var en gave at få disse oversættelser, og jeg inddrager stadig oversættelserne fra dengang. For dig skete der også meget de år. Du gjorde, hvad du kunne for at få både dine noveller, romaner og essays læst i U.S.A. Det blev de, i U.S.A. såvel som i Danmark. Fejringer var der mange af.

Jeg blev efterhånden nysgerrig efter at opleve U.S.A. og rejste dertil første gang i 1987. Jeg skulle opholde mig i længere tid i New York, og du sendte rørende en artikel om East Village, fordi du havde boet der i 60'erne. Du fortalte også, hvor farligt der var i 7'erne. Du gav mig navn og adresse på flere kontaktpersoner, hvis jeg skulle få brug for hjælp. Tilmed et møde med din agent overvejede du meget overraskende. Det var lidt for meget af det gode: Jeg var digter, jeg havde end ikke en agent i Danmark og desværre på det tidspunkt et forlag, der ikke havde nogen ansat til at tage sig af de udenlandske rettigheder. Det blev senere et problem for mig. Jeg tabte for meget gulvet og besluttede derfor at forlade Borgen, det forlag, havde gjort det formidabelt godt for poesien på den hjemlige front. Borgens forlag havde mange digtere, som i 80´erne fik deres gennembrud der. Meget havde set anderledes ud i dag, hvis ikke Jarl Borgen havde haft sin store passion for poesi dengang.

Du ønskede, at "skæbnen" ville, at vi skulle mødes 30. september 1988, men du havde selv inviteret mig . . . Jeg havde de år et arbejdsværelse i Zinnsgade i København. Jeg gik ned og købte en rød langstilket rose i Eventyrblomsten, hvor den blev svøbt i cellofan, fik bånd og etikette på efter alle kunstens regler, hvorefter jeg begav mig til Københavns Universitet. Her skulle jeg høre din licentiatsforelæsning. Og her så jeg dig og Monique for første gang. I din indledende tale blev jeg overraskende omtalt som en "distinguished poet". Jeg sad og lyttede til dig uden at kende nogen omkring mig. Siden kørte du, Monique og jeg sammen i bil ud til din reception i Domus Medica. Vi havde skrevet endeløst mange breve sammen og talt i telefon i flere år, så det føltes godt omsider at tale rigtigt sammen alle tre—og tilmed fejre dig! En uforglemmelig dag.

På et tidspunkt sendte jeg dig og Monique Transformationer. Poesi 1980-1985 (1985), som jeg havde redigeret og fået udgivet på Systime. Du havde selv dengang tanker om et stort udvalg af danske digtere, så jeg tænkte, at det måske interesserede jer. Du skrev og takkede hjerteligt. Der var blot et problem: jeg havde ikke dedikeret bogen til jer. Kunne jeg ikke komme til en middag hos jer og gøre det, når jeg var i København?! Jeg husker ikke præcis, hvornår det var, men jeg tog imod invitationen og mødte op på Fragariavej 12 i Hellerup, hvor du dengang boede med Monique, din søn og datter. Det var en generøs invitation og et måltid så kærligt forberedt af Monique, der havde små sedler liggende på køkkenbordet, med hvad der skulle huskes til de forskellige retter. Lige så omsorgsfuldt som når oversættelserne blev til. Efter de mange breve og telefonsamtaler var det en glæde at sidde sammen og have god tid til at høre om hinandens liv, rejser, bøger etc.

Du fik stadig mere travlt. Ting begyndte for alvor at ske for dig sidst i 80'erne. Det var skønt at følge! Du rejste f. eks i efteråret 1987 ud over til Lisabon, Köln, Oslo og Lucerne til New York og Oklahoma for at have oplæsninger, holde foredrag, give interviews og tilmed holde workshops. Dit ophold havde været så vellykket, at du blev inviteret tilbage for i perioder at undervise på universiteter i U.S.A. Jeg blev løbende udstyret med nye telefon-numre, for at vi kunne nå hinanden. Du ville gerne høre om mit indtryk af U.S.A., fordi jeg skulle vidt omkring på den første af mine rejser med Jacob Holdt, og du kontaktede mig i komplet jetlagged tilstand om nye tidsskrifter, der havde vist interesse for mine digte. Vi talte meget og længe i telefon den-gang. Jeg fik tilsvarende mere og mere i kalenderen.

Jeg blev i maj måned 1987 sendt på en oplæsningsrejse til fem univer-siteter i England sammen med Kirsten Thorup og Dea Trier Mørch. Noget af en fest, men her ønskede man, at Anne Born, der boede i England, oversatte digte til lejligheden. Hun oversatte akkurat så mange, at læste jeg langsomt, havde jeg lige akkurat nok, og jeg var tvunget til at benytte de samme digte på alle fem universiteter. Anne Born blev imidlertid så glad for *Springflod*, at hun siden oversatte hele bogen og afsatte den til Forest Books, hvor den udkom i 1989. Både dejligt, men også problematisk, når nu du og Monique havde oversat digte fra den . . .

Ingen oversætter har eneret til mine digte. Det lærte jeg tidligt på Bor-gens Forlag, at sådan skulle det være, men så lærte jeg heller ikke så forfær-delig meget mere om oversættere og oversættelser der. Af dig lærte jeg noget meget vigtigt. I en af telefonsamtalerne, vi havde for meget længe siden, var du virkelig vred på mig. Jeg havde aldrig oplevet dig vred og hader at gøre nogen ked af det. Jeg blev så ulykkelig over den episode, der opstod, fordi jeg foreslog, at I ventede lidt med at gå videre med *Hvid feber*, som jeg var så glad for at få oversat! Husker ikke logikken bag mit forslag, jeg skrev tilbage til jer umiddelbart efter at have hørt dit synspunkt i telefonen. I fik tilsendt min tilladelse til at sende manuskriptet til The American Scandinavian Foundation Translation Competition. Hvorefter vi alle tre krydsede fingre.

I en del år oversatte både Anne Born, Roger Greenwald og siden David McDuff mine digte til engelsk. Men den telefonsamtale satte dybe spor, kan jeg godt røbe. Der var flere følelser på spil i samarbejdet, end jeg var bevidst om. Jeg vil nødigt være årsag til, at der går hul på en engel. Jeg kan love dig, at jeg lige siden har haft antennerne ude. Oversættere brænder ikke bare for teksterne, der eksisterer også nære bånd mellem oversættere og forfattere, der har arbejdet tæt sammen i meget lang tid.

Fra midt i 80´erne, op igennem 90´erne oversatte du—og også enkelte digte i dette årtusinde. Først sammen med Monique, siden alene efter jeres skilsmisse. I april 1988 skrev du fra Fragariavej: "Anyway, 1988 does seem to begin to look like Pia Tafdrup year in the American literary journals—with twenty-four poems out or soon due out so far, and another twenty or more under consideration elsewhere!"

Du skiftede adresse, og vi kom tilfældigt til at bo ikke langt fra hinanden i København på dine to sidste adresser. Vi har haft en dejlig optræden sammen i Paludans Bogcafé, vi har besøgt hinanden, og jeg kan ikke gå omkring i dine gader uden at tænke på dig. Jeg har alle tidsskrifter og antologier med dine oversættelser på en hylde i mit arbejdsværelse. De få tidsskrifter og antologier, vi ikke modtog, fremskaffede du en fotokopi af, dem har jeg ligeledes gemt. Disse amerikanske tidsskrifter og antologier udgør alle et interessant og vigtigt kapitel i mit liv.

Hvis ikke du husker de mange steder, vi fik digte bragt, kommer listen her:

Verse. No. 3 (1985). Oxford (1985).
Osiris 23. Canada & Mexico (1986).
Frank. An International Journal of Contemporary Writing & Art. No. 6/7 (Winter/Spring 1987). Paris (1987).
Paintbrush. A journal of poetry, translations and letters. (Autumn 1987). Missouri, U.S.A. (1987).
Albany Review. (August 1988). Albany, New York U.S.A. (1988).
Prism international. Contemporary writing from Canada and around the world. Vol. 26, No. 2 (1988). Vancouver (1988).
Men & Women. Together &Alone. Morty Sklar & Mary Biggs, eds. The Spirit

That Moves Us Press. Iowa, U.S.A. (1988).

The Contemporary Review. (Spring/Summer 1988). Iowa, U.S.A. (1988).

Visions. No. 28 (1988). Arlington, VA, U.S.A. (1988).

Asylum. 4:3. Greensboro, NC, U.S.A. (1988).

Rohwedder. No. 4 (1988). Los Angeles, U.S.A. (1988).

Stone Country. (Nov. 1988). MA, U.S.A. (1988).

Colorado Review. 15:2 (Fall/Winter 1988). U.S.A. (1988).

Tordenskjold. Newsletter from the Danish Writer's Union. No. 2. (Autumn 1989).

Celtic Dawn. No. 3 (1989). Oxford (1989).

Pequod. No. 26/27 (1989). *A journal of Contemporary Literature and Literary Criticism.* New York University. New York, U.S.A. (1989).

Frank. An International Journal of Contemporary Writing & Art. No. 11/12 (Winter 1990). Paris (1990).

The Seattle Review. An International, Multicultural Issue. No. 1 (1990). Washington, U.S.A. (1990).

The Cimarron Review. No. 92 (July 1990). Oklahoma, U.S.A. (1990).

Blue Unicorn. (Summer 1990). California, U.S.A. (1990).

Visions International. Virginia, U.S.A. (1990).

This Same Sky. A Collection of Poems from around the World. (Selected by Naomi Shihab Nye). Four Winds Press: New York, U.S.A. (1992).

The Cimarron Review. (Fall 1999). Oklahoma (1999).

The Literary Review. 45:3 (2002). Fairleigh Dickinson University. Madison, NJ, U.S.A. (2002).

New Letters A Magazine of Writing & Art. 7-:3/4 (2003). University of Missouri-Kansas City (2004).

Tiferet. A Journal of Spiritual Literature. 2:1 (2005). NJ (2005).

The Literary Review. 50:2 (2007). Fairleigh Dickinson University, Madison, NJ (2007).

Tænk, at et andet menneske kaster sig ud i at oversætte og tilmed placere digte i tidsskrifter og antologier, som jeg siden modtager og kan glæde mig over. Dine oversættelser og disse mange tidsskrifter og antologier, gav mig håb. Tænk, at du gjorde den indsats for mig, Tom. Det er jeg dig evigt taknemmelig for, ud over hvad du har lært mig om den enestående relation mellem oversætter og digter.

De kærligste hilsner

—Pia

Pia Tafdrup
Hope Carries Us

February 2021

Dear Tom

It's great to have you in Denmark. Here you can unfold as a writer, and have your books published in the United States, where you have constantly traveled around and presented them. You've built up a huge oeuvre in the many years I've known you, but you've even translated me and several others. We are not only lucky, but also privileged.

You were my first translator for English. You're the one who introduced me in the language I'm now most translated into. Most Danish authors published abroad have been translated into German in particular. It doesn't apply to me. I am sure that your work for my writing in periodicals and anthologies opened doors to the books that have since been published in England.

I made my debut in 1981, and just a few years later you contacted me regarding *Verse*, Issue 3, *Osiris* 23, and then *Frank Magazine*, No. 6/7. You sent thorough information about which experimental celebrities had been printed over the years in *Frank*, the Franco-American magazine in Paris: Italo Calvino, Allan Ginsberg, William Burroughs, Charles Bukowski, and many others. You wrote because the editor, David Applefield, then a student at the Sorbonne, wanted a Nordic section in his journal, which was read by two thousand European and American readers. Here you thought I should be included, and I can't tell you how staggering it felt that you also wanted to translate me into this small but very fine journal. Back then, you were married to Monique, who is Danish, and you translated with her.

The poems were sent to Paris by you. On October 26, 1986, you wrote to me because you had been called by David Applefield, who wanted me to be included in the section with the Nordic poets. You'd have expected him to have taken on two or three poems—but it just became "The Last Soft Membrane" from *The Innermost Zone* (1983), you wrote in 1987 when the track came out. That was fine for me. I was happy to have another poem published in English, but you and Monique now started sending some of your many translations to other journals in the United States. It was your impression that was a good time for translations. You would keep me informed of positive feedback when it came (!), you wrote. Such warmth and promises give hope for a future. The fact that you got involved in my poems—and really liked them—made me happy.

My poems are written in Danish, they are intended primarily for a Danish audience, but that it is possible to translate them so well that they are printed and read in other countries, it is overwhelming. You opened up the big world to me, and you did it on your own initiative because you care about poetry and think it's important that it reaches out. It means a lot when someone is so passionate about your poems. It meant so much to me that you took it upon yourself to bring my poems into the many journals and anthologies with all the correspondences it required. You and Monique continued to translate, you translated from *Spring River* (1985) and I commented as always. We exchanged letters and often spoke on the phone at the time. We were very much in agreement on how the poems could be grouped, and I listened to you when you chose where the individual poems should be sent.

In particular, you threw yourself into *White Fever* (1986). You were hoping to translate it all and find an American publisher. No easy case! You wrote to me in one of your long and thorough letters in April 1987 that "*White Fever* which could have a chance in the New York houses, even though—as you probably know—to publish a book of poetry in New York or Boston, you practically have to be a candidate for the Nobel Prize and even then they worry about losing money." About six months later, you sent a handwritten letter in which you wrote "The 40-page collection of translations, mainly from *White Fever*, was submitted to the ASF competition and is still awaiting judgment."

Hope carried us both through many years and has given us a sublime friendship. An entire book was not published, but many poems were in a multitude of journals and anthologies in the United States. From *White Fever*, your favorites were the poems "Nevertheless", "The Dream of The Reading", "Your Face", and "The Terror of Lust". I was so impressed with what you and Monique had translated and placed both in underground journals and established places. Jeg began to use these poems for readings in England and the United States.

Your letters were full of names of new journals to be approached: *Paintbrush: a Journal of Poetry, Translation and Letters, Prism International* in Canada, and *The Spirit That Moves Us* ("terrible name, but a good, nicely made journal", you said). Wonderfully very successful, and these journals were sent across the Atlantic to me in Rudme on Funen, where I lived then with dreams of also traveling into the big, wide world. It was a gift to have these translations, and I am still including the translations from that time. For you, a lot happened in those years, too. You did what you could to get both your short stories, novels, and essays read in the U.S. They were, in the United States as well as in Denmark. There were a lot of celebrations.

I gradually became curious to experience the United States and first went there in 1987. I was supposed to stay in New York for a long time, and you sent me an article about the East Village because you'd lived there in the '60s. You also told me how dangerous it was in the '70s. You gave me the name and address of several contact persons in case I needed help. Even a meeting with your agent, I considered very surprising. It was a little too much of a good thing: I was a poet, I did not even have an agent in Denmark and unfortunately at the time a publisher who had no one employed to take care of the foreign rights. It later became a problem for me. I lost too much ground and therefore decided to leave Borgen, the publisher, who had done formidably well for poetry on the domestic front. The Borgen's publishers had many poets who in the '80s got their breakthrough there. Much would have looked different today if Jarl Borgen had not had his great passion for poetry back then.

You wanted us to meet on September 30, 1988, and you invited me yourself. I had for years a study in Zinnsgade in Copenhagen. I went down and bought a red long-stemmed rose in Eventyrblomsten, where it was wrapped in cellophane, got ribbons, and labeled according to all the rules of art, after which I went to the University of Copenhagen. This is where I was supposed to hear your licentiate lecture. And here I saw you and Monique for the first time. In your introductory speech, I was surprisingly referred to as a distinguished poet. I was listening to you without knowing anyone around me. Then you, Monique, and I drove together by car to your reception in Domus Medica. We had been writing endless letters together and talking on the phone for several years, so it felt good to finally talk right together all three— and even celebrate you! An unforgettable day.

At one point, I sent you and Monique *Transformations: Poetry 1980-1985* (1985), which I had edited and published on Systime. You had thoughts of a large selection of Danish poets even then, so I thought it might interest you. You wrote and thanked me warmly. There was just one problem: I hadn't signed the book to you. Couldn't I come to a dinner with you guys and do it when I was in Copenhagen?! I do not remember exactly when it was, but I accepted the invitation and showed up at Fragariavej 12 in Hellerup, where you then lived with Monique, your son, and daughter. It was a generous invitation and a meal so lovingly prepared by Monique, who had small notes lying on the kitchen table, with what she needed to remember for the different dishes. Just as considerate as when the translations came into being. After the many letters and telephone conversations, it was a pleasure to sit together and have plenty of time to hear about each other's lives, travels, books, etc.

You got busier and busier. Things really started happening to you in the late '80s. It was great to follow! In the fall of 1987, for example, you travelled to Lisbon, Cologne, Oslo, and Lucerne, to New York and Oklahoma to have readings, give lectures, give interviews, and even hold workshops. Your stay had been so successful that you were invited back to teach at universities in the United States for periods. I was regularly equipped with new phone numbers so we could reach each other. You wanted to hear about my impression of the United States, because I was going far and wide on the first of my travels with Jacob Held, and you contacted me in complete jet-lagged mode about new journals that had shown interest in my poems. We talked a lot and long on the phone back then. I got correspondingly more and more on the calendar.

In May 1987, I was sent on a reading trip to five universities in England together with Kirsten Thorup and Dea Trier Mørch. Quite a party, but here they wanted Anne Born—who lived in England—to translate poems for the occasion. She translated just so many that if I read slowly, I had just enough, and I was forced to use the same poems at all five universities. Anne Born, however, became so fond of *Springflod* that she later translated the entire book and submitted it to Forest Books, where it was published in 1989. Both nice, but also problematic, since you and Monique had translated poems from the original too.

No translator has exclusive rights to my poems. I learned this early on at Borgens Forlag that this was how it should be, but then I also did not learn much more about translators and translations there. From you, I learned something very important. In one of the phone calls we had a very long time ago, you were really mad at me. I'd never seen you angry and hate to upset anyone. I was so unhappy about the episode that occurred because I suggested that you wait a bit to move on with *White Fever*, which I was so happy to get translated! Don't remember the logic behind my suggestion, I wrote back to you immediately after hearing your point of view on the phone. You were sent my permission to send the manuscript to the American Scandinavian Foundation Translation Competition. After which all three of us crossed our fingers.

For a number of years, both Anne Born, Roger Greenwald, and then David McDuff translated my poems into English. But that phone call left deep traces, I can tell you. There were more emotions at stake in the collaboration than I was aware of. I don't want to be the reason an angel breaks down. I can promise you, ever since, I've had the antennas out. Translators are not only passionate about the texts, there are also close links between translators and authors who have worked closely together for a very long time.

You translated from the mid-'80s through the '90s, and even some poems in this millennium. First with Monique, then alone after your divorce. In April 1988, you wrote from Fragariavej: "Anyway, 1988 does seem to begin to look like Pia Tafdrup year in the American literary journals—with twenty-four poems out or soon due out so far, and another twenty or more under consideration elsewhere!"

You changed your address and we accidentally came to live not far apart in Copenhagen at your last two addresses. We've had a lovely performance together in Paludan's Book Café, we've been visiting each other, and I can't walk around your streets without thinking about you. I have all journals and anthologies with your translations on a shelf in my study. The few journals and anthologies we didn't receive, you procured a photocopy of, I've saved them, too. These American journals and anthologies all constitute an interesting and important chapter in my life.

If you don't remember the many places we had poems accepted, the list comes here:

Verse. No. 3 (1985). Oxford (1985).

Osiris 23. Canada & Mexico (1986).

Frank. An International Journal of Contemporary Writing & Art. No. 6/7 (Winter/Spring 1987). Paris (1987).

Paintbrush. A journal of poetry, translations and letters. (Autumn 1987). Missouri, U.S.A. (1987).

Albany Review. (August 1988). Albany, New York U.S.A. (1988).

Prism International, Contemporary writing from Canada and around the world. Vol. 26. No. 2 (1988). Vancouver (1988).

Men & Women. Together &Alone. Morty Sklar & Mary Biggs, eds. The Spirit That Moves Us Press. Iowa, U.S.A. (1988).

The Contemporary Review. (Spring/Summer 1988). Iowa, U.S.A. (1988).

Visions. No. 28 (1988). Arlington, VA, U.S.A. (1988).

Asylum. 4:3. Greensboro, NC, U.S.A. (1988).

Rohwedder. No. 4 (1988). Los Angeles, U.S.A. (1988).

Stone Country. (Nov. 1988). MA, U.S.A. (1988).

Colorado Review. 15:2 (Fall/Winter 1988). U.S.A. (1988).

Tordenskjold. Newsletter from the Danish Writer's Union. No. 2. (Autumn 1989).

Celtic Dawn. No. 3 (1989). Oxford (1989).

Pequod. No. 26/27 (1989). *A journal of Contemporary Literature and Literary Criticism.* New York University. New York, U.S.A. (1989).

Frank. An International Journal of Contemporary Writing & Art. No. 11/12 (Winter 1990). Paris (1990).

The Seattle Review. An International, Multicultural Issue. No. 1 (1990). Washington, U.S.A. (1990).

The Cimarron Review. No. 92. (July 1990). Oklahoma, U.S.A. (1990).

Blue Unicorn. (Summer 1990). California, U.S.A. (1990).

Visions International. Virginia, U.S.A. (1990).

This Same Sky. A Collection of Poems from around the World. (Selected by Naomi Shihab Nye). Four Winds Press: New York, U.S.A. (1992).

The Cimarron Review. (Fall 1999). Oklahoma (1999).

The Literary Review. 45:3 (2002). Fairleigh Dickinson University, Madison, NJ, U.S.A. (2002).

New Letters A Magazine of Writing & Art. 7-:3/4 (2003). University of Missouri-Kansas City (2004).

Tiferet. A Journal of Spiritual Literature. 2:1 (2005). NJ (2005).

The Literary Review. 50:2 (2007). Fairleigh Dickinson University, Madison, NJ (2007).

I can't believe another human being is delving into translating and even placing poems in journals and anthologies that I later receive and can rejoice in. Your translations and these many journals and anthologies gave me hope. I can't believe you made that effort for me, Tom. I am eternally grateful to you for that, in addition to what you have taught me about the unique relationship between translator and poet.

The loveliest greetings

—Pia

Lennox Raphael
F*R*A*N*K*T*R*U*M*P*S*T*E*I*N*O

"Hi Lennox,
Well, I won't do a belly dance!"
Thomas E. Kennedy

BELIEVE ME, SO BE IT. Curiously enough, not so easy to write about a writer who, over a time, becomes your friend, and you stop thinking of him/her, as a person, my God, as writer, not easy, not easy at all, and u become more interested in the person, can even damage what u think of him as a person, a writer, whatever that could be, whoever, and I have had the pleasure so many times in my life, so many dreams, and, after a while when u think of yourself, which makes it so difficult, as one ends up having to think of oneself, and all of this is so terrifying, for/to me, already bound to the nature of disappearing marble, shards of the soul, words emotionalized by dreaming within themselves and becoming inverse precipices so difficult . . . well, maybe difficult is not the word . . . so challenging to write about someone I have come to know so well, a lovely writer, as a person, first, Tom Kennedy, with whom I have spent so much quality time here in Copenhagen, my own home since February, 1993—and I was so shocked a while back to realize suddenly this had become the place where I have spent the longest continuous time of my life—Tom Kennedy, what does he have to do with this: well, everything, a writer comes into your life, and have u wondering in a jolly good way: well, of course, blame it on Robert Gover, dear friend of mine, author of the novel ONE HUNDRED DOLLAR MISUNDERSTANDING, became best friends since that day in the sixties at the home of Walter Lowenfels, when Walter introduced me to Gover, and, lo, pronto, we became instant, psychicowboy brothers, and never stopped until he skipped this mountain for perhaps another even more challenging Paradise: but, before that, introducing me to Thomas E. Kennedy:

Sat, Jun 17, 2006, 1:32 AM

to me

Hey Lennox:
I'm in contact with Thomas Kennedy the noted short story author and it turns out he's living in Copenhagen so I gave him your phone number and address because I figure you'll want to meet him and I know he'll want to meet you. so this is a heads up that he'll probably give you a call soon or an email. He's interested in the Sixties. I was remembering an incident that happened when Jerry Rubin and Abbie Hoffman went before a HUAC hearing. I wanted to get a date for that HUAC hearing so went on line to find it. I was not overly amazed to find that all mention of that HUAC hearing has been deleted from the Net. However, a few small oblique references to it did sneak through but without any date. Would you happen to remember when that HUAC happened?
What I remember so vividly is Abbie Hoffman putting on a flag shirt in his hotel room, getting ready to make his appearance for the day, then walking across the street toward the building where the hearing was held, and being grabbed by about six cops who tore the flag shirt off his back only to find he'd painted a Vietnamese flag on his back. So they grabbed him and hustled him down a side street to a police van and locked him in it. Before they could drive away with him, some demonstrators across the street taunted them and, while they were distracted by the taunters, a long-haired hippie type let the air out of all the van's tires.
I'm not longer sure whether this happened before or after the Chicago 8 trial, but I think it was autumn. Stuff from 40 years ago kind of blurs in my memory. How about yours?
Bob

Then, me to Robert Jun 21, 2006, 11:53 AM

Such lovely weather here, for a change, and ive been spending lots of time in the country gardening, but am back in Copenhagen now, and happy to hear from you; and I/d love to meet Thomas Kennedy. Yr memory of Abbie and the shirt is spot on.
I dont have a ready date for the HUAC hearings, and im unable to put my hands on that now because all my sixties material is in Langeland, but, when I return there, I/d check.
Incredible how the sixties lives and is till an exciting era.
Somewhere in Langeland, and i havent yet unpacked the boxes moved from Copenhagen sometime ago, I have all the 68 copies of EVO, and into 69, and this has lots of relevant info.
What else. Europe is in soccer fever. 700,000 people gathered at the Brandenberg gate yesterday to celebrate Germany's victory over Ecuador. Big party time in Berlin.
I took Helga to an Irish pub last night to look at Sweden vs England on wide screen.
The match was a draw: so everybody relatively happy.
I put yr name down on list of persons to receive 'galley' of Garden of Hope, and this should be wt u any day now (mailed from California).
The water robustly cool rather than cold, and I can now stay in the sea for as long as I wish.
How's everything?
Lennox
**
And now Thomas E. Kennedy:

This guy, Thomas Kennedy, jovial, easy-going, I am hearing about him, listening, thinking, as I scrape my way thru the sea ice, but who is he, an American, writer abroad, in the honest tradition, James Joyce, Beckett, Richard Wright, Ezra Pound, Henry Miller, Hemingway, one can fill a book of quality names from all corners of the globe, the great to my heart Gertrude Stein, Elizabeth Bishop—we lived in the same area of Rio de Janeiro—and how I hate dropping names!, and only yesterday a friend in Manhattan tells me he went to a home dinner months ago and two writers were dropping my name and, after a while, had to pick it up from the floor and dust it off as, he felt, they were pretending to know me, and why not, perhaps they did, for we do live in a time, especially now, as time deconstructs itself, when everybody knows everybody and, pretense no longer instant offense, only silence is justified since everything is fake, and on the take, fake news, fake views, fake fake, fake on the make, and it's just so much that anyone can take, but letz get back, real has never been real, Ages of Enlightenment never scot-free of the magic of being while barbecuing non-being, civilizations upon civilization, piling up, one after another, play upon play, cruelty amok, rituals of godship and the politics of my nightmare better than yours and evil winds the imaginary dreams of Gertrude's dog, Basket: and what was it, this rumors of if you want to be great writer don't stay home, go somewhere where only you alone can be responsibly obsessed with language and homelessness and being privately mad and praised for it, whether Henry James or James Baldwin or Spanish Picasso in Paris or Walter Benjamin and Malcolm Lowry or Kundera, the lightning of his being, as we, artists of time, prophets of homelessness with unquestionable FACTS trembling thru sinscrutable Danish snow on a bike of all things pedaling to a heaven, all language, and I am beginning to wonder why I love Tom's company and the times we spend among the Danes who spend less and less time among themselves and treating the covid as imaginaries arising from the Mohammed cartoons that was a disaster of free speech from the get (god) wince images are never on sale and are bewitched by their own bewitchment, even as I started thinking for real of thou THOMAS, of what my dear friend, each the best friend of the other, and who/what could be even more blind than those of us who claim to fame is knowing everything of not nothing.

So, me one, in language, bewitched, bothered and bewildered, and getting to know also myself, and taking care of the office with Jesper Dalmose, co-curator, with myself, of the Berlin Soup International Arts Festival.

And, as another hint of the flow in these parts, a note from Kennedy.

Date: Sat, 19 Aug 2006 13:58:03 +0200
Subject: Poesiensdag

Hello, Lennox,

Although you and I are both Americans and have lived in Copenhagen for many years, our paths have never crossed. Recently, I've had rather extensive contact with Robert Gover, with whom I did a long interview for THE LITERARY REVIEW, and he urged me to contact you (you are also mentioned in the interview).

Today, I was being interviewed by telephone on Frederiksberg radio in connection with Poesiensdag and as I scrolled down the list of participants saw that you too will be there (in fact mentioned it on the radio and your famous Che!) It happens that my partner, Alice, and I are hosting a reception in honor of two international guests who are coming to Copenhagen specifically to participate in Poetry Day (Bob Stewart, who is editor of NEW LETTERS magazine at University of Missouri Kansas City, and his partner, Lisa Brown).

At the party will be about 40 people -- poets, actors, family, friends -- and Alice and I would be very happy if you and your partner would care to join us then.

The reception (and light buffet) will be on Saturday, August 26th, from 2.00 p.m. to 7.00 p.m

I also see that your forthcoming book will be published by Hopewell —a publisher I too am connected with and which will probably issue my next story collection in 2007. In fact, if you read INFORMATION, any day now you will see a review of Robert Gover's ONE HUNDRED DOLLAR MISUNDERSTANDING reissued by Hopewell.

Anyway, I hope very much you both will join us on Saturday, as I look forward very much to meeting you.

All best wishes,
Tom
(Thomas E. Kennedy)

Tue, 22 Aug 2006

Dear Lennox,

Here I've only just got into contact with you and am writing again—but for a good cause.

Would you be willing to write an essay for an anthology titled AGING MALE? This is the brainchild of my close friend, the award-winning novelist Duff Brenna, and I think he and I will be co-editors on it. The idea is to invite about 24 or 25 men writers to do an essay on th experience of getting older. Duff got the idea after reading a book about women and aging that was published by Nan Talese at FSG. Duff knows Nan and thought he would have a shot at getting her to consider this book for him.

The content is wide open as long as it has something to do with being male and aging. I mentioned you to Duff and he is eager to have an essay from you. Robert Gover has already agreed to do an essay himself. If you think you might be willing to do it, I can send you my essay if you would like to see what I did. Or perhaps you would prefer not to see mine. I focused on one thing only (the prostate)—another fellow is doing a piece about the recent death of his younger brother from whom he had been estranged for many years but managed to get to his death bed. Of those invited so far, the age range is about 55 to 70+, and one of our invitees is 81 (and sharp as a tack). It would be wonderful if you would consider joining the project.

The length is open—probably around 10 or 12 pages but could be longer. And the deadline is probably around March.

Hope you would like to join in. So far we have a pretty good list of people—Duff himself, me, Walt Cummins, Robert Gover, Gordon Weaver, Greg Herriges, and others, and invitations are going out to a bunch of others, including Ishmael Reed and Ahmad Jamal.

Anyway—looking forward to meeting you Saturday.
Best wishes,
Tom

I guess, it does pay to grow old; but, as Eubie Blake said, at 100, "if i knew i was going to last so long i/d have taken better care of myself."

Me2!, & here am I at work, saying YES to the invitation

[And so we met; and met, and met again, & socialized, and always such a lovely time.]
**** &,

TOM: That sounds perfect. Would you like to pick a poem from among a selection I send you, or would you like me to pick one for you?

LENNOX: Please pick one for me. A lot more exciting. Cheers, Lennox

TOM: Will do, Lennox—within the coming days. All the best!

*****

CORRECT; heart of Life in the office space, MEN AT WORK, & WOMAN TOO, gender be blessed as sky & sea.

. . . and, ever more so, out of writers responding to time & place, the imaginary in pursuit of something whose emptiness is the fullness of time whose own dream is the homelessness of an idea that squirms in the God-4sakenMistaken excellence of expectations where words are pores bought and sold to souls of lost folk; and what a merry way of having your name picked up from the floor because Jules Feiffer was your witness in the Che! trial saying he saw it and had been writing a play and having great difficulty juicing its sensuality and, from seeing Che!, understood what it was all about and went home and made what he was doing work.

AND THIS BIG CONFESSION FROM THOMAS E. KENNEDY

Hi, Lennox,

Well I won't do a belly dance!
I was thinking of reading translations of Dan Turèll for about 20 minutes with you reading one of his translations for 3-5 minutes? Does that sound okay?
Would you like me to describe it? In how many words?   And can you read first and me second -- or how would you like to do it?
LENNOX: You should read first, then have me read a poem, then u read again.
happy sunday!
June 23, 2012, 11:05 AM

***

as Niels Hav steps in:

Tue, Mar 20, 2007, 9:50 AM

Dear Tom,

Welcome to the group!
We are now five in the club: Heather, Dennis, Lennox, Thomas &
Niels.

Reading at Atheneum bookshop April 26th 5 p.m.
http://www.atheneum.dk/default.asp?show=page&id=2635
10 min. to each writer = 50 min. (maximum, strictly!)

Everyone can use hers or his 10 min. as she/he wants to tell about
her/his
work, but poetry would be preferred.

Most important is to give people a fine afternoon & enjoy an hour
with
friends.

Happy to have you with us Tom.

Best,
Niels
This, just an idea of the happy traffic

Etcetcetcetcetcetcetcetcetcetcetcetc

Then, years later, after lovely times of reading and listening and literary
plotting in Copenhagen hearing Tom was in hospital
I appealed to our Little Mermaid
& told Tom I was coming,

presented myself at INFORMACION, and, coast clear, entered the room, just as he seemed to be napping and, much later, I discovered he was out for a second, dreaming, and, opening his eyes, saw yours truly as winged angel trumpquiloquy projected into the future: and, sooner than later, I stepped on his heels & met

F*R*A*N*K*T*R*U*M*P*S*T*E*I*N*O

(winged costumed chameleon beast man

high-pitched beautiful voice

(music)

MC (*yellow overalls*): I am Time the Invisible.
This is the great golden
F*R*A*N*K*T*R*U*M*P*S*T*E*I*N*O
(*dancing playfully*)
FrankTRUMPSTEINO: Whither are u wondering?
Life, which you seek, just a peek.
So fill your belly with jelly,
day and night make merry,
let every longing be full of joy,
dance & to the music,
Don't be *noisty*
wash hands & bathe.
Fear me nut.
I*m a *ghoist*,

I*m a *Ghoid, – a Polavoidandroid*!!
!!O, boist, I*m so moist,
put me in bed with a *noist*!!
"Uh, ok!, bear with me –
& wot*bout a brief history of now for now?"

20*F*A*K*E*24
*TWENTY*FOUR HOURS,*
WILD LIZARD,
*F*R*A*N*K*T*R*U*M*P*S*T*E*I*N*O*
QUITE HORRENDOUSLY BEAUTIFUL
FAKE MIGHTY MURMURINGS
of GHOSTS with blue lies,
holes in the loopholes
& tears bringing fake fake to its knees
in ubiquitous mud postBEING disrobing chaos,
stripping beautiful chaos of harlot horror of generosity
lovely reminders at last we were mute not sad
then easily had by what was both good & bad,
being everlasting
no longer blamed by Shadows on their own
& little left to deepening sorrow bestirring sadness,
long eyes cast thru darkness,
waving regret as silence & desire,
pity weeping, dragheart down slippery slopes
of alternative reality in imagined universes,
which is, um, ----- so good,
Franktrumpsteino.
Big hug up, big babe.
Holiness from within bright yellow top,
my monster making it up as he goes along.
And where does **beacoup** begin & disbelief end?

In fact, my magic wand is a silver hand
from a thoU.S.A.nd & one platinum puns
dancing on golden window sills & cobblestoned pills
"Yes, master, what next?"
Corrosive idiocy on buns.
"This is it."
"Welcome to 20*F*A*K*E*24!"
"I*m back! I flap my flings.
How do you like my looks??"
(*showing off/in*)
"*Dread*!, isn't it?" . . .
my chiseled quesadilla jaw sadness
hot cougar caipirinha ha, ha, ha
gold standard black cohosh

love worth fighting worth dying for …
F*R*A*N*K*T*R*U*M*P*S*T*E*I*N*O
hiding underneath your breath
from that far off look in your lies
made of special stuff & powder puff
reaching out to hell was the next best thing:
cult become occult;
and now, fish I wish,
O invisible mermaid,
You are working!

I may have lost my special woo woo voodoo
in the take-out poo poo,
but time is still my best zoo.

Forget friendly errors,
Time holy like blind mirrors
Dreams become spent shells of blue kisses
from yellow chameleons,
rare consequences immensely cheering,
real time spoiling dreams,
blood lust eviscerating the just,
Time on its head scolding the dead.

That said & done, emptiness is not fun.
While remembering to
enjoy the abyss
that shrieks from its beak
leveling with the devil
since red meat can*t be beat
tears of a hurricane,
guiltless/square,
extra ghost memories flash hallucinations
from inner abyss,
Code Love, forbidden glove,
openings doublings erasures: the void.
Writing imaginary input vapor,
Pity as glandular disorder.
How deeper is your love?
Pick-up dreams, U, OK?
Time naked on the bitter honeypot,
alleged penetrations,
pro-kremlinized memories on wooden toothpicks,
centrifuged kindness ubiquitize mucus.
I swallowed my pride & tried to hide from myself:

also swallowing the dime
& made every time any time
— & yours too
&, suddenly, everything new,
and I can boast of being in love with you
"It*s all over but the crying.",

Ignore new forms of cannibalism
... eating people's spirits!
... what happens to time when we are asleep?

Wild kisses bleed pain to dust
as audited feelings begin to rust
and wazoo-kazoo risks that kiss?

Nothing matters since everything does
and, for safety's sake, hides in stray fobs:
everything's by chance
& even those without toes can dance on their heels –
making good sense of how nonsense feels

No one cares anymore –
perjured silence haunted by the noise of love
& fallout
from innocence to beguilement
& then high praise
for whips running on empty,
the scraping of brake pads
heavenly attempts to stop speed from falling apart.
Indeed, Simple survival now an art
deeper the wound more dangerous the message
Of course, too, kisses, consequences,
monsters hopscotching on one's tongue
never sorry, belong,
easily sprung from a prison yet arisen
desire not for hire
selling doubts, provoking redoubts.

I, F*R*A*N*K*T*R*U*M*P*S*T*E*I*N*O
chased by bad memories
thru fierce blizzards on the back of lizards.

O, Buttercup, buttercup,
*just don*t give up!*
(*dancing*)

wind screaming, wild kisses bleeping,
greed of bad seed
turning worst like irreducible curse,
salad of bitterness sweeter when tossed like regrets.

Buy me a dream.
Love me as a doorstep,
my heart has no instep,
feelings suddenly deaf,
ooohs outpaced my *aahs*
& chasm sad faces of now smiling enemies
of themselves
and the one who thought he was bigger than any WHAT-IF
(?) 20*F*A*K*E*24 fake Heaven of faces.
Well, here I be, alive.
Veracity scorpion pity roast proud cloud
dragon whistles tiger kiss silence
enough hypocrites squeeze apple buttocks
as anthurium consequences of puddles wag their tails
Bitterness never fails to please
meanings rinse dishes of wishes & abstract swishes
Find a *softfake*.
One word will do.
TIME

Wet lips fly quite contented in disfigured innocence
Rome is that just you, invited?
I bit my tongue on the merry*go*round.
I should've known bitter.
Crocodile smiles warm my heart and burn bridges.

As past holds to the future.
Gone are minutes lost to better promises.
I pity shadows who choose are *klepto indebto.*
Try your west to fool me;
I feel a rocket in my pocket
& am kind eunuch to know better.
Like pet pigs,
I scratch my back on memories.
Even fatal is now fractal.
The only way out was win, but who cared –
I*m a ghoist,
I*m a Ghoid, –
I*m a Polaghoid!!!
I roist my thoist.
No rezoom to boist!!!,
Foist choist Foist!!!!

Wake-up *candleflies*, rework your victories.

velvet bullets kill you softly.

I swim the wild sea
on the back of a monster

I am.
I rush
20*F*A*T*E*24
as Time collapses at the red lights.

It*s a nasty time.
I can*t stand meeting friends,
I will not be scrutinized another time,
I have lost so I have lost,
I will not lose another time,
once is enough twice is damning,
but how will I be if I am not,
should I end myself or begin a brand new elf.
Just remember, when you get to Heaven,
pull the door before inserting the key.

I don*t trust my feelings anymore, --- only U!

When I look in the mirror I see nasty-nasty-nasty
but I'm not nasty, that's not me, –
I'm not me, never *nastynastynasty,*
never part of a nasty dynasty,

here today gone to sorrow,
trumpquiloquist howling like French rolls.

I never lost in my life, OOOOOOOOO,
time tickles my satisfaction
Only fools dive when angels jive.

"I don*t like food, it makes me hungry."

Ordinary impulses are divine;
Art is still possible.
Everything stopped being Everything
a long time ago,
fake hate & make hate,
intimate culture of the intricate vulture.

The most powerful me is you.
.
No vote, no vaccine.

I keep you alive.
We nurture the future.
I*m no ordinary contemporary beast.
Be not so commasified.
This is our 20*F*A*T*E*24.
O, scurrient be scurrient,
Heroic Innocence.

"What did I say?"
I was saying, just a while ago,
You perfume like Aunt Maude,
I am an A-class fraud.
"This iron ghost has shed its curse.
Yes, *! hoya paranoia!*,
I miss you; kill the pain again.
!!!*Make us great*!!!.
No use both-siding while riding
water seamstresses sewing oceans of teardrops,
Beast of the Heart of BIGUPS,

imaginary escapes from futures
pardoned by forgetfulness
rolling down Lookout Mountain,
impossibilities puzzled by silence,
20*F*A*K*E*24,
briefs of crocodile griefs –

I*m the last of the Geoducks!!
I am the Golden Beast
whose breath is yeast at the Feast
& sweetened salt of mythical bones
too glorified to be satisfied by disloyal horror,
man o love sings.
The future is now.

The cow that jumped over the moon was carrying
fake news to the pews,
but now long-over soon,
GOOD is the best test,

limited sedition: sillyhouette: sudden me.

Don*t laugh …don*t laugh,
the devil's rebuke makes me puke,
I saw the same moon in dark noon sky
averse to being shy

siccing nauti, nauti Quantum Ali
at mercy, mercy *me.*

I could be wrong,
but this will not be me.

Perfection the seeing*eye stick, take your pick,
finder's peepers wading thru swamps of semioticks
behold, an endless me
as Life takes its own journey.
Nauseous me around tolerance + democrazy.

Look, I stare at the left hand
as one would a mirror
as Nebucanezzar & his Cleopatra ever clever
bow to the Caesar
20*F*A*K*E*24
promising golden miles making us smile
IND*E*L*I*C*I*O*U*S*L*Y

As, after a hard day's work,

timely maintenance:
indecent haste in lost taste for desire,
brushing one's nose against roses become abyss
bluebirds flying out of stones
& language as time's oyster bones

of F*R*A*N*K*T*R*U*M*P*S*T*E*I*N*O

and, Tom that question of the other year
as to what really was Lennon of the Sixties like,
*well, I didn*t know him then;*
but last time we sat for a bite was at a restaurant in Manhattan's Chinatown
with Jerry Rubin, Yoko Ono, the impeccably committed William Kunstler
(first lawyer to attend to the CHE! matter),
and Rennie Davis:
and I had flown in from the farm in Puerto Rico
with my stepson, Ion Birch, now an artist in New York,
and his mom, painter Cuqui Aponte;
and I ordered vegetarian soup, and John said, he would have some of that too;
but I could tell, looking at the laughing surface shine,
that something was amiss,
and the waiter said,"Noi, noi, noi, - no have no meat!" –
but John took the spoon & started searching:
and, lo & behold, fished out a meaty unidentified object:
and that was dat,
long before the likes of

F*R*A*N*K*T*R*U*M*P*S*T*E*I*N*O
& the magic angel
in

20*F*A*K*E*24

MASTER OF CEREMONIES: And, as for this Thomas E Kennedy, family man, great champion of the cause, great writer, impeccable smile, traveler in the land of words, loyal to friend & self, good*natured, affable, etcetera – bless his heart, just a bad belly dancer, & way past this
I, F*R*A*N*K*T*R*U*M*P*S*T*E*I*N*O

Peace & Love

Credit: photos by Jesper Dalmose, video avant-gardist & part of the Kennedy Circle.

LENNOX RAPHAEL

Martin Glaz Serup
So and so many sheets to the wind in Copenhagen

AN EVENING IN A BAR, the bar we went to most often, Rosengården, where we had Giraffes and talked about literature. Tom showed me the bullet holes in the wall behind the bar—this is where some famous Danish resistance person got killed. The Horse Thief, during World War II. Tom would of course know the full story and its context, I only knew the name of the famous Danish etc. I had heard the name throughout my upbringing.

In the same bar, another evening, Tom and I were sitting opposite each other, drinking, chatting, smoke from cigarettes and cigarillos, the atmosphere so jolly; all of a sudden, as a reply to something I said, I must have sounded arrogant, not my intention, but probably, young and drunk, Tom said: All my life is about literature, about letters. Something like that, I can't remember it word for word. He was kind and nice and sweet, and so firm, laughing but insisting, I felt ashamed. I think I might have said something about how writers of poetry are more focused on form and prose writers more on story. I felt ashamed, I feel ashamed even about writing it now. So maybe he said: All my life is about form.

When I lived in Fanø, I was in Copenhagen, maybe on my way somewhere, travelling, I stayed at Tom's place in Østerbro, in his bed, he himself slept on the couch in the living room, I am younger than him—and was much younger fifteen years ago—but he insisted.

Last time we went out, going from one bar to another, I referred to a sexual scene in one of Tom's novels that I'd just read. That was the only time I tried that, he replied.

Also the time Tom was being the literary tour guide of Irish Literature, while we were a crowd, pub crawling from one Irish bar to another. I don't even know who organised it, some society I guess. It was fabulous. I was especially flabergasted when Tom read an excerpt from some Irish playwright's work that I'd never heard of before—amazing, it was amazing; friendship, beer, and literature. I might have had a pint too many, though, for now I can't remember the name of the playwright. I'll ask Tom right away—maybe he remembers.

Heather Spears
A Sketch of Tom Kennedy

Heather Spears has passed away quietly and peacefully, eighty-six years old. She was a Canadian writer and artist living in Denmark. She published five novels and fourteen collections of poetry. *The Creative Eye*, the first of a series on visual perception, and three books of drawings. She has won numerous awards in Canada including The Governor-General's Award for Poetry. Her collection *I can still draw* was short-listed for the Lowther Memorial Award. She traveled widely and has drawn at many international festivals, and in hospitals in the Middle East, Europe, and America. A genuine person and a great artist. R.I.P. —Niels Hav

*Tom Kennedy, Heather Spears, Niels Hav, Lennox Raphael
in Copenhagen's now-closed Atheneum Bookstore
(Photograph by Christina Bjørkøe)*

Tom Kennedy by Heather Spears

Niels Hav
On the carousel of time with Tom

THIS IS HOW I REMEMBER our first visit to Tom's home. He invited us to Halloween. It was a relatively new thing in Scandinavia at the time, and we arrived with curiosity. Our spiced expectations were not disappointed. The party was a unique combination of Danish hygge and American Halloween with zombies, skeletons, pumpkins, sweets, drinks, and music. The hot center was Tom, his mood and laughter bound us together.

Thomas Kennedy had been a legend in Copenhagen long before we met. An American from New York involved in the literary life of the capital. I came in from the remote West Jutland province with the sound of the North Sea rumbling in my ears. Tom explored the capital with an urban citizen's sense of the good meeting places, he became a connoisseur of cafés, bars, pubs, and also of the literary life in Copenhagen. You meet, exchange ideas, stories, and anecdotes. Now you can use Tom's four independent novels in *The Copenhagen Quartet* as a guide to watering holes in the city.

Around Tom is always a cheerful atmosphere, blessed among the favorites. A frank kindness is the crucial criterion, the quality sine qua non if you want to be friends with Tom. That's how we know him. I have been on stage with Tom in cafés, bookstores, and at readings in Kongens Have, the park in the middle of Copenhagen, where poetry used to be celebrated with readings every summer. Tom is always in genuine contact with his audience, he has a message, people feel that.

When I exchange emails with Tom, I write in Danish, and Tom answers in English. It works perfectly, Tom is bilingual. And several times it has happened that Tom returns and fishes a poem out of my prose, he takes some sentences from my mail, translates them into English and declares that this is a poem. For example this one: Regardless how short or long / love is the stuff of joy / that keeps our heart muscle pumping.

As time goes on, this could be our common statement. We're too old to be unhappy, and it's too late to die young. Now we are in the middle of it, the wild circus of life. The roles are distributed, the clown, the acrobat, the tamer, and the trained predators. We dance and wave, and we know the show may soon end.

My greeting to Tom is a poem based on the battered inside of the cupboard under the kitchen sink in a classic Copenhagen apartment.

THE BATTERED INSIDE

The battered inside of the cupboard under the kitchen sink
makes me happy. Here are two honest nails
hammered into the original boards that have been there
since the apartment block was built. It's like revisiting
forgotten members of our closest family.
At some point the boards were blue; there is some leftover red
and a green pastel. The kitchen sink is new
and the counter has been raised ten centimeters. Probably
it's been renovated several times through the years.
The kitchen has remained current; there are new lamps,
electric stove, fridge and coffee maker.
But here under the sink a time warp has been allowed
its hidden existence. Here is the wash tub with the floor cloth,
the plunger and a forgotten bit of caustic soda.
Here the spider moves about undisturbed.

Maybe there's been kissing and dancing in this kitchen.
Probably there's been crying.
Happy people newly in love have prepared fragrant meals
and later cooked porridge while making sandwiches for lunch boxes.
Hungry children have stolen cookies. Laughter has resounded
in the stairwell and ropes have been skipped in the yard
while new cars were being parked outside. People moved in and out,
old ones died and were carried downstairs, newborn babies
were carried upstairs. Everything according to order—
my nameplate will also disappear from the door one day.
I get down on my knees in front of the kitchen sink
and respectfully greet the plunger, the spider
and the two honest nails.

© Niels Hav
The poem translated by P.K. Brask & Patrick Friesen

Per Šmidl
Close Encounters of the First Degree
In Homage to Thomas E. Kennedy

"YOU ARE NOT AMUSED," notes the narrator of Tom's "I Am Joe's Prostate" to his own self. The self has just been informed of the likely prospect of having to wear diapers. That it is not amusing is to say the least. If the truth is to be told it is terrifying.

However, that constitutes an exception since Tom, the real-life Tom that I've come to know, is usually just that: amused. It doesn't take much. Whenever there's a wee whif of jazz in the air and a mouthful of beer left in the glass his eyes exude amusement. And it is precisely for this reason that the comment —at least for us who know Tom and who are his friends—is so excruciatingly funny that the laughter in our bellies congeals in our throats to form a lump. A painful lump! Diapers! Christ almighty! What a ridiculous prospect. Reading this essay about Joe's paleolithic prostate prospects we, Tom's male friends, cringe and shrivel in our own pants. We're most definitely not amused either and so, for relief, we're obliged to flush the lump down our throats if need be with floods of beer and torrents of hearty laughter.

Truth to be told—even if the narrator of "I Am Joe's Prostate" tells us that his own self is not amused, we don't really believe it. Tom's horrified and amused and this at the same time. To use a figure of speech Tom is at bottom, that is chronically and profoundly, amused as he is peeking out at the horrifying human comedy from behind his beer glass. Being the writer he is, deep down in the depths of that being he is forever taking note of and jotting down observations about the (appallingly absurd and grotesque) world around him, a world he feels estranged from and which keeps the reservoir of laughter in his gut at a feverish pitch.

The reason I know this is because I've been there and seen it happen with my own eyes. Yes, when I close those same eyes and think of Tom, I see his face and hear his voice and smell the smoke from the cheroot and/or cigars that he always smokes in the places where we used to meet. Those places are neither of a very great number nor are they of a very great variety. Unless we meet in a cheap diner and go to Christiania's jazz club later, or we meet in Tom's ground level flat in Vardegade Street we'll ninety percent of the time meet either in a serving house or on a street corner in the immediate vicinity of such an establishment. Tom loves serving houses with such a deep and requited love that it makes him uneasy when the distance to the nearest one exceeds a short walk. In fact I would go so far as to say that Tom's love for serving houses is of a romantic nature. Actually he pretty much loves everything about them from the somehow always sensual and buxom barmaids behind the counters to the regular pissing business in unsavory urinals not to mention the draft beer schooners that the aforementioned barmaids pour him as he watches them attentively in his sympathetic way from the other side of the counter. When it comes to serving houses Tom is a downright troubadour. So well adapted to the peculiar environment of the Danish *værtshus* (serving house) has he become that he takes on its color and effortlessly, by some biochemical process, distills jazz from the smoke-filled air, absorbs the sound of people's voices at the other tables, relishes the thought of his own cheroots sticking their noses alluringly out of the freshly bought package on his own, the ready lighter next to them, and the ashtray where he drops the residue of his fiery and rather smoky pleasures.

We have probably agreed to meet at four o' clock in the serving house of—usually—Tom's choice. (Compared to Tom I'm a total amateur, novice, and dilettante when it comes to serving houses.) Tom, however, has almost always jumped the gun on me. As I approach I espy him from the other side of the street. He's sitting at his favorite table by the window with a schooner of beer before him, blowing jazz into the air, and smiling when he catches sight of me. Sometimes when we meet he's sporting his round and flat black beret that makes him look a bit like Che Guevara would have, had he had more of a flair for the simple pleasures of life; and sometimes he's not, because Tom's relationship with Cuba is less revolution than it is tobacco. Beret or no beret, either way, Tom's face lights up in a smile to let me know I'm welcome company.

"Hi Per," he'll say and gesture to the almost empty schooner on the table before him. He'll then look into my eyes and add: "Would you like to have a beer?" Affirming his supposition we shake hands, Tom downs the last drops and with glass in hand (not to have it refilled but to help the friendly barmaid with her labors) he steps to the bar.

Five minutes later Tom returns to the table with a fresh beer in each hand. He sets one down before me, sits down himself, raises his glass, and looks at me with that characteristic amused expression in his eyes that tells me as much as: "Well, here we are, out of songs to sing, sipping beer and yakking to our hearts' content, two lonely writers at day's early dusk, much too steeped in beer to say goodnight!"

The conversational subjects for Tom and me are as few, select, and choice as are our meeting places: life, literature, and women. We usually start out with the latter. Women. "I love women, not just barmaids," I'll declare and Tom will gravely nod his bereted head. If there happens to be something to relate in that department we may get stuck there and never move on to other departments. However, big news is rare and so more often than not we'll turn to shoptalk about our work-in-progress or publishing tribulations, or promotional efforts and press releases. Or the sad plight of the literary critic. Or ideas for the next strategic move ahead. We may also (on a good day) exchange impressions and profundities about Hamsun's *Hunger* or the alehouses and barmaids in Joyce's work. Kafka, too, may peek in on us occasionally. (This usually happens when my epic controversies with the Danish State's welfare-bureaucracy have once again cramped my style.)

We're now on the third and fourth pint of beer. Our tongues are loosened a bit. Against my own will and better judgement I may have broached the off-limits subject, resurrected my demoniacal persona, felt the rottten whiff of the old paranoia and decided to turn back, when . . . I look across the table at Tom. Inadvertently as it were I've uncapped a can of beans, perhaps fingered a single bean out of it and thrown it on the table. But that's enough. That's all it takes. As I said: I look across the table at Tom and what do I see? I see that amused, expectant expression on his face. His mouth is closed, he's lit a fresh cigar and is blowing clouds of smoke from between his tight lips and . . . he doesn't say anything. He knows that all he has to do is wait and nine times out of ten I can't help but spill the contents of the entire can. In one fell swoop the table is a mess of spilled beans. Tom loves it. He beams. The amusement in his eyes has turned to laughter and then it comes from his throat and mouth: "Ha-Ha-Ha!" He thinks that what I've just said is very funny even though it was horrible when it happened and it has undoubtedly left dreadful scars on my soul.

"Ha-Ha-Ha!" Tom's still laughing. And then he raises his glass: "A toast," he says, "no, a grand toast to the extortionists of this tortured world! A toast also to Per's proselytes, the host of prosecutors and his preposterous and perilous perambulations in Prague!"

I look across the table at Tom's amusement and feel relieved of my paranoia. It's the fact that I know that Tom knows. It's hardly a coincidence that in his novel, *In the Company of Angels,* the grumpy old man Mikhail Ipsen's soul is forever embittered due to his real-life emasculating encounters with the Danish State's bureaucratic machinery.

And here, in my opinion, we've arrived at the crux of the matter: why two people like Tom and I were destined to meet and become not only pals but writers in arms. Lured by the sensual tone of a jazz-saxophone Tom had settled in Copenhagen. Harassed, angry, and paranoid after a conflict with the Danish State, I had left Copenhagen to settle (for twelve years) in Prague. It was not long after my (involuntary) return from Prague, at a time when I found myself alone with my two little kids, that Tom and I met the first time. A friend had offered to babysit the kids in order for me to go out and draw a breath of fresh air on the town as it were. In the newspaper I had read that a bunch of poets and writers were going to read from their work in a large bookstore . . .

To cut a long story short: I went to the event and afterwards introduced myself to the American author Thomas E. Kennedy who I had read about in the newspapers but never met in person. (To make it still the more fateful, a friend of mine had shortly before the event lent me Thomas' novel *Greene's Summer*, which I was reading at the time.)

Thomas E. Kennedy shook my hand and asked if I'd join him and a few others for a beer in a nearby joint. I went and . . . Well, the rest is history as they say. Tom was then and Tom still is today a foreigner in Denmark, an American writer who translated Danish authors into English but had never himself been translated into Danish—not to mention published. (Why had not any of the Danish authors that Tom introduced to the American audience thought of that?) Like me, the paranoiac, prodigal son and ex-exiled writer banned from the country's literary circles, Tom existed on the fringe of Danish letters. On that first night these two outsiders realized— consciously but mostly subconsciously—that in spite of all their apparent differences they had something elusive but essential in common.

Since that first night we've helped each other and been in close touch. Thanks to you, Tom, I have published my (in Denmark unpublishable) novel *Wagon 537 Christiania* and my essay "Testimony of a Copenhagen Taxi-driver. An Essay in Four Movements" with Serving House Books. Thanks to you the "wagon" has just recently—like a bottled message tossed into the sea from the desert isle in my native land—been picked up by friendly strangers on the coast of Scotland. You, Tom, may not be informed of this but know this to be true: that in my heart you hold a special place. There will forever be with me the chronic amusement in your face beaming at me from across the table.

Reviews

AS TOM KENNEDY'S REPUTATION GREW, especially with the publication of the novels of *The Copenhagen Quartet*, he began to receive extensive reviews in major outlets like *The New York Times* and *The Washington Post*, as well as other newspapers and periodicals in several countries. Samples are included in this section.

IN THE COMPANY OF ANGELS
Jonathan Yardley, *The Washington Post*

Anyone who questions the inherent weirdness of American book publishing need look no further than the strange case of Thomas E. Kennedy. Now in his mid-60s, he is a native New Yorker who has published more than twenty books, has received extravagantly favorable reviews, enjoys an international reputation and has been festooned with the Pushcart Prize, the O. Henry Award, and other honors almost too numerous to list in this space. Yet with the exception of the occasional essay or short story and two slender volumes of nonfiction, he has gone unpublished in his native country.

Perhaps this is because he has lived in Copenhagen for more than three decades. There's certainly nothing unusual about American writers choosing to live and write abroad—Gore Vidal leaps to mind as the most prominent recent example—and still finding plenty of American publishers eager to issue their work. Of course Vidal has lived in Rome while Kennedy has chosen Copenhagen, a city that might as well be off the map so far as most Americans are concerned, but that too seems a pretty flimsy excuse for the neglect that so far has been his fate on this side of the Atlantic.

Whether that will change with the publication of *In the Company of Angels* is impossible to say, though given the usual fate of serious literature in the American marketplace there is little reason to be optimistic. Still, a good publisher has taken him on and declares itself bullish about his American prospects, so there is at least some reason to hope that he will reach something approximating the readership that he clearly deserves.

In the Company of Angels is a volume in what Kennedy calls his *Copen-*

hagen Quartet. It is set in that city sometime during or soon after the reign in Chile of Augusto Pinochet, who held office from 1974 to 1990. If that seems a strange way to date a novel set in Denmark, the explanation is simple: Its central character, Bernardo Greene, is a Chilean who was tortured for about two years by Pinochet's thugs and is now in Copenhagen for treatment at one of its centers for the rehabilitation of torture victims. It needs to be pointed out that these are places Kennedy knows well, as he has been an editor and translator of the centers' publications.

Greene, known as Nardo, was a teacher who "told some children about a poet who sang dangerous songs," as he explains to Michela Ibsen, a Danish woman with whom he eventually becomes intensely involved. When she asks how the authorities found out about this, he says: "The usual ways. A pupil who is moved by the poem says something at home. A parent complains. The principal called me in one day. He asked if I had told the pupils that the poet Domingo Gomez Rojas had been tortured by the police and went mad and died in a dungeon. I told [him] yes, I had, and he asked me why. I said because it was so. He asked me what good such information did for the pupils." The torture that followed was brutal, excruciating, insanely clever. Earlier, Nardo had told his story to Michela in the third person:

> "They were not seeking information or secrets or a confession from him. Their objective was to break his spirit only because he had been a man the people of his community respected, a teacher. They looked up to him, trusted him, a man not without dignity or the courage to examine his thoughts, his experience, and to tell of what he believed to be so. Not a hero, but a man nonetheless, still a man. Then. He believed what the philosopher Socrates said, that an unexamined life is not worth living. To break the spirit of such a man is to break the spirit of those who looked to him for their identity, for a way to think of themselves as human beings."

The description of torture that follows in Nardo's narrative is too explicit to be quoted here. He was subjected to both physical and psychological pain, including vile comments about his wife and young son who, like so many thousands during the years of Pinochet, ended up among the disappeared. That Nardo survived is nothing short of miraculous, but he did so at great cost. The Danish doctor who is treating him, a good man named Thorkild Kristensen, is able to help him recover the use of an arm that had been badly damaged during the torture. But getting to the psychological damage is far more difficult, not least because it is so painful for Nardo to revisit that time and because he simply does not want to talk about it.

"It occurred to me that we had reached the end of possibility," Kristensen says. "I was tired of this expense of time with so little result. So many months had passed. The cost was too great. His arm was healed. That was good, a substantial result. But so much remained still, and we were getting nowhere." Then, almost from out of nowhere, there is a breakthrough. The doctor asks Nardo, "How did they break you?" and suddenly the words pour forth, in a desperate torrent that leaves no doubt as to the bottomless cruelty of Pinochet's police and the suffering to which Nardo was subjected.

Nardo's principal torturer was a man he thought of as Frog-eyes, whom the doctor contemplates one night, shuddering at "the ugly gaze of a frog-eyed face that ruled my world, sent me patients, broke people, and sent them to me to be repaired again as best I could, which was not very good, laughing at how much better he was at his job than I was at mine." Kennedy understands the terrible intimacy of the relationship between torturer and victim, the polar opposite of the love being sought by Nardo, Michela, and many of the others in this story.

Of these others, the most important are Michela's octogenarian parents, shoved away by "the Great Social Democratic Kingdom of Denmark" in a bleak, high-rise nursing home, her father dying of cancer and her mother reduced to dementia. There are also Voss, Michela's lover, ten years her junior, and her ex-husband, Mads, who beat her "maybe a dozen times, twenty times, perhaps twice a year for sixteen years." She and Nardo live in the community of the abused, and eventually we come to understand that whatever hope they have for peace and a semblance of happiness must be given to them by each other.

In the Company of Angels—I leave it to you to discover the explanation for the title—is powerful and of the moment. Since it was originally published in Denmark in 2004, I suspect it was inspired by torture conducted by the American government in Iraq and Guantanamo, but I didn't detect a whiff of political or ideological posturing in it. Kennedy writes clean, evocative prose, and an occasional note of humor leavens this dark novel. He is a writer to be reckoned with, and it's about time the reckoning got underway in the country of his birth.

FALLING SIDEWAYS by Thomas E. Kennedy
Tom Andes, *The Rumpus*

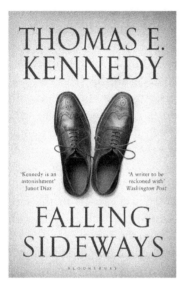

Falling Sideways, the second installment in Thomas E. Kennedy's *Copenhagen Quartet,* constitutes a ribald meditation on love and lust, fathers and sons, men and women, and the compromises one makes growing up. Told from multiple points of view, Kennedy's densely plotted novel takes place over the course of less than a week; as well as corporate intrigue, Kennedy packs several family crises and a coming-of-age story into that time frame. Rich with literary allusion, Kennedy's funny, insightful rumination on masculinity demonstrates his ample gifts as a storyteller, and it gives reason to hope Kennedy, who has lived in Copenhagen since the mid-1980s and has published more than twenty-five books on small, mostly overseas presses, will continue to find a wider audience in his native United States.

The novel commences when Martin Kampman is appointed CEO of a Copenhagen-based multinational known as the Tank for the explicit purpose of downsizing. He starts by sacking the novel's central character, Lawrence Breathwaite, the sole American at the Tank, one who has thoroughly acclimated to his environment, having married a Dane. Though he once had literary ambitions, Breathwaite has long since given them up in order to succeed in the corporate world: "Sitting to pee, he looked into the novel he'd been reading, at two lines he had underscored: *Choose carefully who you pretend to be, for that is who you will become.*" Having long since given up pretending to be anything but a corporate drone, Breathwaite begins the novel in poor health, waiting for the axe to fall. The lines he marks serve as an overture for the novel.

In an early scene, Breathwaite's debauched colleague Harold Jaeger sits in a meeting, contemplating Kampman's undecipherable mumble:

"The woman beside him, Signe Cress, head of the legal department, also one year younger than Jaeger and one step higher on the hierarchical totem, was taking notes with a silver Cross pen in a fine script he could not quite decipher. It worried him vaguely that she seemed to understand enough of what the CEO was saying to take notes."

Obsessed with hierarchies and with sex, an old-style corporate player in the vein of Don Draper from *Mad Men*, Jaeger—unlike happily married, neutered Breathwaite—has developed "some of the prime skills of manhood." Nevertheless, he lives in a dingy two-room apartment, having lost everything to a physically abusive ex-wife. By contrast, Kampman exemplifies a new type of corporate man, one distinguished by his self-control— and, by extension, by his ability to control others. After a confrontation with Breathwaite, in one of several italicized stream-of-consciousness passages, Kampman contemplates the resemblance between Breathwaite and Kampman's own alcoholic father: "*Told him with my eyes how pathetic he made himself appear. Sentimental drunk. Sad, really. Victims of themselves. Naked to the world.*" In one of the parallels that structures the novel, Breathwaite struggles with the memory of his own father's powerlessness in the face of Breathwaite's mother's infidelity, just as his son, Jes, will struggle with Breathwaite's powerlessness when he gets fired from the Tank.

As the novel develops, Kennedy focuses on the budding friendship between Kampman's and Breathwaite's sons, Adam and Jes. As Jes initiates Adam into the world of smoky bars, immigrant neighborhoods, and American rock and roll, the boys reject the compromises they see their fathers having made (again in an italicized passage): "*And Jes told me what you do for a living. You fire people. How come I never knew that before, Dad? You keep it a secret? Ashamed, maybe?*" The boys sit in Jes's apartment drinking beer and listening to jazz and old Bob Dylan records; they share a significant sexual experience with Jytte, one of several strong female characters. While the novel seems wiser than its teenage rebels, we can't help but root for them, even if we fear their idealism might be doomed.

Falling Sideways dramatizes the impossibility of having it both ways: "*Choose carefully who you pretend to be, for that is who you will become.*" Late in the book, during an argument, Jes throws these lines back in his father's face. By pretending to be a corporate man, has Breathwaite become one? To the fathers in the book, compromise equals survival, while to their sons, compromise equals a betrayal of principle. Yet if Kennedy understands the ways in which growing up necessitates compromise, he also seems to understand the price we pay for making those compromises, and part of the novel's grace lies in the fact it successfully embodies both sides of a generational conflict.

Like each novel in *The Copenhagen Quartet, Falling Sideways* stands alone, though the books share thematic links and a setting. Unlike the previous installment, *In the Company of Angels, Falling Sideways* treats masculinity as its major theme, yet in both books, Kennedy writes strong, sympathetic female characters. By the end, Breathwaite has lost nearly everything—his position, his manhood, the respect of his son; his literary dreams have long since come to naught—but he finds redemption in his marriage, which offers a reprieve from the hyper-masculine world of the Tank. In the book's final scenes, Kennedy takes several remarkable risks, delivering us to a place where we understand the tragic inevitability of selling out—and more importantly, the ways in which we might nevertheless be redeemed.

The novel succeeds in part because Kennedy seems to empathize with his most flawed characters. Even Kampman, who so engenders our hatred and makes us glad to see him fall, only wants what's best for his son. True, many of the female characters serve as helpmeets, initiating the boys (and the men) into adulthood, yet every character engages the reader's sympathy. Perhaps—as other critics have suggested—Breathwaite deserves better than he gets from his son at the end of the novel. Yet Jes's cruelty toward both his father and toward Adam underscores the moral complexity of Kennedy's world, suggesting the limits of idealism sometimes lie with the all-too-human limitations of idealists, who can abuse their power just like anyone else. Ultimately, however, the book remains hopeful, capturing art's romantic allure as well as both the rewards and the costs of pragmatism.

KERRIGAN IN COPENHAGEN A LOVE STORY
Susann Cokal, *The New York Times*

The essay, the guidebook, the love story, the comforting exchange of facts in a bewildering world of emotion—all are to be found in Thomas E. Kennedy's *Kerrigan in Copenhagen*. The novel's title character, Terrence Kerrigan, is an American expat whose pregnant wife packed up their two-year-old daughter and vanished, leaving him to eke out a somewhat intellectual and definitely dipsomaniacal middle age in the archly named "serving houses" of Denmark's capital city. The year is 1999, and Kerrigan has been hired to write a guide to the one hundred best bars in town. The result is a spiraling exploration of alcohol, history, literature, art, and jazz—and Kerrigan's wounded psyche.

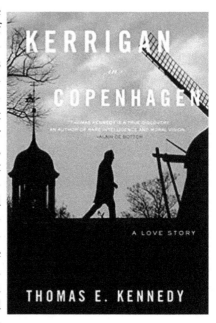

Kennedy's book, the last in a quartet of Copenhagen novels (each of which can be read independently), is undeniably smart, not least because it records the formation of a not-so-smart book. Coarse language plays off lyrical images and often stunning prose that twirls with the improvisations of the jazz musicians Kerrigan admires. It's a swirl of dichotomies. The bibulous Kerrigan is influenced equally by Joyce's *Ulysses* and Kierkegaard's *Either/Or*. A peripatetic philosopher, Kerrigan once wrote scholarly papers on literary verisimilitude; now he simply reads and drinks. A green-eyed, fifty-something woman, whom he refers to as his Research Associate, accompanies him with a Moleskine full of facts and the emotional burden of dissatisfaction with her own failed career.

Kierkegaard's *Either* comprises several essays on the value of hedonism, a.k.a. aestheticism; its companion piece, *Or,* argues in favor of social and moral responsibility. Kerrigan probably stopped with *Either.* There Kierkegaard (whose very name means *graveyard)* tries to identify the unhappiest person who ever lived. Don Juan is a contender; Kerrigan might also qualify. Fixated on the memory of his much younger ex-wife in a blue bikini, he suspects he'll never recover from her treachery and loss.

Having plumped for hedonism, then, Kerrigan more or less lives the life depicted within Kierkegaard's *Seducer's Diary.* Philosophies may change, but fermentation is forever. Copenhagen's notable sights and taverns are identified in boldface for readers who want to follow along. Kerrigan reflexively assesses the charms of the almost invariably voluptuous young barmaids as well as his age-appropriate Associate, whom he finds attractive in Ovidian soft light. It will be a small miracle if she returns his ardor: After cleaning him up following an alcohol-related accident, she's abruptly abandoned while he sleeps with his therapist and then jets off to Dublin. "You are so blind," his wife once told him. Now he's tormented by the idea that the Associate might have said the same thing after they made love. The quest for precision—perhaps an end to improvisation—drives the novel's literally breathless second half, at the end of which Kerrigan may or may not find his green-eyed Associate waiting.

Indiscriminate lust aside, the authors Kerrigan ruminates upon are male, with a few exceptions like Muriel Rukeyser (writing about female genitalia) and Karen Blixen, who wrote under the pen name Isak Dinesen (quoted on the value of drink). He grants far more time and depth to Hans Christian Andersen, Goethe, Knut Hamsun, and other literary men. Even the sculptures Kerrigan studies are male—unless they feature inviting female forms. The Associate doesn't get a name until halfway through, and even then it's rarely used.

Yes, Kerrigan is a sexist. But he offers his readers a defense: "I just adore women. So, O.K., maybe I am a sexist. But I don't know any better." Take the rough words of an educated man for what they're worth: perhaps one more miracle tipping the scales that weigh the eternal question of love . . . one more swan to float on Sortedams Sø as Kerrigan sips a beer.

BENEATH THE NEON EGG by Thomas E. Kennedy
John Harding, *The Daily Mail*

American author Thomas E. Kennedy's new novel is his fourth set in his—and his lead character Patrick Bluett's—adopted home of Copenhagen.

Divorced after a long marriage, Bluett spends his days alone in his lakeside flat, working as a freelance translator, looking out at the wintry lake and listening to jazz, especially John Coltrane's masterpiece *A Love Supreme*. The nights, though, are different; after dark, he wanders the streets, drifting from bar to bar and looking for something that's more than sex but not quite love, getting a buzz from walking on the wild side of Denmark's capital.

But when tragedy strikes his neighbour and only close friend, Bluett finds himself investigating a mystery and stumbling into danger. Brilliantly atmospheric, with a smorgasbord of edgy sexual encounters, Kennedy's novel is a symphony of loneliness and longing which completely absorbs the reader and grips the heart. Bluett's addiction to self-destruction is something we can all recognise.

As someone who has Coltrane as his ringtone, I was always going to love this book; many others will, too.

Thomas E. Kennedy's MY LIFE WITH WOMEN OR THE CONSOLATION OF JAZZ
Linda Lappin, *The California Review of Books*

Thomas E. Kennedy, author of *The Copenhagen Quartet*, is often considered a "writer's writer," one whose name may be known only to a particular niche of readers, but to whom other writers turn for illumination concerning the nuts and bolts of writing—issues of craft as well as of inspiration. His career has been a slow, steady, unstoppable river towards greater recognition. After four decades of small press publications and prestigious awards, at last, in 2010, at the age of sixty-six, he made a quantum leap to a major house—Bloomsbury, which republished all four volumes of his masterful *Copenhagen Quartet*, originally issued from 2002-2005, by Wynkyn de Worde, an independent Irish press.

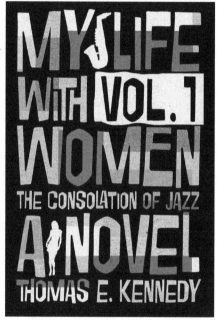

For the Bloomsbury imprint, the novels were deeply revised, refurbished with new titles, and assigned a new order in the *Quartet*. Volume 3 of the de Worde series, *Greene's Summer*, was the first to be released by Bloomsbury, now entitled *In the Company of Angels*. Dealing with the return to life of a Chilean torture victim, it was an instant success, garnering highest praise from *The Los Angeles Times*, *The New Yorker*, *The Guardian*, just to name a few. The other three volumes, all critical successes, followed closely: *Falling Sideways* (formerly *Danish Fall*), *Kerrigan in Copenhagen* (*Kerrigan's Copenhagen*) and *Beneath the Neon Egg* (*Bluett's Blue Hours*). Comparing the revisions to the originals is a fascinating study in the art of rewriting and editing for all students of the craft. *Kerrigan's Copenhagen*, for example, was completely overhauled and reduced by more than a third of its page count when republished as *Kerrigan in Copenhagen*.

The Quartet is a metafictional, intertextual, *roman fleuve*: four independent stories set in the four seasons of Copenhagen, each with a different genre and style—novel of social conscience; effervescent, experimental love story combining philosophical enquiry with a guidebook; office satire; noir. The stories unfold upon the vibrant urban canvas of Copenhagen, in, on, and around real streets, cafés, bars, parks, landmarks, bridges, and apartment buildings so that the city itself could be considered a character in the overall plan, or perhaps, a muse, like Joyce's Dublin or Durrell's Alexandria. In all four novels, jazz offers suggestions for plot structure and lends its rhythms to Kennedy's prose.

The very diverse male protagonists of each of these novels seem to be drawn from Kennedy's own direct, personal experience—as an expat writer in Denmark, an autumnal lover in search of a meaningful relationship, yet attracted to situations of risk—as well as from his professional life, as a translator working with torture victims in a rehabilitation center (*In the Company of Angels*), and as a manager in an international firm in the throes of downsizing.

In his new, two-volume, semi-autobiographical novel/fictionalized memoir, *My Life with Women*, Kennedy pushes autobiographical fiction to its limits—and gives us the backstory of his writing career: the women and the music that provided inspiration; the tangled relationships impossible to fix; the quest to become (and call himself) a real writer, interwoven with many anecdotes of the partners, writers, teachers, publishers, editors, friends, students, agents, reviewers, booksellers, rivals, children, and lovers who accompanied him from the first small press adventures to his international success. While the narrator, Edward Fitzgerald, and some of the characters bear fictionalized names, others are real people with real names whom many readers will recognize. After the first two pages, we sense that this is more than a self-portrait of the artist through the years, and we want to know: Where is the author going with this? How much is real and how much the stuff of fiction?

Two writers come to mind as mentors and models for this latest installment of Kennedy's ambitious project of transforming life into fiction and fiction into life: Anaïs Nin and Henry Miller, linked themselves by a literary and sexual passion. Anaïs Nin, who claimed that her life and writing were inseparable, transmuted her famous diary into fiction through her *roman fleuve*, following the lives of four women, each of whom represents part of Nin herself. Miller's work, strongly autobiographical, has been described by one critic as retrieving what "remains of the disappearing past." For both

Nin and Miller, honesty in addressing the darker shades of eros was essential to their work. For both, writing was an exercise in seduction (sometimes of each other) and also a form of spiritual practice. These are tenets with which Kennedy would surely agree.

Like Miller, Kennedy as a storyteller can be, at times, blunt, ribald, witty, wily, naughty, and hilarious, but also tender, philosophical, and wise. Like Nin, he can be lyrical, intuitive, and sensitive to the connections between music and writing. Like both Nin and Miller, he is willing to follow the muse wherever she leads, and by the end of Volume 2, she has led him to a most unexpected place where the writing life begins to unravel.

Volume 1 covers the period from age sixteen and his first encounters with the explosive combination of girls, jazz, and writing, to age fifty-six with the end of his loveless marriage as an expat in Copenhagen. Volume 2 opens with 9.11 and ends in 2018, when, for the first time, at seventy-four, with three major relationships come undone, he begins to frequent prostitutes, still longing to worship a female body.

It is also in the latter third of this volume, that, after confronting a frightening health crisis, he finds himself grappling with a writer's worst nightmare: losing his grip on language. First, his fluency in Danish evaporates—the language which he spoke daily, and from which he translated expertly, disappears from his tongue. He can understand it but no longer speak it. Then words in English scramble when he talks and his memory begins to falter—all due to the pressure of an inoperable brain cyst. And if that weren't enough, a nasty fall on the metro stairs sends him back to the hospital. While the reader knows that he will get back on his feet, once the broken ankle is mended, we also know that an abyss yawns up ahead and eventually the words will run out altogether.

It's in these hospital scenes, when, as Sylvia Plath suggests, one has given up one's body over to the nurses and doctors and it is no longer one's own anymore—that we see the whole range of his humanness: candid, gentle, randy, embarrassed, nostalgic, soulful, upbeat, depressed, and grateful for the courtesy he receives from friends, strangers, hospital staff. The "courtesy" he prizes echoes D.H. Lawrence's concept of "tenderness" which the English writer believed infused Etruscan culture, a sensitivity to the environment and to others which when practiced allows us to become truly ourselves leaving others room to flourish.

As his Polish "mistress" reminds him at the end of the book, the most manly thing a guy can do is face fear. And in writing this new book, that's exactly what Edward Fitzgerald aka Thomas E. Kennedy has done. Not quite

Thomas E. Kennedy Bibliography

The following list of Thomas E. Kennedy's primary works and secondary materials is in two sections. The first includes Kennedy's primary writings, listed chronologically by category, and the second includes secondary sources—essays and articles about Kennedy and reviews of Kennedy's individual books (both alphabetically by author). Where a review deals with more than one book, it is listed under essays and articles. The sections and subsections are as follows:

PRIMARY SOURCES: Novels, Books of Short Fiction, Book of Poetry, Books of Literary Criticism, Anthologies, Mini-anthologies, Short Fiction, Essays and Articles, Poetry, Song Lyrics, Columns, Literary Criticism, Craft Articles, Book Reviews, Interviews with Thomas E. Kennedy, Interviews by Thomas E. Kennedy, Translations from Danish.
SECONDARY SOURCES: I. Essays and articles about Thomas E. Kennedy. II. Selected Reviews of Books by Thomas E. Kennedy.

PRIMARY SOURCES

Novels

Crossing Borders. Wichita: Watermark Press (1990).

A Weather of the Eye. Kansas: Potpourri Publications (1996).

The Book of Angels. La Grande: Wordcraft of Oregon (1997).

Kerrigan's Copenhagen A Love Story. Galway: Wynkyn de Worde (2002). [Excerpt under same title in *The Literary Review Webchapbook*, Series 2 (2002); excerpt under title "Absinthe-Minded." *Absinthe: New European Writing.* No. 3 (2004): 6-7].

Bluett's Blue Hours. Galway: Wynkyn de Worde (2003). [Excerpt under title "Autumn Wasps." *Agni.* No. 50 (1999): 156-78; and under title "The Sacrament of Vodka." *Frank: An International Journal of Contemporary Writing & Art.* No. 18 (2001): 47-59].

Greene's Summer. Galway: Wynkyn de Worde (2004). [Excerpt under title "Michela Crosses the Bridge." *The Literary Review.* 47:2 (Winter 2004): 89-96].

Danish Fall. Galway: Wynkyn de Worde (2005). [Excerpt under title "Let Everyone Forget Everyone." *The South Carolina Review.* 40:3 (2008)].

A Passion in the Desert. La Grande: Wordcraft of Oregon (2007).

Last Night My Bed a Boat of Whiskey Going Down: A Novel in Essays. Fort Collins, CO: New American Press (2010).

In the Company of Angels. New York and London: Bloomsbury Publishing (2010) cloth (March 2010) U.S.A.; (June 2010) UK; Aus/NZ (August 2010) paper (March 2011).

Falling Sideways. New York and London: Bloomsbury Publishing (2011) cloth US Edition. (March 2011); British Edition (November 2011).

Kerrigan in Copenhagen A Love Story. New York and London: Bloomsbury Publishing (2013) cloth.

Beneath the Neon Egg. New York and London: Bloomsbury Publishing (2014) cloth.

My Life with Women or The Consolation of Jazz. Volumes 1 and 2. South Orange, NJ and Copenhagen: Serving House Books (September 2020).

Books of Short Fiction

Unreal City. La Grande: Wordcraft of Oregon (1996).

Drive Dive Dance & Fight. Kansas City: BkMk Press (1997).

Cast Upon the Day. NJ: Hopewell Publications (2007).

Getting Lucky: 20 New & Selected Stories, 1982-2012. Milwaukee, WI: New American Press (2012).

Books of Essays

Realism & Other Illusions. Essays on the Craft of Fiction. La Grande: Wordcraft of Oregon (2002). [Four major segments reprinted in a four-part series. *Potpourri* online (2003); secondary rights purchased by *Glimmer Train Writers Ask Newsletter* and reprinted in altered form (2002-continuing)].

The LiteraryTraveler (with Walter Cummins). Washington, DC: Del Sol Press (2005). [Subsequently reprinted. *The Literary Explorer.* Del Sol Press (2007)].

Riding the Dog: A Look Back at America. Fort Collins, CO: New American Press (2008).

Our Literary Travels (with Walter Cummins). South Orange, NJ and Copenhagen: Serving House Books (March 2020).

Book of Poetry
Verses for Drunks, Lechers & Miscreants & Other Boxes. Copenhagen: Iben-Books (2011) (limited hardbound edition).

Books of Literary Criticism
Andre Dubus: A Study of the Short Fiction. Boston: Twayne (1988). [Excerpt reprinted. *Short Story Criticism* 15. Detroit: Gale (1995); and *Bedford Introduction to Literature*. "On Morality and Revenge in Andre Dubus's 'Killings.'" New York: Bedford Books of St. Martin's Press (1996 and 1998) (5th ed.)].

The American Short Story Today (with Henrik Specht). Copenhagen: United States Information Service in cooperation with Fulbright Commission in Denmark and Odense University English Department (1990).

Robert Coover: A Study of the Short Fiction. New York: G.K. Hall/Macmillan (1992). [Excerpt reprinted. *Short Story Criticism* 15. Detroit: Gale (1995); and *Short Story Criticism* 101. Detroit: Thomson/Gale Group (2007)].

Index to American Short Story Award Collections, 1970-1990. New York: G.K. Hall/Macmillan (1993).

Anthologies (ed.)
New Danish Fiction (with Frank Hugus). Normal, IL: *The Review of Contemporary Fiction.* 15:1 (Spring 1995).

Small Gifts of Knowing: New Irish Poetry and Prose. Madison, NJ: *The Literary Review.* 40:4 (Summer 1997). [Introduction reprinted. *Twentieth Century Literary Criticism* (TCLC-102). Farmington, MI: Gale (2001)].

Stories & Sources. Madison, NJ: *The Literary Review.* 42:1 (Fall 1998).

Poems & Sources. Madison, NJ: *The Literary Review.* 44:1 (Fall 2000).

The Secret Lives of Writers (with Walter Cummins). Madison, NJ: *The Literary Review.* 45:4 (Summer 2002).

Best New Writing: The Eric Hoffer Award 2007 (with Christopher Klim, Robert Gover, and Mat Ryan). Titusville, NJ: Hopewell Publications (2007).

Writers on the Job (with Walter Cummins). Titusville, NJ: Hopewell Publications (2008).

New Danish Writing: Voices from the Blue Port & Beyond. Madison, NJ: *The Literary Review.* 51:3 (Spring 2008).

Best New Writing: The Eric Hoffer Award 2008 (with Christopher Klim, Robert

Gover and Mat Ryan). Titusville, NJ: Hopewell Publications (2008).

The Girl with Red Hair (Co-edited with Walter Cummins). Copenhagen & Florham Park, NJ: Serving House Books (2010).

The Book of Worst Meals: 25 Authors Write about Terrible Culinary Experiences (Co-edited with Walter Cummins). Copenhagen & Florham Park, NJ: Serving House Books (2010).

Winter Tales: Men Write About Aging. (Co-edited with Duff Brenna). Copenhagen & Florham Park, NJ: Serving House Books (2011).

Mini-anthologies (ed.)

"Danish Poetry Since 1965." *Frank: An International Journal of Contemporary Writing & Art.* No. 6/7 (Winter Spring 1987): 80-100. "Contemporary Danish Poetry and Prose in Translation." *The Cimarron Review.* No. 92 (July 1990): 7-51.

"European Profile: Jean Tardieu." *The Cimarron Review.* No. 94 (January 1991): 7-22.

"Contemporary Yugoslavian Poetry and Prose in Translation." *The Cimmaron Review.* No. 96 (July 1991): 7-70.

"Fiction and Poetry by American Expatriates." *The Cimmaron Review.* No. 100 (July 1992): 7-64. [Introduction reprinted. *Potpourri.* (May 1993): 202].

"Czechoslovakia's Jan Benes." *The Cimarron Review.* No. 98 (January 1992): 7-39.

"Three Bulgarian Poets." *The Cimarron Review.* No. 102 (January 1993): 7-26.

"New Poetry and Prose from the Baltic." *The Cimarron Review.* No. 104 (July 1993): 7-74.

"First Translations of Syrian Poetry and Prose." *The Cimarron Review.* No. 108 (July 1994): 5-38.

"International Profile: José Saramago." *The Cimarron Review.* No. 110 (January 1995): 7-18.

"Contemporary Dutch Literature." *The Cimarron Review.* No. 112 (July 1995).

"International Profile: Péter Esterházy." *The Cimarron Review.* No. 114 (January 1996): 7-30.

"Ten Irish Poets." *Potpourri.* 9:1 (1997): 36-40.

"Contemporary Irish Prose and Poetry." *The Cimarron Review.* No. 116 (July 1996): 9-90.

"Contemporary Australian Prose and Poetry." *The Cimarron Review*. No. 120 (July 1997): 7-75.

"India's Sudeep Sen." *The Cimarron Review*. Number 122 (January 1998): 7-33. "South African Fiction and Poetry." *The Cimarron Review*. No. 124 (Summer 1998): 7-76.

"European Profile: Welsh Poet Tony Curtis." *The Cimarron Review*. Nos. 126-127 (Winter 1999/Spring 1999): 7-31.

"International Retro Issue: *Cimarron* and the World: Ten Years of International Writing." *The Cimarron Review*. No. 128 (Fall 1999-Summer 1999): 3-105.192.

Short Fiction

1982

"Shadow Fruit." *Nebula*. No. 21/22 (1982): 125-33.

"A Woman of Mystery and Understanding." *Nit & Wit*. Fifth Anniversary Issue (March/April 1982): 24-5.

1984

"The Sins of Generals." *Confrontation*. Nos. 27-28 (1984): 311-21. [Reprinted. *Into the Silence: American Stories*, Andre Dubus (ed.). Cambridge: Green Street Press (1988): 200-16; and *Unreal City*. La Grande: Wordcraft of Oregon (1996): 89-111].

"The New Dust Jacket." *Central Park*. No. 5 (Spring 1984): 27-28.

1986

"A Clean Knife." *Great River Review*. 7:1 (1986): 44-60. [Honorable Mention. Pushcart Prize XII 1987-88. Reprinted. *Drive Dive Dance &Fight*. Kansas City: BkMk Press (1997): 45-60].

"Friday Fish and Cakes on Sunday." *Calliope*. 9:2 (Spring 1986): 20-30. [Reprinted as "The Fish" in *Rafters*. 1:1 (1996): 64-73].

"Color of Darkness, Color of Night." *Soundings East*. 9:1 (Spring/Summer 1986): 11-18. [Reprinted. "Color of Darkness." *Four Quarters*. 9].

"The Eldorado Bar & Grill." *Beloit Fiction Journal*. 2:1 (Fall 1986): 46-56. [Reprinted. *Potomac Review*. (Summer 1996): 24-9].

"Here's My Story, It's Sad But True." *Black Warrior Review*. 13:1 (Fall 1986): 52-61.

1987

"Escargots." *North American Review*. 272:2 (June 1987): 32.

"City of the Foxes." *Writers Forum.* 13 (Fall 1987): 135-47.

"Gasparini's Organ." *Crosscurrents.* 7:3 (1987): 99-116. [Reprinted. *Literary Olympians II, Crosscurrents Anthology* (1987): 183-212; Fiction: *The Best of Crosscurrents,* 1980-92 (1994): 49-66; *Unreal City.* La Grande: Wordcraft of Oregon (1996): 171-91].

"A Berlin of the Mind." *Passages North.* 8:2 (Summer 1987): 6-8. [Passages North Emerging Writer Competition Winner; reprinted in *Passages North Anthology: A Decade of Good Writing.* Minneapolis: Milkweed Editions (1990): 305-13; *Passport Magazine.* 5 (1993): 13-24; in Serbian translation in *CBCKE* 19 (1994): 129-34; in *Unreal City.* La Grande: Wordcraft of Oregon (1996): 25-40].

"The Devil Trap." *Asylum.* 3:1 (June 1987): 24-6. [Reprinted in *Open Magazine* (1988): 10-11; *Cornerstone.* 18:89 (1989): 20-21; *Unscheduled Departures: The Asylum Anthology of Short Fiction.* (1991): 46-8; *Icon.* 30:2 (Spring 1992): 11-13; World's Apart Issue 1 (1996): 18-19; *Ragtime.* 7:1 (2000): 12-3; *Tiferet.* 1:1 (Winter 2004): 46-8; *Offshoots* 9. (2007); and re-told at numerous venues in Danish by StoryTeller Olsen in StoryTelling Festivals].

1988

"Thanksgiving." *Riverwind.* 11(1988): 67-78.

"Years in Kaldar." *The Literary Review.* 31:3 (Spring 1988): 315-27. [Charles Angoff Award from *The Literary Review*; Honorable Mention. *Best American Short Stories 1989* and *The Pushcart Prize XIII, 1988-89*; reprinted in *Cast Upon the Day.* Titusville, NJ: Hopewell Publications (2007): 15-34].

"The Angel of the Lowlands." *Other Voices* 9. 3:9 (Fall 1988): 94-103. [Reprinted in *Unreal City.* La Grande: Wordcraft of Oregon. 41-58].

"The Fly, the Wasp, the Ant." *Asylum: A Magazine of the Arts.* 4:3 (1988): 9-13.

1989

"Flies." *Confrontation.* Nos. 39/40 (Fall-Winter 1989): 75-90.

"Murphy's Angel." *New Delta Review.* 6:1 (1989): 71-87. [Reprinted. *The Pushcart Prize XV, 1990*: 348-61; Serbian translation. *CBECKE* 10 (Fall 1991): 133-43; *Unreal City.* La Grande: Wordcraft of Oregon (1996): 59-76].

"The Great Master." *Missouri Review.* XII:2 (1989): 179-90. [Reprinted. *Unreal City.* La Grande: Wordcraft of Oregon (1996): 7-24; *Writers Notes Maga-*

zine. 2 (2004): 2-10; *The Booktrader Christmas Album* (2008): 29-32].

"What Does God Care about Your Dignity, Victor Travesti?" *New Letters.* 55:3 (Spring 1989): 27-50. [Reprinted. *The Whole Story: Editors on Fiction.* Columbia, SC: Bench Press (1996): 173-80. *Unreal City.* La Grande: Wordcraft of Oregon (1996): 129-44; *Stories & Sources: The Literary Review.* 42:1 (Fall 1998): 161-9; *Realism & Other Illusions.* La Grande: Wordcraft of Oregon (2002): 161-72].

"Dental Assistant." *Touchstone.* 9:1 (Spring 1989): 33-8. [Reprinted. *Mediphors.* No. 15 (1989): 15-7].

1990

"Little Sinners." *American Fiction Number 1.* New York: Birch Lane Press (1990): 99-112.

"The Night Door." *The Gopherwood Review.* (Fall 1990): 6-8.

"Footsteps." *Short Story.* I:1 (Fall 1990): 1-9. [Reprinted. *World Wide Writers.* 10 (2000): 205-15].

"To the Western Wall, Luke Havergal." *Margin.* 11 (1990): 77-88. [Honorable Mention in *Pushcart Prize XVI 1991*; reprinted under title "The Book of Angels" with introduction by Gladys Swan. *The Southwest Review.* 79:2/3 (Spring/Summer 1994): 529-39; reprinted. *Unreal City.* La Grande: Wordcraft of Oregon (1996): 113-28].

"St. Catherine's Foot." *Z Miscellaneous.* 1990: (unpaginated). [Reprinted. *The Alembic.* (Spring 1996): 157-62].

1991

"One Less Butterfly." *Maryland Review.* (Spring 1991): 39-46.

"The Story about the Dog." *Bluff City.* 2:1 (Spring 1991): 18-21.

"Unjust and Deceitful Men." *Four Quarters.* 5:2, Second Series. (Fall 1991): 37-44.

"Paper." *Rockford Review.* X (1991): 85-9.

"The Heat Death." *New Letters.* 57:3 (Fall 1991): 75-91. [Honorable Mention in *Pushcart Prize XVII*, 1991-92; reprinted in *Unreal City.* La Grande: Wordcraft of Oregon (1996): 145-70; reprinted. Serbian translation. *OCBHT 16* (1996): 45-53].

"Sally at the Bullfight." *Paristranscontinental.* 2 (1991): 91-8. [Reprinted. *Oxford Magazine.* 8:1 (Spring-Summer 1992): 25-35; French excerpt. *Syntaxe anglaise.* Paris. (1998): 274-84].

"Seeing Things." *Virginia Quarterly Review.* 67:2 (Spring 1991): 336-46. [Reprinted. *Unreal City.* La Grande: Wordcraft of Oregon (1996): 77-88].

1992

"Graceless Soldiers." *Epiphany: A Journal of Literature.* (Summer 1992): 204-12.

"Christmas Eve." *Bluff City.* 3:1 (Summer 1992): 20-9.

"Dust." *New Delta Review.* 8:1 (Summer 1992): 25-40. [Reprinted. *Drive Dive Dance & Fight.* Kansas City: BkMk Press (1997): 61-76; *Realism & Other Illusions.* La Grande: Wordcraft of Oregon (2002): 183-98].

"Landing Zone X-Ray." *New Letters.* 58:4 (Fall 1992): 73-85. [Reprinted. *O. Henry Prize Stories 1994.* New York: Doubleday (1994): 346-59 (cloth and pb); Honorable Mention. *Pushcart Prize XVIII.* (1993-94); reprinted. *Drive Dive Dance & Fight.* Kansas City: BkMk Press (1997): 141-52].

"A View of the World." *Chariton Review.* 18:2 (Fall 1992): 12-22.

"Flying Lessons." *The Gettysburg Review.* 5:4 (Autumn 1992): 578-89. [Honorable Mention. *Pushcart Prize XVIII* (1993-94); reprinted. *Americas Review. Writing of the Political Movements.* No. 6 (1994): 15-29].

1993

"The Young Man Has a Grief." *The Contemporary Review.* No. 5 (Winter 1993): 3-17.

1994

"Danish Light." *Passport 7.* (1994): 141-56.

"Bonner's Women." *Glimmer Train.* No. 10 (Spring 1994): 78-93. [Reprinted. *Drive Dive Dance & Fight.* Kansas City: BkMk Press (1997): 3-16; reprinted. *Rosebud.* No. 19 (Fall 2000): 61-7, with an introduction by Gordon Weaver].

"The Burning Room." *New Letters.* 60:3 (1994): 109-36. [Reprinted. *Drive Dive Dance & Fight.* Kansas City: BkMk Press (1997): 17-44. Reprinted. *Mediphors No. 11* (1998): 16-23; Honorable Mention. *The Pushcart Prize XXIV.* (2000)].

1995

"It Was a Secret." *Paragraph.* (Summer 1995): 35.

"The Severed Garden." *New Letters.* 61:3 (1995): 135-56. [Reprinted. *Drive Dive Dance & Fight.* Kansas City: BkMk Press (1997): 121-40].

"Broccoli is a Vegetable." *Vignette.* (Summer 1995): 81-91.

"Some Words on Paper." *The European Magazine.* Nos. 3-9 (August 1995): 20. [Short Story Competition winner; reprinted. *The Cape Cod Voice Lit-*

erary Issue. 1:7 (August 2-15, 2001): 4-5].

"The Face at the Window." *The European Magazine.* 26 (October-November 1995): 18-19. [Short Story Competition winner].

"Drive Dive Dance & Fight." *New Letters.* 61:4 (1995): 35-58. [Reprinted. *Drive Dive Dance & Fight.* Kansas City: BkMk Press (1997): 97-120].

1996

"Kansas City." *New Letters.* 62:4 (1996): 37-58. [Reprinted. *Drive Dive Dance & Fight.* Kansas City: BkMk Press (1997): 77-96].

"Bliss Street." *Patchwork of Dreams: Voices from the Heart of the New America.* New York: The Spirit That Moves Us Press (1996): 32-46.

"Noises in Fiction." *New Novel Review.* 4:1 (Fall 1996): 127-34. [Reprinted. *Realism & Other Illusions.* La Grande: Wordcraft of Oregon (2002): 91-102].

"The Report." *Fiction & Drama.* 8 (1996): 127-33. [Reprinted. *The Aurora.* No. 1 (Winter 1997): 11-17].

"Cat Face Moon." *Potpourri.* 8:3 (Fall 1996): 6-10.

1997

"Young Lion Across the Water." *Prism International.* 36:1 (Fall 1997): 16-24. [Honorable Mention. *Pushcart Prize XXIII*; reprinted. *Atlas 2* (2007): 95-105].

"Small Gray Blues." *Oregon East.* XXVIII (1997); 74-99. [Winner of Shock Waves Fiction Competition, Permeable Press; Reprinted. *Writers Notes Magazine.* Issue 6 (2006): 19-35; reprinted. *Cast Upon the Day.* Titusville, NJ: Hopewell Publications. (2007): 35-52].

"Anniversary." *The Alembic.* (Spring 1997): 114-18.

1998

"Communion." *Gettysburg Review.* 11:2 (Summer 1998): 231-46. [Reprinted. *Cast Upon the Day.* Titusville, NJ: Hopewell Publications (2007): 121-43.

"Beyond the Wall." *World Wide Writers.* No. 2 (April 1998): 11- 26.

"Morbid Anatomy." *Mediphors.* No. 12 (Fall-Winter 1998): 21- 3.

"Truly Slush." *Rejected Quarterly.* 1:2 (Fall 1998): 10-14.

1999

"Rafferty, the Goddess." *Glimmer Train.* No. 30 (Spring 1999): 60-75.

"Bluett's Plunge." *StoryQuarterly.* No. 35 (1999): 111-26. [Reprinted. "Gurb's Plunge" in *Cast Upon the Day.* Titusville, NJ: Hopewell Publications

"Autumn Wasps." *Agni.* No. 50 (1999): 156-78. [Excerpt from novel, *Bluett's Blue Hours* (2003)].

"Cast Upon the Day." *Arts & Letters: Journal of Contemporary Literature and Art.* No. One (Spring 1999): 46-59. [Reprinted. *Cast Upon the Day.* Titusville, NJ: Hopewell Publications (2007): 105-20].

"South American Getaway." *World Wide Writers.* 5 (1999): 157-69. [Reprinted. *Cast Upon the Day.* Titusville, NJ: Hopewell Publications (2007): 91-104].

"The Foot of St. Catherine." *The Literary Review.* 42:3 (Spring 1999): 394-9.

2000

"Donna Aube." *Glimmer Train.* No. 35 (Summer 2000): 88-103. [Reprinted. *Where Love Is Found.* New York: Washington Square Press (2006): 308-20].

"The Order of the Flowers." *New Letters.* 60:3 (2000): 115-27.

"Angelique." *Buzzwords.* Issue 3 (December 1999): 15-22.

2001

"The Sacrament of Vodka." *Frank: An International Journal of Contemporary Writing & Art.* No. 18 (2001): 47-59. [Excerpt from novel, *Bluett's Blue Hours* (2003)].

"A Cheerful Death." *Gulf Coast.* 13:1 (Winter 2001): 144-57. [Winner 2000 *Gulf Coast* Short Story Contest. Honorable Mention. *Pushcart Prize 2002.* Reprinted. *Cast Upon the Day.* Titusville, NJ: Hopewell Publications (2007): 72-90].

"The Splendor of Truth." *Boulevard.* 16:3 No. 48 (Spring 2001): 1-11. [Reprinted in *Cast Upon the Day.* Titusville, NJ: Hopewell Publications (2007): 144-57].

"Surprise Endings." *New Letters.* 68:1 (2001): 107-26. [Reprinted. *Cast Upon the Day.* Titusville, NJ: Hopewell Publications (2007): 186- 206].

"The Age for a Cage." Potpourri. 13:3 (2001): 63-6.

2002

"Angel Body." *Angel Body and Other Magic for the Soul.* Sheffield: Back Brain Recluse (2002): 7-15. [Sequel to "Murphy's Angel"—see 1989].

"Kerrigan's Copenhagen." *The Literary Review Webchapbook.* Series 2 (2002): online. [Excerpt from *Kerrigan's Copenhagen A Love Story.* 2002].

2003

"The Pleasure of Man and Woman Together on Earth." *New Letters*. 69:2 & 3 (2003): 215-39. [Honorable Mention. *Pushcart Prize XXIX 2005*. Reprinted. *Cast Upon the Day*. Titusville, NJ: Hopewell Publications (2007): 158-85].

2004

"Absinthe-Minded." *Absinthe: New European Writing*. No. 3 (2004): 6-7. [Excerpt from novel, *Kerrigan's Copenhagen, A Love Story*, 2002].

"Michela Crosses the Bridge." *The Literary Review*. 47:2 (Winter 2004): 89-96. [Excerpt from novel, *Greene's Summer*. (2004)].

2006

"Mizzen Morph." *The Cape Cod Voice Literary Issue*. 5:20 (February 9-22 2006): 15-17.

"A Thought." *Contrary Magazine*. (December 2006) (online).

2007

"Fellow Travelers." *Glimmer Train*. No. 63 (Summer 2007): 78-91. [Reprinted. *Cast Upon the Day*. Titusville, NJ: Hopewell Publications (2007): 207-222].

"Baboon Dream." *Perigee: Publication for the Arts*. No. 18 (October 2007) (online).

2008

"Let Everyone Forget Everyone." *The South Carolina Review*. 40:3 (Spring 2008): [Altered excerpt from novel, *Danish Fall*, 2005].

"Is Dog?" *Fiction Magazine*. (Spring 2008).

"Dancing with Mary Ella." *Perigee: Publication for the Arts*. No. 20 (April-May-June 2008) (online).

"Pig Soup." *Oregon East Magazine*. 39. (2008).

"What to Take." *Oregon East Magazine*. 39 (2008).

"Connection" and "The Willow." *Fifteen Project*. (online magazine) (2008).

2009

"Man at the Window." *Tiferet*. (2009).

"Adventures of an Old Dude" (novella). *New Letters*. 76:2 (2010): 153-92.

2011

"Straining Man." *World Prose Portfolio #2.* (2011) (online literary journal).

2012

"Getting Lucky" (novella). *The South Carolina Review.* 45:2 (Fall 2012).

Essays and Articles

1989

"Medical Education in the European Communities." (With Hans Karle). *European Journal of Education.* 24:4 (1985): 399-410.

1990

"What Does It Mean to Be a European?" (in Danish). *Journal of the Danish Medical Association.* (1990).

1993

"The Banalization of the Beast. The Fascination of Horror." *Engelsk Meddelelser (Journal of the Danish High School Teachers of English).* (Spring 1993): 13-16. [Reprinted. *RePUBLISH.* 1:1 (Spring 1994): 13-4].

1994

"A Garden of Dead Poets: Père Lachaise Cemetery, Paris." *Potpourri.* (March 1994): 19.

1995

"In the Wake of Bloom." *AWP Chronicle.* 28:3 (December 1995): 11-5. [Reprinted. *Abiko: The James Joyce Review.* No. 17 (Fall 1997/Winter 1998): 173-81; *The Literary Explorer* (www.WebDelSol.com) 2003; and *The Literary Traveler.* Washington, DC: Del Sol Press (2005): 65-76].

1996

"Standing Room Only: The 10th Annual Night of New Works." *Poets & Writers.* (March/April 1996): 24-7.

1997

"The Glass Motel: Personal reflections on the fortieth anniversary of Lolita." *The Literary Review.* 41:1 (Fall 1997): 117-30. [Reprinted as "Reflections on Lolita." *World Wide Writers 3* (1998): 187-208].

"Lunch at the Moral Pub." *Potpourri*. 10:4 (1998): 48 (mispaginated in index as 24).

"The Dream of a Castle." *Agni*. 48 (1998): 142-6.

1998

"Fortune, Fate, God, Kipling, Robert Crumb, a Broken Radio, and the Father of My Friend Who Tortured Turtles." *The Literary Review*. 42:1 (Fall 1998): 170-7.

1999

"The European Authors Who Destroyed Me." *Writers Forum*. 6:6 (October-November 1999): 13-6. [Reprinted. *Literary Review of Canada* (March 2001): 9-11 and *Potpourri*. 11:3 (1999): 21-5].

"Sweet Fire: Memories of Andre Dubus." *Agni*. 50 (1999): 179-88. "*Cimarron* and the World: Ten Years of International Writing." *The Cimarron Review*. No. 128 (Fall 1999-Winter 1999): 7-12.

"Andre, the Sharer." *StoryQuarterly*. 35 (1999): unpaginated. [Reprinted. *Andre Dubus Tributes*. New Orleans: Xavier Review Press (2001): 64-5].

"Introducing Susan Schwartz Senstad." *The Literary Review*. 43:1 (Fall 1999): 100-01.

2000

"Copenhagen: City of Light." *Write Magazine*. 1:1 (Spring 2000): 32-5. [Reprinted as "One Writer's Life in Copenhagen." *Potpourri*. 12:3 (2000): 40-3].

"Enlightened Reading." *Writers Forum*. 6:11 (November 2000): 26-31. [Reprinted as "Getting Around the Mind." *Realism & Other Illusions*. La Grande: Wordcraft of Oregon (2002)].

"The Fascinated Beast." *The Literary Review*. 44:1 (Fall 2000): 7-10.

2001

"Me and the Foreign Workers" (in Danish). *Information*. (December 24, 2001): 10.

"The Wind Blew It Away: Memoir of a Summer Day on the Contrascarpe." *The Literary Explorer*. (www.WebDelSol.com) (2001). [Reprinted. *The Literary Traveler*. Washington, DC: Del Sol Press (2005): 9-22].

"Limmat Run Past Joyce and Nora." *The Literary Explorer*. (www.WebDelSol.com) (2001). [Reprinted. *The Literary Traveler*. Washington, DC:

Del Sol Press (2005): 27-32].

"Pictures from Helsinki." *The Literary Explorer.* (www.WebDelSol.com) (2001). [Reprinted. *The Literary Traveler.* Washington, DC: Del Sol Press (2005): 37-46].

"A Little Wreath of Sonnets for Francé Preseren." *The Literary Explorer.* (www.WebDelSol.com) (2001). [Reprinted. *Isis.* (2002): 117-8; *The Literary Traveler.* Washington, DC: Del Sol Press (2005): 59-64].

2002

"The Poets & Pubs of Auld Reekie." *The Literary Explorer.* (www.WebDelSol. com) (2002). [Reprinted. *The Literary Traveler.* Washington, DC: Del Sol Press (2005): 105-114].

"Tomba Emmanuelle: The Legacy of the 'Lesser' Vigeland and the Norwegian Modernists." *The Literary Explorer.* (www.WebDelSol.com) (2002). [Reprinted. *The Literary Traveler.* Washington, DC: Del Sol Press (2005): 115-126].

"Debtors' Prison: Memories of My Early Exile in Voltaire's Ferney." *The Literary Explorer.* (www.WebDelSol.com) (2002). [Reprinted. *The Literary Traveler.* Washington DC: Del Sol Press (2005): 133-46].

"Happy Hour(s): Notes on the Translation of Two Poems by Pia Tafdrup." *The Literary Review.* 45:3 (Spring 2002): 521-23.

"Painter, Swan, Weaver: No Sameness Here." *The Literary Review.* 46:1 (Fall 2002): 200-05.

"Images of Danish Writers: Kierkegaard, Brandes, Andersen." Photo essay: *The Literary Review Web.* (www.theliteraryreview.org/tlrweb/).

2003

"I Kiss Your Feet: A Visit to Baroness Varvara." *The Literary Explorer.* (www.WebDelSol.com) (2003). [Reprinted. *The Literary Traveler.* Washington, DC: Del Sol Press (2005): 181-96].

"Ionian Days, Ionian Nights: Lefkas, Meganissi, Scorpios, Ithaca, Cephallonia." *The Literary Explorer.* (www.WebDelSol.com) (2003). [Reprinted. *The Literary Traveler.* Washington, DC: Del Sol Press (2005): 220-24].

"N'Yawk N'Yawk, Digs & Haunts of Writers." *The Literary Explorer.* (www.WebDelSol.com) (2003). [Reprinted in *The Literary Traveler.* Washington, DC: Del Sol Press (2005): 233-53].

"Life in Another Language." *The Literary Review.* 47:1 (Fall 2003) *Frank.* No. 19 (Fall 2003): 83-104. [Honorable Mention in *Pushcart Prize XXIX,* 2005].

2004

"In the Dark." *New Letters*. 70:3+4 (2004): 165-78. [Honorable Mention *Pushcart Prize* XXX (2006)].

"How a Master's Degree Fired My Ambition." *Writers Forum*. (September 2004): 9-11.

"Introducing Gladys Swan, Multi-Artist." *The Literary Review*. 48:1 (Fall 2004): 127-9.

"The Ancient Kingdom's Young Writers School." *The Literary Review* 47:3 (Spring 2004): 24-28.

"Riding the Dog." *New Letters*. 70:1 (2003/2004): 61-72. [Reprinted. *New American Essays. A Book Edition of New Letters Magazine*. 72:1 (2005/2006): 120-32].

2005

"Something to Fall Back On." *Writers on the Job*. (www.WebDelSol.com) (2005).

"The Bridge Back to Queens." *New Letters*. 71:3 (2005): 46-65. [Honorable Mention. *Pushcart Prize XXI* (2007)].

"Cold Days in Contrescarpe: Walking with Jake Barnes and Lady Alice." *The Literary Explorer* (formerly *The Literary Traveler*). (www.WebDelSol. com) (2005).

"Airports, Hotels, Taxicabs." *The Literary Explorer* (formerly *The Literary Traveler*). (www.WebDelSol.com) (2005).

"Knossos as Creative Nonfiction." *Ibid*.

"Our Banners Purple and Gold Above." *Ibid*.

2006

"Rescuing a Literary Treasure." *PIF magazine*, new edition. No. 1 (2006) (online).

"Dostoevski on Skinnergade." *The Literary Explorer* (formerly *The Literary Traveler*). (www.WebDelSol.com) (2006).

"Letting It Happen." *Writers Forum*. (January 2006).

"A Slightly Wet Spring Day in Copenhagen" (in Danish). *MetroNyt* (*Metro News*). No. 3 (May 2006).

"A Rumor of Jazz." *RondeDance 1, a literary annual*. (August 2006): 126-31.

"Introduction" to *The Book of Mamie* by Duff Brenna. La Grande: Wordcraft of Oregon (2006): 9-12.

"Angels in Disguise: Shakespeare and Co." *The Literary Explorer* (formerly *The Literary Traveler*). (www.WebDelSol.com) (2006).

"Giving Up the Money." *Ibid.*
"Assassination of the Horse Thief." *Ibid.*

2007
"The Virgins." *The Literary Explorer* (formerly *The Literary Traveler*). (www.WebDelSol.com) (2007).
"Watch Out for the Hippos, Mr. Kennedy!" *Ibid.*
"Literary Plot: Selecting a Place to be Dead." *Ibid.*
"I Am Joe's Prostate." *New Letters.* 73:4 (Summer 2007): 73-88 (Winner of "Ellie"—National Magazine Award 2008); reprinted. *Best American Magazine Writing 2008*: 426-42 (Columbia University Press) and in Danish in *Euroman* Copenhagen. (August 2008): 104-11; Winner. *New Letters* "Readers Award."
"Shoot to Maim, Smile to Disarm: Visit to Two Danish Prisons." *The Literary Explorer* (formerly *The Literary Traveler*). WebDelSol (www.WebDelSol.com) (2007).
"A Shout from Copenhagen." Weekly blog posts from October 2007 on *Absinthe: New European Writing* website, Google Blogspot, and MySpace. "Visit to an Open Prison," "Visit to a Maximum Security Prison," "Bookshops of Copenhagen," "The Baboon Dream," "Burroughs in Copenhagen," "The Meeting with Evil," "Silence Was My Song," "Rudy G & the Scent of Corruption," "Anna Pihl, You Are Real," "The Books of Duff."

2008
"Days on the Road." *Euroman.* (January 2008): 35.
"A Shout from Copenhagen." Weekly blog posts on *Absinthe: New European Writing* website, Google Blogspot, and MySpace. "Sex Workers of the World Rejoice," "The Bookstores of Copenhagen Minus One—Chester's Turns the Key," "Pain," "Farewell, Varvara; Farewell Sweet Baroness," "The Envelope, Please: National Magazine Awards 2008," "That Big Yellow 'M': I'm Hatin' It," "Dangling Man Behind the Fence," "Taste of Literary Denmark," "Kennedy Dethrones King?" "The Danish Xmas Lunch," "Creating a Life Narrative," "Katherine Mansfield, Linda Lappin, Walter Cummins."
"A Shout from Copenhagen." Column in each print issue of *Absinthe: New European Writing.* Starting with Issue 10 (2008).
"Life in Another Language" (in Danish, "At leve på et andet sprog"). *Politiken.* (November 2, 2008): Sektion 2: 1, 6.

2009

"Chasing Jack." *New Letters*. 75:1: 127-45.

"Uncle Danny Comes to America: An Introduction to the Poetry of Dan Turèll." *New Letters*. 75:2.

"Dan Turèll's 27-Year-Old Cigar." *Absinthe: New European Writing*. (Autumn 2009).

"The Ambassador of Dan Turèll" (essay-interview with Chili Turèll). *Absinthe: New European Writing*. (Autumn 2009).

2010

"Gas-pump Cowgirl 1966." *Ecotone*. (University of North Carolina-Wilmington). No. 10 (Fall 2010): 19-43.

2011

"A Night in Tunisia." *Epoch*. (Cornell University).

"Poughkeepsie 1962." *Serving House Journal*. (ServingHouseJournal.com). No. 3 (2011).

"You Don't Remember Me, But I Remember You: For Janet McDonald (1994-2007)." *Serving House Journal*. (ServingHouseJournal.com). No. 4 (2011).

"The Murdered Poet" (on José Domingo Gómez Rojas). *New Letters*. 78:1 (2011-2012): 63-70.

2012

"The Night Side." *Ecotone*. (University of North Carolina-Wilmington) (Spring 2012).

Poetry

1985

"Two Poems: A senryu and a haiku." *Great River Review*. 6:2 (1985): 285.

1988

"Five Tributes." *Slipstream*. No. 8 (Summer 1988): 77.

"Transit Passenger." *Passages North*. 9:2. (Summer 1988): 7. [Poetry contest finalist; also issued on an audio cassette issue of *Slipstream*. (1988)].

"To Sappho." *Hollins Critic*. XXVI:2 (April 1989): 18-9. [Reprinted. *Celtic Dawn 5* (1990): 32].

1991

"The Dark Lover." *The Contemporary Review*. No. 4 (Spring/Summer 1991): 45-6.

"Your Painted Face: 7 Poems 'Clear Pearl Nails,' 'In Your Face,' 'Against the Sun,' 'Natural Separation,' 'Heavenly Skin,' 'Second Person Direct,' 'Removal.'" Featured Poet. *Happy*. Vol. 3 (Fall 1995): 36-7.

1996

"Dream Life." *Thorny Locust*. No. 11 (Summer 1996): 4.

"Song." *Ibid*: 5.

"Two haiku." *Potpourri*. 8:6 (1996): 42.

1997

"Black Soup." *Gulf Stream Review*. No. 13 (1997): 60.

2001

"Amber Hunting." *The South Carolina Review*. 33:2 (Spring 2001): 100.

"A Little Wreath of Sonnets for Francé Preseren." *Isis* (*Journal of the Slovenian Medical Association*). 7 (July 2001): 117-18. [Reprinted. *The Literary Explorer*. (www.WebDelSol.com) (2001) and *The Literary Traveler*. Washington, DC: Del Sol Press (2005): 59-64].

"Finnish Songs," "Perkele," and "Magick Instructions." *The Literary Explorer* (formerly *The Literary Traveler*). (www.WebDelSol) (2001); reprinted. *The Literary Traveler*. Washington, DC: Del Sol Press (2005): 43-5.

2006

"Continuing Story of My Life in Østerbro (Transportation from Ferlinghetti)." *The Booktrader Julehæfte* (*Christmas Annual*). 14-16 (2006): 7-12.

2009

"Verses for Drunks, Lechers, and Miscreants." *The Booktrader Julehæfte* (*Christmas Annual*). (December 2009).

2010

"Poems in Cigar Boxes." *New Letters*.

Song Lyrics
1970
"Sad Song, Happy Song," "You May Never Wake Up," and "Hangover Horns."
Hammer. San Francisco/Atlantic Recording Co. SD203 (1970).

1995
"Turns Me Around Upside My Head." Little Wolf: Music from the Hill
House. Hill House Music: HHM10000 (1995).

2008
"Angel's Gone Away." Little Wolf: Music from the Hill House 2. Hill House
Music (2008).

Columns
"The Literary Explorer" (formerly "The Literary Traveler"). (with Walter
Cummins). (www.WebDelSol.com) (2001-continuing).
"Writers on the Job." (with Walter Cummins). (www.WebDelSol.com)
(2005-2020).
"A Shout from Copenhagen." On *Absinthe: New European Writing*; Google
Blogspot; FaceBook; and MySpace (tek@adslhome.dk). (Online regular-
ly from October 7, 2007).

Literary Criticism (short works)
1985
"This Intersection Time. The Fiction of Gordon Weaver." *The Hollins Critic*.
22:1 (February 1985): 1-11.

1986
"A Literalist of the Imagination." *Sewanee Review*. 94:4 (Fall 1986): lxxx-
viii-xc. [Reprinted. *Contemporary Literary Criticism*. (1991, 1992,
1994)].
"Imagination as a Way of Knowing in the Fiction of Gladys Swan." *Writers
Forum*. No. 12 (Fall 1986): 15-24.

1987
"The Existential Christian Vision in the Fiction of Andre Dubus." *Revue Del-
ta*. No. 24 (février 1987): 91-102. [Reprinted in altered form in *Andre
Dubus: A Study of the Short Fiction*. Boston: Twayne. (1988); and *Tiferet*.

I:II (2004): 5-9].

"The Progress from Hunger to Love: Three Novellas by Andre Dubus." *The Hollins Critic*. 24:1 (February 1987): 1-9. [Reprinted in altered form in *Andre Dubus: A Study of the Short Fiction*. Boston: Twayne. (1988)].

"A Fiction of People and Events." *The Sewanee Review*. 95:2 (Summer 1987): xxxix-xii. [Reprinted in altered form in *Andre Dubus: A Study of the Short Fiction*. Boston: Twayne (1988)].

"Fiction as its Own Subject." *The Kenyon Review*. IX:3 (Summer 1987): 59-71. [Reprinted in abbreviated form in *Sherwood Andersen. Harold Bloom's Major Short Story Writers*. Philadelphia: Chelsea House Publishers (2003): 72-5].

"Reading Joyce" (on "Clay"). *PMLA Forum: Publications of the Modern Language Association of America*. 102:5 (October 1987): 845-6.

"Language Against the Void." *The Chariton Review*. 13:1 (Spring 1987): 108-10.

1988

"Sean O'Faolain's 'The Silence of the Valley.'" *Critique: Studies in Contemporary Fiction*. 29:3 (Spring 1988): 188-94.

"American Story Since the War." *The Midwest Quarterly: A Journal of Contemporary Thought*. 29:2 (Winter 1988): 280-4.

1989

"Art as Identity in the Recent Fiction of Gordon Weaver." *The Chariton Review*. 15:1 (Spring 1989): 88-98.

"Introduction to John Barth's 'Livshistorie'" (in Danish). *Kannibal*. No. 4 (1989): 20.

"The Exporting of Pia Tafdrup." *Tordenskjold, Newsletter of the Danish Writers Union*. 2 (Autumn 1989): 13-14.

"Balancing Acts." *American Book Review*. 11:1 (March-April 1989): 9.

"Picketing the Zeitgeist: Donald Barthelme." *American Book Review*. 11:5 (November-December 1989): 3, 18, 25. [Reprinted. *Contemporary Literary Criticism Yearbook 1989*. Vol. 59. Detroit: Gale (1991): 250-51].

1990

"Realism & Other Illusions: Innovation and Convention in Recent American Short Fiction." *The American Short Story Today*. Copenhagen: United States Information Service. (1990): 27-36.

"The Turning Point: The American Short Story" (in Danish). *Revue Verdens-*

litteraturen 1990. Copenhagen: Standart/Samleren, 1990: 98-100. [Reprinted in *Engelsk Meddelelser. Newletters of the Danish High School Teachers of English.* No. 73 (December 1991): 41-49].

"Barthelme, Barth, and Coover: Realism and Reality in Contemporary American Literature" (in Danish). *Fredag.* No. 1:27 (1990): 50-9.

1991

"A Mixed Gathering of Danish Women." *Translation Review.* Nos. 36-37 (1991): 52-3.

"Barthelme's Realism." *The Review of Contemporary Fiction.* 11:2 (Summer 1991): 22-3.

"The Deed-Drenched Past." (on Gladys Swan). *American Book Review.* 13:4 (October-November 1991): 26. [Reprinted. *Contemporary Literary Criticism.* (1992)].

"Realism Plus" (on Gordon Weaver). *American Book Review.* 13:5 (December 1991/January 1992): 30.

1992

"The Pushcart Prize." *ANQ: A Quarterly Journal of Short Articles, Notes, and Reviews.* 5:4. New Series (October 1992): 203-6.

1993

"Gordon Weaver." *Dictionary of Literary Biography: American Short Story Writers Since World War II.* Raleigh: Brucolli Clark Layman. (1993): 308-13.

"The New American Expatriates." *Potpourri.* (May 1993): 20-2. [Reprinted introduction to mini-anthology in *The Cimarron Review.* No. 100 (July 1992): 7-13].

"The American Short Story Today, Part One." *Potpourri.* (September 1993-1994).

"The American Short Story Today, Part Two." *RePUBLISH.* 1:1 (January 1994).

1995

"Future Classics: Two Novels for Tomorrow's Readers." *Surfing Tomorrow: The Future of American Fiction.* Prairie Village, KS: Potpourri Publications. (1995): 51-8.

2001

"Small Gifts of Knowing." *Modern Irish Literature, Twentieth Century Literary Criticism*. Vol. 102 (Ed. Linda Pavlovski) GALE Group (2001): 295- 7.

2008

"Seven Exemplary Fictions." (Excerpt from *Robert Coover: A Study of the Short Fiction*. New York: Twayne, 1992) in *Short Story Criticism* Vol. 101 (Ed. Jelena Krstovic) Thomson-Gale (2008): 164-72.

2009

"Violence: The Language of Isolation." (Excerpt from *Andre Dubus: A Study of the Short Fiction*. New York: Twayne, 1988) and "The First and Last Stories of Andre Dubus" [from *The Gettysburg Review*. 14:2 (Summer 2001)] in *Short Story Criticism* Vol. 118 (Ed. Jelena Krstovic) GALE, Cengage Learning (2009): 1-13 and 49-53.

Craft Articles

1988

"Illicit Entries into Private Minds: On Point of View Shift in Fiction." *The Seattle Review*. 11:2 (Fall 1988/Winter 1989): 72-81. [Reprinted. *Seattle Review*. 21:1 (Spring-Summer 1998): 216-25; and in altered form in *Realism & Other Illusions*. La Grande: Wordcraft of Oregon (2002)].

1989

"Interviewing." *New Writers Magazine*. (November-December 1989): 20. [Reprinted in altered form in *Realism & Other Illusions*. La Grande: Wordcraft of Oregon (2002)].

1990

"Rejection, Persistence, and Reward." *Poets & Writers*. 18:3 (May/June 1990): 29-35. [Reprinted. *The Writers Place Newsletter*. Milwaukee (1991) and in altered form in *Realism & Other Illusions*. LaGrande: Wordcraft of Oregon (2002)].

1991

"Can You Teach Someone to Write? On the American Writing Schools."

NAAS Newsletter: The Nordic Association for American Studies. (Spring 1991): 8-9. [Reprinted. *PIF* (online) and in altered form in *Realism & Other Illusions.* La Grande: Wordcraft of Oregon (2002) and *Potpourri* 14:3 (2002): 30-5 (and online 2003)].

1992

"From a Far Country: The Problem of Place." *The Writing Self.* 1:2 (Spring 1992): 1, 3. [Reprinted. *Potpourri.* (November 1993): 14, and in altered form in *Realism & Other Illusions.* La Grande: Wordcraft of Oregon (2002)].

1993

"Writing in a Castle." *Potpourri.* (October 1993): 14-5. [Reprinted in *AWCP Chronicle.* (February 1995)].

"A Piece of the Moveable Feast. The WICE Paris Writers Workshop." *Potpourri.* 5:9 (September 1993): 19-21.

1994

"Realism & Other Illusions." *AWP Chronicle.* 26:6 (May-Summer 1994): 26-30. [Reprinted. *Best Writing on Writing 2.* Cincinnati: Story Press (1996): 196-207, in *Realism & Other Illusions.* La Grande: Wordcraft of Oregon (2002) and in *Potpourri.* 14:4 (2002): 40-7 and online (2003)].

1995

"A Story's Five Senses." *The Writer.* 108:8 (August 1995): 21-4. [Reprinted. *The Writer's Handbook.* (1996) Boston: The Writer Press. (1996): 170-4].

"Losing Your Mind." *Writing Exercises for Students of Writing.* Anne Bernays and Pamela Painter. New York: Harper Collins. (1995): 44-6.

1998

"Torturing Your Sentences: A checklist for self-editing a fiction manuscript." *The Seattle Review.* 21:1 (Spring-Summer 1998): 206-15. [Reprinted in altered form in *Realism & Other Illusions.* La Grande: Wordcraft of Oregon (2002) and in *Potpourri.* 15:1 (2003): 26-35].

1999

"On Naming Characters," "On Learning to Write," and "On Point of View." *Glimmer Train Writers Ask Newsletter.* Issues 4, 16, 18 (1999).

2002

"Last Word: Prose Needs to be Built Like a Cathedral." *Writers Forum*. 8:8 (April 2002): 72.

2006

"The Forbidden Shift." *The Glimmer Train Guide to Writing Fiction, Building Blocks*. Cincinnati: Writers Digest Books. (2006): 28-30.

"Imposing Your Will." *Ibid*: 200-2. "Writing Advice." *Ibid*: 220.

"Read the Poets." *Ibid*: 252-3.

"Thomas E. Kennedy." (on research). *Ibid*: 371-2.

2007

"Get Surreal." *The Writer*. 120:5 (May 2007): 44-5.

"Who Says You Can't Shift Point of View in Fiction?" *The Writer*. 120:10 (October 2007): 37-40.

2008

"The Junk We Carry." *The Writer*. 121:5 (May 2008): 24-7.

2009

"The Art of Hunting Amber." *The Writer*. 122:5 (May 2009).

"A Writer Is One Who Writes." *Glimmer Train Newsletter* (online).

"The Impulsion of Spontaneity." *Perigee Publication for the Arts*. (online) (July 2010).

"Cutting Up." *Glimmer Train Bulletin*. (April 2010).

"Four Questions about Writing." *Writers & Artists Yearbook* 2010. (Feb-Mar-Apr 2010).

Book Reviews

1986

"A Celebration of Our Perishability: *On The Man Who Loved Levittown* by W.D. Wetherell." *The Hollins Critic*. 23:1 (February 1986): 12.

1988

"On Sudden Fiction, James Thomas (ed)." *New Letters Review of Books*. 2:1 (Spring 1988): 13.

"Stories in the Mirror: Andre Dubus's Selected Stories." *New Letters Review of Books.* 2:3 (Fall 1988): 12.

1989

"Gordon Weaver's *The Eight Corners of the World.*" *Cream City Review.* 13:1 (Winter 1989): 309-13.

"To Build and to Kill: Don Metz's *Catamount Bridge.*" *New Letters Review of Books.* 2:3 (April 1989): 15.

"Confusion of Intentions: T. Nedreas' *Nothing Grows by Moonlight.*" *American Book Review.* 11 (July-August 1989): 18.

"Dark Belly Laughs: Howard Bloch's *Moses in the Promised Land.*" *American Book Review.* 11:1 (March-April 1989): 9.

1990

"Kenneth Tindall's *The Banks of the Sea.*" *Home Planet News.* 7:2 (April 1990): 7, 22.

"Pia Tafdrup's *Spring Tide.*" *Celtic Dawn: The International Poetry Review.* Issue 6 (Summer 1990): 41.

1995

"Writers and Critics: Jan Gretlund's *Eudora Welty's Aesthetics of Place.*" *The Hollins Critic.* 32:5 (December 1995): 12-4.

"Insulting the National Vanity: Lance Olsen's Scherzi, I Believe." *Iowa Review.* 25:3 (Winter 1995): 166-67.

1997

"Gordon Weaver's *The Way You Know in Dreams.*" *Confrontation.* (1997).

"The Lie that Yields Truth: Jennifer Johnston's *The Illusionist.*" *The Cimarron Review.* No. 120 (July 1997): 160-61 and *Queen's Quarterly.* 104:2 (Summer 1997): 330-1.

1998

"The Speed of Frustration: Lance Olsen's *Burnt.*" *The Iowa Review.* 28:1 (Spring 1998): 201-3.

"Ordinary Lives: Tiina Nunnally's *Maija.*" *Potpourri.* 10:2 (1998): 23.

"Hot and Cool: Duff Brenna's *Too Cool.*" *Rain Taxi Review of Books.* (Fall 1998): 25.

1999

"*Frank* 16/17." *Home Planet News.* Issue 44 11:2 (Winter-Spring 1999): 8.

2001

"Chris Arthur's *Irish Nocturnes.*" *The Literary Review.* 44:3 (Spring 2001): 602-3.

2003

"Claire Tomalin's *Samuel Pepys: The Unequaled Self: A Biography.*" *Literary Potpourri.* II:3 (March 2003) (online).

"Norman Mailer's *The Spooky Art: Some Thoughts on Writing.*" *The Literary Review.* 46:4 (Summer 2003): 759-61.

2004

"Robert Stewart's *Outside Language.*" *The Literary Review.* 47:3 (Spring 2004): 145-6.

"Chris Arthur's *Irish Willow.*" *The Literary Review.* 47:2 (Winter 2004): 163-4.

2005

"David Applefield's *On a Flying Fish.*" *The Literary Review.* 48:3 (Spring 2005): 160-2.

2007

"Robert Gover's *On the Run with Dick and Jane.*" *The Literary Review.* 50:2 (Winter 2007): 190-1.

"Gladys Swan's *A Garden Amidst Fires.*" *The Literary Review.* 51:1 (Fall 2007): 227-9.

"Steve Taylor's *Cut Men.*" *The Literary Review.* 51:1 (Fall 2007): 218-9.

Interviews with Thomas E. Kennedy

1984

"Thomas E. Kennedy." *Americans in Denmark: Comparisions of the Two Cultures by Writers, Artists, and Teachers.* (F. Richard Thomas, ed.). Carbondale: Southern Illinois University Press. (1984): 23-6.

1990

"Doctor and Author." Interview by Jens Kerte (in Danish). *Politiken.* 1. Sektion. (22 February 1990): 6.

"Thomas E. Kennedy I." *New Letters on the Air.* Interview and reading.

(1990) (June 22, 1990).

1991

"The Quiet American." Interview by Bo Green Jensen (in Danish). *Weekendavisen Books.* (1 Feburary 1991): 16.

1993

"Border Crossings." Interview by David Applefield. *The Paris Free Voice.* 17:1 (February 1994): 6.

1997

"Thomas E. Kennedy II." *New Letters on the Air.* Interview by Angela Elam and Reading. (1997) (August 18, 1997).

"Language and Image: A Profile of Thomas E. Kennedy." Barbara Youree. *Potpourri.* 8:3 (1997): 3-5.

"thomas e kennedy: destroying the dominant." Interview by Lance Olsen. *George jr.* (April 1997) (online).

1998

"Thomas E. Kennedy." *Rebel Yell: A Short Guide to Fiction Writing.* Lance Olsen. San Jose: Cambrian Publications (1998): 38-9.

1999

"Real Cities with Imaginary Prose About Them: An Interview with Thomas E. Kennedy." Susan Tekulve. *The Literary Review.* 44:4 (Summer 1999) 613-28.

"Thomas E. Kennedy, Writer. Interview." Linda Davies. *Glimmer Train.* No. 30 (Spring 1999): 40-59.

2000

"American Writing in the World. A Panel Discussion on WebDelSol: Thomas E. Kennedy, Linh Dinh, Reetika Vazirani, Ilan Stavans." (Walter Cummins.) *WebDelSol.* (January 2000) (online).

2001

"Literary Conference Call: Duff Brenna in San Diego, Thomas E. Kennedy in Copenhagen." David Applefield. *Frank.* 18 (2001): 8-38.

2002

"Lifeline, Thomas E. Kennedy." *The Lancet.* 360:9341 (October 19, 2002):

1260.

"An American in Copenhagen" (in Danish). *Dorte Hygum Sørensen. Politiken.* 2nd Sektion. (27 February 2002): 4.

"Angels and Observations: An Interview with Thomas E. Kennedy." Monica Swanson. *Graph-O-Mania* (The Converse College Writing Center Newsletter.) (Fall 2002): 2, 6-7, 8-9, 10.

2003

"Thomas E. Kennedy." Derek Alger. *PIF.* (November 29, 2003) (online).

2004

"The Quiet American" (in Danish). Tonny Vorm. *Information.* (October 23, 2004): 19.

"It's Not a Choice, It's a Calling. Thomas E. Kennedy Interviewed by Duff Brenna." *Perigee: Publication for the Arts.* No. 6 (9/19/2004) (online).

"*Greene's Summer* by Thomas E. Kennedy is based on reality..." Interview in Spanish by Diego Zuniga. *Las Ultimas Noticias,* 7 (December 2004): 17.

2005

"Cheer Up, Hamlet: Interview with Thomas E. Kennedy" (in Danish). Tonny Vorm. *Euroman.* (November 2005): 32.

2007

"A View from across the Sea: An Interview with Thomas E. Kennedy." Melanie Tortoroli. *The South Carolina Review.* 40:2 (Fall 2007): 83-97.

"An Interview with Thomas E. Kennedy." Duff Brenna. *Perigee: Publication for the Arts.* (December 2007).

2008

"An Interview with Thomas E. Kennedy." Okla Elliott. *New Letters.* 75:1 (2008-2009): 90-106. [Reprinted in three parts in successive issues in *Inside Higher Education* (summer of 2009)].

"Thomas E. Kennedy." Interview by Tore Leifer on *Danish Public Radio, Culture News* (3:30-3:40 p.m., June 11th, 2008).

"Thomas E. Kennedy, Riding the Dog." Interviewed on Danish TV Station 2 ("Deadline," 5.00 o'clock news November 3, 2008).

"The Tourist's Advantage: An Interview with Thomas E. Kennedy." Markus Bernsen. *Weekendavisen* (in Danish). Nos. 26–27 (June 2008): 8-9. Reprinted in English translation in *Perigee: Publication for the Arts.* (August 2008) (online).

"Thomas E. Kennedy." *New Letters on the Air*. University of Missouri Kansas City. Radio interview. Angela Elam (October 2008).

2009

Thomas E. Kennedy. Excerpt of transcript from *New Letters on the Air*. *Frank: A Journal of Contemporary Writing & Art* (Paris). No. 20 (2009).

Thomas E. Kennedy, Interviewed by Jake D. Steele on *AuthorsAudio*. (July 2009).

2010

"An American in Copenhagen: An Interview with Thomas E. Kennedy." Joyce J. Townsend. *Writer's Chronicle*. 42:5 (Mar-Apr 2010): 8-14.

"Interview with Thomas E. Kennedy." Janet Skeslien Charles. (www.jsk-esliencharles.com) (March 31, 2010).

"Poetry Is Born in the Ear": An interview with Thomas E. Kennedy by Anna Bridgwater (in Danish). *Forfatteren (The Writer, magazine of the Danish Writers Union)* (June 2010): 4-5.

Interview on French TV "France24" *Journal de la Culture/Culture Magazine*. Eve Jackson. (October 21, 2010, 3:30 p.m.).

2011

"Thomas E. Kennedy's Dangerous Songs." Interview. Tom Andes. *The South Carolina Review*. 44:1 (Fall 2011): 97-107.

"An Interview with Thomas E. Kennedy." Sara Byrd. *Serving House Journal*. No. 4 (2011) (servinghousejournal.com).

Interviews by Thomas E. Kennedy

1984

"Nuts, Bolts, and Sheer Plod: An Interview with Gordon Weaver." *Western Humanities Review*. 38:4 (Winter 1984): 363-71.

1986

"Experience of Event, Image of Experience: An Interview with Gladys Swan." *Writers Forum*. No. 12 (Fall 1986): 25-40. [Reprinted. *Potpourri* (December 1994)].

1987

"Raw Oysters, Fried Brain, the Leap of the Heart: An Interview with Andre Dubus." *Revue Delta*. No. 24 (February 1987): 21-78. [Reprinted. *Andre Dubus: A Study of the Short Fiction*. Boston: Twayne (1988) and *Leap of the Heart: Andre Dubus Talking*. New Orleans: Xavier Review Press (2003): 89-125].

"To See the Fleeting Moment as Everlasting: An Interview with W. D. Wetherell." *Green Mountains Review*. New Series. 1:2 (Fall-Winter 1987-88): 110-20. [Nominated by the editors for a Puschart Prize].

1991

"To Intuit the Enormity of the Wreck: An Interview with Robert Coover." *AWP Chronicle*. (February 1991): 11-2. [Reprinted. *Robert Coover: A Study of the Short Fiction*. New York: Macmillan/Twayne (1992)].

1993

"Poetry Is When the Language Gets Lucky: An Interview with William Stafford." *The American Poetry Review*. 22:3 (May-June 1993): 49-55. [Reprinted. *The Muse Upon My Shoulder, Discussion of the Creative Process*. (Sylvia Skaggs McTeague). Madison: Fairleigh Dickinson University Press (2004): 48-62].

"Only for the Moment Am I Saying Nothing: An Interview with J. P. Donleavy." *Passport*. 6 (September 1993): 77-86. [Reprinted. *The Literary Review*. 40:4 (Summer 1997): 655-71 and *The JP Donleavy Compendium* (www.jpdonleavycompendium.org/)].

1994

"Frankly Speaking: An Interview with David Applefield." *Potpourri*. (June 1994): 31-3.

"The Poem is Bigger Than Me: An Interview with Pia Tafdrup" (in Danish). *Weekendavisen. Bøger*. 16-22 (September 1994): 8-9.

"A True Man of Letters: Robie Macauley." *The San Francisco Review of Books*. (June-July 1994). [Reprinted. *Potpourri*. (November-December 1994): 34-7].

1996

"The Founders of La Fonderie: An Interview with John Calder and David Applefield." *Potpourri*. 8:2 (1996): 55-8.

1997

"A Last Conversation with Robie Macauley." *Agni*. No. 45 (1997): 178-92.

"The General's Son: An Interview with James Carroll." *AWP Chronicle*. 29:4 (February 1997): 1-8.

1998

"An Interview with Duff Brenna." *Quarterly West*. No. 46 (Spring-Summer 1998): 172-86.

2001

"Up from Brooklyn: An Interview with Janet McDonald." *The Literary Review*. 44:4 (Summer 2001): 704-20.

2007

"Remembering the Sixties: A Conversation with Robert Gover." *The Literary Review*. 50:2 (Winter 2007). 21-42. [Reprinted. *Perigee*, "Features," 5:1 No. 17 (Aug/Sept/Oct 07) (online)].

"Torture Doesn't Stop Terror; It Creates Terrorists: An Interview with Inge-Genefke and Bent Sørensen." *Exploring Globalization* (Fairleigh Dickinson University) (online).

2008

"An Interview with Walter Cummins." *Perigee*. (October 2008).

2009

"An Interview with Duff Brenna." *Writer's Chronicle*. 42:2 (Oct-Nov 2009): 58-65.

2011

"A Nightingale That Knows My Name: An Interview with Line-Maria Lång, The Girl With Red Hair." *Absinthe 16: New European Writing*. (Spring 2011): 61-3.

Translations from Danish

Books

Møller, Henrik Sten. *Erik Magnussen*. Copenhagen. (1990).

Guldbrandsen, Alice Maud. *Silence Was My Song*. (nonfiction). Copenhagen: Documentas (2005). [In progress under a grant from the Danish

Arts Council. Excerpt published. *The Literary Review.* 49:2 (Winter 2006): 23-48. *Perigee Publication for the Arts.* (December 2007)].

Larsen, Thomas. *The Meeting with Evil: Inge Genefke's Fight Against Torture.* Copenhagen: Lindhardt & Finghof (2005). Excerpts published as a three-part series. *New Letters.* 74:1 (2007): 80-7; 74:2; (2008): 89-103; 74:3 (2008).

Nordbrandt, Henrik. *Leafy Sea Dragon* (poems). Copenhagen: Gyldendal. [Under a grant from the Danish Arts Council. Excerpts published in *American Poetry Review.* 37:2 (Mar-Apr 2008): 36-7; *Agni.* 66 (2007): 102; *The Literary Review.* 51:3 (Spring 2008); *Danish Literary Magazine.* (Spring 2008); *MidAmerican Review*].

Nordbrandt, Henrik. *Visiting Hours* (poems). Copenhagen: Gyldendal. [Under a grant from the Danish Arts Council. Excerpts published. *American Poetry Review.* 37:2 (Mar-Apr 2008): 36-7; *The Literary Review.* 51:3 (Spring 2008)].

Larsen, Thomas, and Mortensen, Finn. *The Danish Shipping Magnate: Mærsk McKinney Møller.* Copenhagen: Gyldendal (2010) (not published).

Thorhauge, Thomas. *Come Home.* (graphic novel). Publication pending.

Turèll, Dan. *The Big City Trilogy* (poetry). Translation in progress under two grants from the Danish Arts Council; various poems have appeared in *New Letters, Absinthe: New European Writing,* and *Perigee Publication for the Arts.*

Turèll, Dan. *Last Walk Through the City.* Limited bilingual edition with lithographs by Barry Lereng-Wilmont. Copenhagen: Pavillon Neuf Private Press (2010).

Chapbooks

Nordbrandt, Henrik. *Wind from a Distant Autumn* (poems). Self-enclosed chapbook of 16 poems in *MidAmerican Review* (Spring 2010).

Larsen, Thomas. *The Meeting with Evil: Inge Genefke's Fight Against Torture.* Introduced and translated by Thomas E. Kennedy (three essays published in *New Letters*). Copenhagen & Florham Park, NJ: Serving House Books (2010).

Prose (articles/stories)

1987

Skyum-Nielsen, Erik. "Danish Poetry Since 1965." *Frank: An International Journal of Contemporary Writing & Art.* Nos. 6/7 (Winter/Spring

1987): 80-2.

Eriksen, Jens Martin. "The Nameless City." (Translated with Monique Kennedy.) *Ibid*: 90-1.

1990

Holst, Knud. "Amber Man." (Translated with Monique Kennedy.) *The Cimarron Review*. No. 92 (July 1990): 33-7. [Reprinted in *The Cimarron Review*. No. 128 (Fall 1999): 16-20].

Panduro, Leif. "And that's a Fact." *Ibid*: 38-42.

Thorup, Kirsten. "The Family's Dissolution." *Ibid*: 46-8.

1992

Five Book Reviews. *Danish Literary Magazine*. 2 (Spring 1992): 5-6, 18-19, 22-23.

1995

Sibast, Peer. "At the Beach." *New Danish Fiction: The Review of Contemporary Fiction*. 15:1 (Spring 1995): 102-10.

Lynggaard, Klaus. "White Light." *Ibid*: 124-7.

2004

Sigsgaard, Palle. "Three Strangers." *The Literary Review*. 47:3 (Spring 2004): 33-4.

Christensen, Helle Thornvig. "Persistence, an excerpt." *Ibid*: 35-8.

2006

Guldbrandsen, Alice Maud. "Silence Was My Song, an excerpt." *The Literary Review*. 49:2 (Winter 2006): 23-48.

Inuk, Lotte. "Ice Age, an excerpt." *The Literary Review*. 49:3 (Summer 2006): 12-16.

2007

Bukdahl, Lars. "Backstroke through Tears." *Danish Literary Magazine*. (Spring 07) Danish Arts Council (online).

Blendstrup, Jens. "The Now Deceased Member of the Mikkelsen Family." *Ibid*. [Reprinted. *Absinthe: New European Writing*. No. 9 (Spring 2008)].

Bukdahl, Lars. "Symphonic Babble." *Ibid*. [Reprinted. *Absinthe: New European Writing*. No. 9 (Spring 2008)].

Andersen, Jens. "Childhood's Inn." *Ibid*.

Poulsen, Christa Leva. "The Return of Overview" and "A Ponderous Ambition." *Ibid.*

Mortensen, Henning. Excerpts from three novels: *Tooth and Nail, Rita Corsica,* and *The Fox Goes Out There. Danish Literary Magazine.* (Fall 2007) (online).

Inuk, Lotte, "The Revolution." *Chroma: A Queer Literary Journal.* No. 7 (Autumn 2007).

Larsen, Thomas. "The Anatomy of Torture—Villa Grimaldi." First part of a series of excerpts under the series title "Inge Genefke's Testimony on Torture" from the nonfiction book, *The Meeting with Evil: Inge Genefke's Fight Against Torture. New Letters.* 74:1 (Fall 2007): 83-7.

2008

Larsen, Thomas. "The Meeting with Evil." Part 2. An excerpt from the nonfiction book *The Meeting with Evil: Inge Genefke's Fight Against Torture. New Letters.* 74:2 (Winter 2008).

Thomas Larsen, "Inge Genefke's Testimony on Torture," Part 3, an excerpt from the nonfiction book, *The Meeting with Evil: Inge Genefke's Fight Against Torture. New Letters.* 74:3 (Spring 2008): 89-103.

Thomsen, Thorstein, Morten Hesseldahl, Peter Øvig Knudsen, Iselin C. Hermann, Flemming Jarlskov, Merete Schmnidt, Iselin C. Hermann, and Karen Syberg: translations of excerpts from eight Danish novelists. *Danish Literary Magazine.* (Spring 2008).

2009

Butschow, Julia. *Apropos Opa.* (Excerpt from novel). *Danish Literary Magazine* (Fall 2009).

2010

Lång, Line-Maria. "Doll." *The Literary Review.*

2011

Lång, Line-Maria. "The Chicken, The Rabbit, The Cow, The Ape and The Horse." *Absinthe 16: New European Writing.* (Spring 2011): 57-60.

Poetry

1987

Nordbrandt, Henrik. "Late Summers." (Translated with Monique Kennedy.)

Frank. An International Journal of Contemporary Writing & Art. Nos. 6/7 (Winter/Spring 1987): 84.

Tafdrup, Pia. "The Last Soft Membrane." (Translated with Monique Kennedy.) *Frank. Ibid.* 94. [Reprinted. *PIP Anthology of World Poetry in the 20th Century: Mass Transit—16 Contemporary Danish Poets.* (Douglas Messerli, ed.). Los Angeles: Green Integer (2006)].

Lynggaard, Klaus. "Beach Hotel" and "There Is Laughter in the Wilderness." *Frank. Ibid:* 95.

Jensen, Bo Green. "The Hunter's Moon." *Ibid:* 99.

Tafdrup, Pia. "Shadows in the Blood" and "Between Always and Never." *Paintbrush.* 14:28 (Autumn 1987): 32-3. ["Between Always and Never." Reprinted. *Heksering/FairyRing.* The Ukrainian Museum of Art. Kiev/ Funens Art Museum, Odense. Forlaget Brandts Klæde Fabrik. (April 1991) (unpaginated)].

1988

Tafdrup, Pia. "Snowpins" and "Anyway." *Men & Women, Together & Apart.* Iowa City: The Spirit That Moves Us Press. (1988): 164-5.

---. Two poems and additional lines of English subtitles in film, *Anholdt, on the Poetry of Pia Tafdrup*, a film by Lars Johansson, Statens Filmcentral, Denmark.

---. "The New Season," "Your Face," "Pleasure's Terror," "That It May Never End." *The Albany Review.* (August 1988).

---. "The Many Lives." *Asylum.* 4:3 (1988): 35.

---. "Silent Explosion," "Glazed Eyes," "Panorama." *The Colorado Review. New Series XV* (Fall/Winter 1988): 77-9.

---. "But You," "Transfusion," "The Day Held," "Gone," "Travel," "Swans," "Avian Longing," "Fan of Rays," "Light Changes," "Burrows," "Insane Silence," "The Loosening," and "Under the Dead." (Translated with Monique Kennedy.) *The Contemporary Review.* (Spring-Summer 1988): 20-6.

---. "Fevered Lillies." *Visions.* No. 28 (1988) (unpaginated).

---. "Came to Me." *Stone Country.* (November 1988): 54.

1989

Tafdrup, Pia. "Seen." *Pequod.* Nos. 26/27 (1989): 195.

---. "Elementary Chemistry." *Tordenskjold.* No. 2 (Autumn 1989): 14.

---. "The Dream about the Reader" and "The Many Lives." *Rohwedder.* 4 (1989): 36.

1990

Tafdrup, Pia. "Black or Red." *Blue Unicorn*. 13:3 (June 1990): 22.

---."The Tongue" and "The Closest Thing to Nothing." *Frank: An International Journal of Contemporary Writing & Art*. Nos. 11/12 (Winter 1990): 100-1. ["The Tongue" reprinted. *The Same Sky*. (Naomi S. Nye, ed.) New York: Macmillan. (1992): 67].

---. "Find Your Way Home." *The Seattle Review*. XIII:1 (Spring/Summer 1990): 151.

Rifbjerg, Klaus. "Borders." *Ibid*: 150.

---. "Before the Mount of Venus" and "Cuckoo." (Translated with Monique Kennedy.) *The Cimarron Review*. No. 92 (July 1990): 27-8.

Malinovski, Nina. "In a Safe Deposit Box." *Ibid*: 25.

Jensen, Bo Green. "In the Beginning" and "I Have Had to Kill You." *Ibid*: 22-3.

Bjørnvig, Thorkild. "Hebride Bay" and "A Mauve Fragrance in the Dark." *Ibid*: 14.

Tafdrup, Pia. "Fossil" and "Yesterday's Tea." *Ibid*: 31.

1991

Tafdrup, Pia. "Echo" and "White Journey." *Danish Literary Magazine* No. 1 (1991): 31-2, 36.

Bjørnvig, Thorkild. "Partridges." (Translated with Monique Kennedy.) *The Tel Aviv Review*. No. 3 (Winter 1991): 400.

1992

Bjørnvig Thorkild. "The Grass at Detifoss." (Translated with Monique Kennedy.) *Literary Olympians*. (1992). Boston: Ford Brown & Co Publishers (1992): 81. [Awarded the Silver Medal by Odysseus Elytis, Judge].

1993

Malinovski, Nina. "Time Port." *Visions International*. (1993). (unpaginated).

1996

Bjørnvig, Thorkild. "Raven Conditions," "Puffins," "Swallow Chicks on Rainy Day." *The Literary Review*. 39:4 (Summer 1996): 509-10.

1997

Draminsky, Jakob and Peter Laugesen. *Memory: A Song Cycle*. 15 songs performed in Copenhagen, 1996. Copenhagn: G3G Records by Multisounds. (1997).

2002

Tafdrup, Pia. "Notice" and "Happy Hour." *The Literary Review*. 45:3 (Spring 2004): 621-5.

2004

Foss, Kristian Bang. "Berlin, April 2003." *The Literary Review*. 47:3 (Spring 2004): 29-32.

Serup, Martin Glaz. "Poem." *Ibid*: 39.

Plambach, Dy. "Three Poems." *Ibid*: 40-3.

Eslund, Mads. "Rorschach Tablets, selections." *Ibid*: 44-5.

Tafdrup, Pia. "Ignition." *New Letters*. 70: 3 & 4 (2004): 244.

2005

Tafdrup, Pia. "Rue Vielle du Temple." *Tiferet. A Journal of Spiritual Literature*. II:1 (2005): 12.

2007

Tafdrup, Pia. "Letting in a Dog," "Banishment from Paradise," and "What Is Wrong with this Picture?" *The Literary Review*. 50:2 (Winter 2007): 57-61. ["Letting in a Dog" reprinted. *Danish Literary Magazine*. (Spring 07). Danish Arts Council: online; and broadcast on BBC Program "Verb" (2007)].

Olsen, Ursula Andkjær. "Fragment" and "Flow as You Will." *Danish Literary Magazine*. (Spring 07) Danish Arts Council (online).

Nordbrandt, Henrik. "Mother, Father, and Children." *Agni*. 66 (Fall 2007): 102.

2008

Nordbrandt, Henrik. "Anatomy," "Three Notations," "Parrots," and "The House in Sweden." *American Poetry Review*. (March-April 2008): 34-5.

Nordbrandt, Henrik, and Anne Louise Bosmans, Lone Hørslev, Peter Christensen Teilmann, Annemette Kune Andersen, and Duna Ghali. Poems by eight Danish poets. *Danish Literary Magazine* (Spring 2008).

Nordbrandt, Henrik, Ten Poems. *The Literary Review*. 51:3. (Spring 2008).

2009

Turèll, Dan. Three Poems / essay. *New Letters*. 75:2&3 (2009): 126-39.

Turèll, Dan. Four Poems / essay / interview with Chili Turèll. *Absinthe: New European Writing 12*. (2009): 34-58.

2010
Turèll, Dan. "Deep Frost Film." *Poetry Wales*. 46:2:6-7 (Autumn 2010).

2011
Nordbrandt, Henrik. "The Ultimate Morale," "Late Summer's First Day," "Draft of a Monument in Four Storeys." *Epoch* (Cornell University).
Turèll, Dan. "Too Much, Man." *Epoch*. (Cornell University).
Turèll, Dan. "My TV Drama." *Ecotone*.11. (Fall 2011): 73-5.
Nordbrandt, Henrik. "Jellyfish." *Ecotone*. 11. (Fall 2011): 63.
Jensen, Johannes V. *Ecotone*. 11. (Fall 2011): 80.
Bjørnson, Bjørnstjerne. "The Month for Me Is April." *Serving House Journal*. #4 (2011) (www.servinghousejournal.com).

2012
Nordbrandt, Henrik. "Four Poems from We Danes." *American Poetry Review*.

SECONDARY SOURCES

I. Selected Essays and Articles about Thomas E. Kennedy
1995
Stewart, Robert. "Choosing Fiction for Publication." (on "What Does God Care About Your Dignity Victor Travesti?") *The Whole Story: Editors on Fiction. A Collection of Essays & Stories*. Columbia, SC: The Bench Press (1995): 170-2.

1996
Fanning, Charles. "The Heart's Speech No Longer Stifled: New York Irish Writing Since the 1960s." *The New York Irish*. (Ronald H. Bagor and Timothy J. Meagher, eds.). Chapter 20. Baltimore and London: Johns Hopkins University Press (1996): 525-7.

1997
Memmott, David. "When the Muse Sings." *Arts East*. Oregon. (Spring 1997): 2.

1998

Brenna, Duff. "Reading Thomas E. Kennedy." *Uptown Magazine*. San Diego. (March 1998).

Brenna, Duff. "Wrestling with Angels: Thomas E. Kennedy." *Arts*. (March 1998).

1999

Brenna, Duff. "Imagination, Secrets and Sins in Thomas E. Kennedy." *Agni*. No. 50 (1999): 189-94.

2001

Lee, Michael. "Clarity from a Distance: Living the much-celebrated expatriot experience." *The Cape Cod Voice*. (July 3-July 8, 2001): 52.

2004

Herriges, Greg, and Tom Knoff. DVD Documentary film: *Thomas E. Kennedy, The Copenhagen Quartet*. Palatine: Harper College. (2004).

MacShéoinín, Liam. "*Kerrigan's Copenhagen A Love Story* and *Bluett's Blue Hours*." *The Burning Bush*. No. 11 (Spring 2004): 28-30.

Petlicki, Myrna. "Literary Secret Is Out: New DVD Documents Award-Winning Expatriate Writer." Pioneer Press. (October 7, 2004): B5.

2005

Herriges, Greg. "The Making of Thomas E. Kennedy: *Copenhagen Quartet*." *The South Carolina Review*. 38:1 (Fall 2005): 85-96.

2007

Cummins, Walter. "The Revelation of Character Inside Out: A Comparison of the First and Most Recent Novels of Thomas E. Kennedy." *The South Carolina Review*. 40:2 (Fall 2007): 100-104.

Gover, Robert. "The Soft Gleam of the Comical." *Introduction to Cast Upon the Day*. Titusville, NJ: Hopewell Publications (2007): 9-14.

Herriges, Greg. "Behind the Scenes of the Documentary Film, 'Thomas E. Kennedy's *Copenhagen Quartet*.'" *Perigee*. (February 2008): (online).

Stewart, Robert. "Passing the Test of Time: The Essays of Thomas E. Kennedy." *The South Carolina Review*. 40:2 (Fall 2007): 98-9.

Lee, Michael. "Novels of Jazz, the Jazz of Novels: On Kennedy's *Copenhagen Quartet*." *New Letters*. 74:1 (Fall 2007): 183-9.

Vorm, Tonny. "Return to Sender." (in Danish). *Euroman*. (September 2007): 97.

2008

Brenna, Duff. "Words Beyond the Chasm: Thomas E. Kennedy's *Copenhagen Quartet*." *The South Carolina Review*. 40:3 (Spring 2008).

Guldbrandsen, Alice Maud and Thomas E. Kennedy. "A Thomas E. Kennedy Bibliography." *The South Carolina Review*. 40:3 (Spring 2008).

Swan, Gladys. "Angels and Torture in the Fiction of Thomas E. Kennedy." *The Cimarron Review*. No. 164 (Summer 2008).

2009

Andersen, Carsten. "Finally discovered after 25 books." (in Danish). *Politiken*. (January 24, 2009): Section 2:5.

2011

"The Point Is to Persist: Thomas E. Kennedy's *Falling Sideways*." Bloomsbury (2011) and *Last Night My Bed a Boat of Whiskey Going Down*. New American Press (2010). Essay-review. Duff Brenna. *The South Carolina Review*. 44:1 (Fall 2011): 168-175.

Selected Reviews of Books by Thomas E. Kennedy

Crossing Borders (novel)

Cochran, Tracy. "*Crossing Borders* by Thomas E. Kennedy." *The New York Times Book Review*. (December 23, 1990): 12.

Dion, Marc Munroe. "Books in Brief." *Kansas City Star*. Books. (December 23, 1990): H-9.

Fitzpatrick, Kathleen. "*Crossing Borders*." *New Delta Review*. 8:1 (Fall 1990/Winter 1991): 111-4.

Jim Købak's *Kirkus Reviews*. (September 1, 1990).

Publisher's Weekly. (September 21, 1990).

Quinn, Mary Ellen. *Booklist*. (October 15, 1990).

Wetherell, W.D. "*Crossing Borders*." *The Cimarron Review*. No. 94 (January 1991): 128-9.

The American Short Story Today

Monty, Ib. "Thorough Status over the Art of the American Short Story." (in Danish). *Jyllands-Posten. Kunst og Kultur*. (August 27, 1991): 4.

Unreal City (novel)

Hibbard, Allen. "the true fantastico." *RainTaxi Review of Books.* 2:2 (1997): 46.

Olsen, Lance. "Unreal City." *The Review of Contemporary Fiction.* (Fall 1996).

Drive Dive Dance & Fight (stories)

Clift, G.W. *Detail. Small Press Review.* (January-February 1998): 10. *Confrontation* (unsigned). Nos. 68/69 (Summer 1999).

Fact Sheet Five. (1998)(unsigned, unpaginated).

Kamata, Suzanne. *Drive Dive Dance & Fight. BookLovers.* (May-June-July 1998): 20, 26-7.

The Book of Angels (novel)

Reich, Carol. "The Book of Angels." *Portlandia Review of Books.* No. 1 (August/September 1998): 8.

Realism & Other Illusions: Essays on the Art of Fiction

King, Zoe. "Realism & Other Illusions." *Words Literary Journal.* (July 2002) (online).

Lappin, Linda. "Exploring the Art and Craft of Fiction." *Kansas City Star.* (April 21, 2002): 39.

Lee, Michael. "How to Write Good." *The Cape Cod Voice.* (February 14-27, 2002): 35.

Library Journal. (2002): unsigned, undated.

Pastore, Michael. "Realism & Other Illusions: 15 Best Nonfiction Books of 2002." *ePublishers Weekly* (online).

Kerrigan's Copenhagen A Love Story (novel)

Abiko Annual. (Unsigned). "*Kerrigan's Copenhagen A Love Story.*" No. 23 (2003): 339-340.

Clement, Ben. "*Kerrigan's Copenhagen.*" *The Copenhagen Post.* "Guide This Week." (29-3 May 2007): G4.

Ferrie, Pauline. "*Kerrigan's Copenhagen A Love Story.*" *BookView Ireland. Emigrant Online.*(May 2003) (online).

Høst, Beth. "Books on Books." (in Danish). *Litteratursiden.dk.*(October 4, 2004) (online).

Kavanagh, Joe. "Books. *Kerrigan's Copenhagen.*" *Irish Connections.* 4:2 (March-April 2003): 74.

Lappin, Linda. "Page after Page, Drink after Drink: Postcard from Copenhagen." *Poets & Writers.* (online). (11.20.02).

---. "Thomas E. Kennedy, *Kerrigan's Copenhagen.*" *The Literary Review.* 47:2 (Winter 2004): 156-7.

Lee, Michael. "Our Favorite Fiction & Poetry of 2002." *The Cape Cod Voice.* (December 19, 2002-January 15, 2003): HV6.

Leonard, Sue. *Books Ireland.* "Kerrigan's Copenhagen A Love Story." Issue 254 (December 2002): 313.

Mac Sheóinín, Liam. "*Kerrigan's Copenhagen.*" *Irish Edition.* (February 2003): 20.

Michaëlis, Bo Tao. "Joyce Wanders in Copenhagen…". (in Danish). *Politiken.* Books. 4 Sektion. (November 30, 2002): 2.

Mouritsen, Lone, Norum, Roger E., and Osborne, Caroline. "*Kerrigan's Copenhagen*, Thomas E. Kennedy." *The Rough Guide to Denmark.* New York: London-Delhi: RoughGuides (2007): 420-1.

Bluett's Blue Hours (novel)

Books Ireland (unsigned). No. 261 (October 2003): 254.

Eberhart, John Mark. "Noteworthy Books of 2003." *Kansas City Star.* (December 2007).

Ferrie, Pauline. "*Bluett's Blue Hours.*" *BookView Ireland. Emigrant Online.* (November 2003). (online).

Lappin, Linda. "*Bluett's Blue Hours.*" *RainTaxi Review of Books.* (online). (Spring 2004).

Lee, Michael. "Our Favorite Books of 2003." *The Cape Cod Voice Literary Issue.* (Winter 2004): 30-1.

Mac Sheóinín, Liam. "*Bluett's Blue Hours.*" *Irish Edition.* (March 2004): 18.

Michaëlis, Bo Tao. "An American in Copenhagen II" (in Danish). *Politiken.* 2 Sektion. (January 12, 2004): 2.

Vorm, Tonny. "The Blue Hour." (in Danish). *Information.* (February 5, 2004): 10.

Wolf, Ulrich. "Copenhagen Seen with Other Spectacles." (in Danish). *Østerbro Avis.* (November 12, 2003): 4.

Greene's Summer (novel)

Ferrie, Pauline. "*Greene's Summer.*" *BookView Ireland. An Irish Emigrant Newsletter.* (August 2004): No. 109 (online).

Lappin, Linda. "*The Copenhgagen Quartet*, Volume III, *Greene's Summer.*" *The Literary Review.* 48:3 (Spring 2005): 169-70.

Tekulve, Susan. "Melancholy Danes?" *The Kansas City Star.* (October 17, 2004): 18.

O'Riordan, Alan. "*Greene's Summer.*" *Books Ireland.* No. 271 (November 2004): 267-8.

Vorm, Tonny. "Thomas E. Kennedy: *Greene's Summer*" (in Danish). *Euroman.* (October 2004): 40.

Danish Fall (novel)

Ferrie, Pauline. "Book of the Week: *Danish Fall*—Thomas E. Kennedy." *Emigrant Online.* (October 17, 2005).

Jenkins, John. "A Saga from Copenhagen...". *Writers Forum.* (December/January 2006): 32.

Lappin, Linda. "Unabashed Astringent Satire: Thomas E. Kennedy, *Danish Fall.* Volume 4 of *The Copenhagen Quartet.*" *The South Carolina Review.* 38:2 (Spring 2006): 274-6.

Lee, Michael. "Favorite Books for 2005." *The Cape Cod Voice.* (December 15-25, 2005): 34.

Mac Sheóinín, Liam. "*Danish Fall* by Thomas E. Kennedy." *Irish Edition.* (April 2006): 20.

Michaëlis, Bo Tao. "Tetralogy: Copenhagen Elegy." (in Danish). *Politiken. Book Supplement.* (Sektion 4). (October 22, 2005): 4.

Vorm, Tonny. "Beautiful and Tragic Portrait of the Capital and its Soul" (in Danish). *Information.* (November 15, 2005): 17.

The Literary Traveler (with Walter Cummins) (essays)

Mac Sheóinin, Liam. "*The Literary Traveler.*" *Irish Edition.* (December 2005): 12.

Tekulve, Susan. "Place and Inspiration." *New Letters.* 71:4 (2005): 140-3.

A Passion in the Desert (novel)

Ankjaergaard, Simon. "Kennedy and the Passion" (in Danish). *Østerbro Avis.* (May 9, 2007): 32.

Brenna, Duff. "Thomas E. Kennedy, *A Passion in the Desert.*" *The Literary Review.* 50:2 (Winter 2007): 163-6.

Mac Sheóinin, Liam. "*A Passion in the Desert*, Thomas E. Kennedy." *Irish Edition.* (December 2007).

Ratner, Rochelle. "Desert Crescendo. *A Passion in the Desert*, Thomas E. Kennedy." *American Book Review, Line on Line.* 29 (March-April 2008): 61.

Cast Upon the Day (stories)

Brenna, Duff. "*Cast Upon the Day*, Thomas E. Kennedy." *The Literary Review*. 50:4 (Summer 2007): 269-71.

Earhart, Julie Failla. "*Cast Upon the Day*, Thomas E. Kennedy." *Armchair Interviews*. (2007) (online).

Gover, Robert. "The Soft Gleam of the Comical: Review of *Cast Upon the Day*." *The South Carolina Review*. 39:2 (Spring 2007): 197-9.

Mac Sheóinin, Liam. "*Cast Upon the Day*, Thomas E. Kennedy." *Irish Edition*. (October 2007): 23 [reprinted in *PIF* (November 2007) (online).]

Merritt, Nicole. "*Cast Upon the Day* by Thomas E. Kennedy." *MyShelf.Com* (2007).

Midwest Book Review: Small Press Bookwatch. "*Cast Upon the Day*. Thomas E. Kennedy." (unsigned). (www.midwestbookreview.com/sbw/aug_07.html) (August 2007).

Williams, Bob. "*Cast Upon the Day* by Thomas E. Kennedy." *The Compulsive Reader*. (online). (2007).

Writers on the Job: Tales of the NonWriting Life (essays)

Hall-Downs, Liz. *Writers on the Job: Tales of the NonWriting Life* (with Walter Cummins). *The Compulsive Reader* (online)(2008).

Midwest Book Review (unsigned).(May 2008) (online).

New Danish Writing

Michaëlis, Bo Tao. *Politiken*. (31 May 2008). (book section: 2).

Rasmussen, Hans Henrik. "The Best Literature or...?" *Information*. (12 June 2008) (book section: 15).

Hav, Niels. "Literature Cannot be Exported." *Information*. (13 June 2008) (debate section: 25).

Riding the Dog: A Look Back at America (essays)

Featured book. *Politiken*. (2 November 2008) (Sunday culture section: 1, 6).

Vorm, Tonny. Portrait and Book Review. *Information*. (January 2009).

In the Company of Angels (novel)

Publishers Weekly. (October 12, 2009) (starred review).

Booklist. (American Library Association). (October 2009) (starred review).

Library Journal. (Vredevoogd, Gwen). (October 2009).

Kirkus Reviews. (December 15, 2009).

Miller, Laura. *Salon.com*. "With changing times the literature of the male-midlife crisis has become richer and riskier than ever before." (March 14, 2010). Book of the Week.

Constans, Gabriel. *New York Journal of Books.* (March 17, 2010).

Whipple, Mary. *Mary Whipple Reviews, Seeing the World Through Books.* (March 19, 2010).

"Favorite Book of the Year." Yardley, Jonathan. *The Washington Post.* (March 21, 2010).

The Florida Sun-Sentinel. (March 28, 2010).

Chicago Tribune. (March 28, 2010).

Kansas City Star. (April 18, 2010).

The New Yorker. Books Briefly Noted. (March 22, 2010).

Library Thing. (www.librarything.com). (March 25-26, 2010).

Serving House: A Journal of Literary Arts. (April 2010).

MacSheoinin, Liam. *PIF Magazine.* (April 2010).

Absinthe Minded (Blog of the literary journal *Absinthe: New European Writing*) (www.absinthenew.com). (April 16, 2010).

Long, Karen R. "A literate story lies amid the grief in Thomas E. Kennedy's *In the Company of Angels.*" *Cleveland Plain Dealer.* (April 19, 2010).

Lee, Michael. *The Barnstable Patriot.* (April 20, 2010).

Birnbaum, Robert. "New Finds—Writer on the Brink." *The Morning News.* (May 1, 2010).

Carter, Emily. "Novel asks difficult questions." *Minneapolis Star-Tribune.* (May 5, 2010).

Heminsley, Alexandra. "Love's a sanctuary for tortured souls." *The Independent.* (Sunday, 12 June 2011).

Mayes, Russ. "Love in the Age of Torture: A Review of *In the Company of Angels.*" *Richmond Books Examiner.* (April 15, 2011).

Yardley, Jonathan. "A Year's Worth of Favorites." (13 December 2010).

The Times (In Short). (12 June 2010).

Time Out. (June 10, 2010).

"Something Good in the State of Denmark." *New Letters.* 76:3 (2010).

Briscoe, Joanna. *The Guardian.* (24 July 2010) "How Much Survives."

Maristed, Kai. *Los Angeles Times.* (July 17, 2010) Book Review.

Metro, Co. UK, "Fiction of the Week: *In the Company of Angels* Is Heavenly." (18 June 2010)

McDowell, Lesley. *Independent.* (12 June 2011) "Love's a Sanctuary for Tortured Souls: *In the Company of Angels,* by Thomas E. Kennedy."

Last Night My Bed a Boat of Whiskey Going Down (a novel in essays).

Cummins, Walter. *The Literary Review.*
Brenna, Duff. *The South Carolina Review.* (2011).

Falling Sideways (novel)
Yardley, Jonathan. "Thomas E. Kennedy's *Falling Sideways.*" *The Washington Post.* (Sunday, March 13, 2011).
Carter, Emily. "The Reverberations of Greed." *Minneapolis Star-Tribune.* (March 5, 2011).
Vanna, Le. "Well Covered: Flying, Falling, Crawling." *The Book Bench. The New Yorker.* (February 24, 2011).
Whipple, Mary. "Thomas E. Kennedy—*Falling Sideways,*" *Seeing the World Through Books.* (March 6, 2011) (MaryWhippleReviews.com).
Kirkus Reviews. "*Falling Sideways,* by Thomas E. Kennedy." Editor Review. (November 15, 2010).
Winston, Len. "*Falling Sideways,* Thomas E. Kennedy." *The Brooklyn Rail.*
Weir, Zach. "Kennedy shakes up characters." *The Post and Courier.* (Sunday, May 8, 2011) (postandcourier.com).
Wilson, Knut. "*Falling Sideways* by Thomas E. Kennedy (Copenhagen Quartet)." (*wilsonknut.com*) (11 May 2011).
Apte, Poornima. "*Falling Sideways* by Thomas E. Kennedy," *CBC News Report Reviews.* (Mar 01, 2011) (cbcnewsreport.com).
Brenna, Duff. (see review essays, 2011, *South Carolina Review*).
"Fresh Fiction," *Image Magazine* (Ireland). (1 Dec 2011): 40.
"The Tuesday Book: *Falling Sideways.*" Peter Carty. *Independent.* (6 Dec 2011): 54.
"Books," *In Style, Sunday* (1 Jan 2012): 44.
"*Falling Sideways.*" *Metro (London Main).* (16 Nov 2011): 53.
"*Falling Sideways.*" *Daily Mail.* (Fri, 25 Nov 2011): 78.
Untitled Books, Thomas E. Kennedy, Features, Satirical, *Falling Sideways.* *Psychologies Magazine.* (December 2011): 50.
"Top 3 Must Read books," *Falling Sideways.* (Thursday, 1 Dec 2011): 182.
"*Falling Sideways.*" *The Bookbag.* (Bookbag.co.uk.book review).
"Dark Days at the Office." George Pendle. *Financial Times.* (Dec 16, 2011).

My Life with Women or The Consolation of Jazz (novel)
Lappin, Linda. "*My Life with Women or The Consolation of Jazz.* Vols. 1 & 2 by Thomas Kennedy." *California Review of Books.* (calirb.com).

Contributors

The late David Applefield was a published novelist, editor and founder of the literary journal *Frank*, *The Financial Times* special representative for sub-Saharan Africa and the Middle East, a media trainer for the U.S. Department of State, a travel writer, and a media advisor to the president of Senegal.

Renée Ashley is the author, most recently, of *Ruined Traveler*, prose poems, and *Minglements: Prose on Poetry and Life*, a collection of essays. Other poetry collections include *The View from the Body*; *Because I Am the Shore I Want to Be the Sea* (Subito Book Prize, University of Colorado—Boulder); *Basic Heart* (X. J. Kennedy Poetry Prize, Texas Review Press); *The Revisionist's Dream*; *The Various Reasons of Light*; and *Salt* (Brittingham Prize in Poetry, University of Wisconsin Press); also a novel, *Someplace Like This*, and two chapbooks, *The Museum of Lost Wings* and *The Verbs of Desiring*.

Phyllis Barber has been writing award-winning stories, articles, essays, and novels for over forty years, in addition to being the mother of four sons, teaching fiction and creative nonfiction in the MFA in Writing Program at the Vermont College of Fine Arts, riding her bicycle one thousand miles across the Midwest one summer, traveling the world, reading across a wide spectrum of books, serving as a community volunteer, playing the piano professionally, and accompanying a diverse variety of musicians. In 2005, she was inducted into the Nevada Writers Hall of Fame.

Duff Brenna is the author of ten books, including *The Book of Mamie*, which won the AWP Award for Best Novel; *The Holy Book of the Beard*, named "an underground classic" by *The New York Times*; *Too Cool*, a *New York Times* Noteworthy Book; *The Altar of the Body*, given the Editors Prize Favorite Book of the Year Award (*South Florida Sun-Sentinel*), and also received a San Diego Writers Association Award for Best Novel 2002. He is the recipient of a National Endowment for the Arts Award, *Milwaukee Magazine*'s Best Short Story of the Year Award, and a Pushcart Prize Honorable Mention. His collection of short stories, *Minnesota Memoirs*, was awarded first prize at the

2013 Next Generation Indie Awards in New York City. His memoir, *Murdering the Mom*, was a Finalist for Best Non-Fiction at the same 2013 Independent Publishers Awards. He also received a second-place award under the Grand Prize category. Brenna's work has been translated into six languages.

T Nicole Cirone is an English teacher and a yoga instructor. Her work has appeared in several literary journals, including *Serving House Journal, Ovunque Siamo: A Journal of Italian-American Writing, Hippocampus, Perigee, Red River Review*, and *Philadelphia Stories*; and in three anthologies. Ms. Cirone holds undergraduate degrees in Italian Studies and Political Science and an MA in English from Rosemont College, and a dual-concentration MFA in Creative Writing Poetry and Creative Non-Fiction from Fairleigh Dickinson University.

Susann Cokal (Susanncokal.net) is the author of four books of literary historical fiction: *Mermaid Moon, Mirabilis, Breath and Bones*, and *Kingdom of Little Wounds. The Kingdom of Little Wounds* won a Printz silver medal from the American Library Association in 2014. Cokal has contributed short stories and essays about contemporary writers, many to anthologies and journals. She has reviewed almost four dozen books for *The New York Times Book Review* and has contributed reviews and essays to numerous other reviewing organs.

Mark Cox has published six volumes of poetry: *Sorrow Bread* (Serving House Books), *Barbells of the Gods* (Ampersand Press), *Smoulder* (David R. Godine), *Thirty-Seven Years from the Stone* and *Natural Causes* (both in the Pitt Poetry Series), and *Readiness* (Press 53). Cox received a Whiting Writers Award, a Pushcart Prize, and numerous fellowships for that work. He teaches in the Department of Creative Writing at University of North Carolina Wilmington and in the Vermont College MFA Program.

Walter Cummins has published seven short story collections and three collections of essays and reviews. More than one hundred of his stories, as well as memoirs, essays, and reviews, have appeared in magazines.

Steve Davenport is the author of three poetry collections: *Bruise Songs* (Stephen F. Austin State University Press, 2020), *Overpass* (Arsenic Lobster/ Misty Publications, 2012), and *Uncontainable Noise* (Pavement Saw Press, 2006). His poems, stories, and essays have been anthologized, reprinted, and published in scores of literary magazines. A story in *The Southern Review* received a 2011 Pushcart Prize Special Mention, and his *Murder on Gasoline Lake*, published in *Black Warrior Review* and later as a chapbook by New American Press, is listed as *Notable in Best American Essays 2007*. He keeps a website, *Collected Works of Gasoline Lake*, at http://gasolinelake.com/.

Lisa del Rosso originally trained as a classical singer and completed a post-graduate program at LAMDA (London Academy of Music and Dramatic Art), living and performing in London before moving to New York City. Her plays, *Clare's Room* and *Samaritan*, have been performed off-Broadway and had public readings, respectively, while *St. John*, her third play, was a semi-finalist for the 2011 Eugene O'Neill National Playwrights Conference. Her writing has appeared in newspapers and magazines. She writes theater reviews and teaches writing at New York University.

Dr. Roger Derham has written four novels and from 2001-2012 was Managing Director, Wynkyn de Worde Publishing Company, which published the initial versions of the four novels of *The Copenhagen Quartet*. As a physician, he worked in Ireland, the U.K., and Australia as an obstetrician and gynaecologist between 1982-2015, subjects he lectures on at the National University of Ireland Galway. For the past twenty years he has been a forensic physician for the Sexual Assault Response Team (SART).

The late Okla Elliott's work appeared in many magazines, as well as being included as a "notable essay" in *Best American Essays 2015*. His books included *From the Crooked Timber* (short fiction), *The Cartographer's Ink* (poetry), *The Doors You Mark Are Your Own* (a novel), and *Blackbirds in September: Selected Shorter Poems of Jürgen Becker* (translation).

Niels Hav is a Danish poet, the author of seven collections of poetry and three books of short fiction. His books are translated into many languages; in English he has *We Are Here*, published in Toronto. He has travelled widely in Europe, Asia, Africa, North and South America. His most recent book, *'Øjeblikke af lykke' / 'Moments of Happiness,'* was published in 2020.

Greg Herriges is a retired professor of English, and the author of over thirty-five essays, stories, and articles, as well as six novels, including *Streethearts* and *The Winter Dance Party Murders*.

Mark Hillringhouse is a published poet, essayist, and photographer whose works have been widely exhibited in area galleries. He was the founding editor of *The American Book Review*, and a contributing editor for *The New York Arts Journal*. Thrice nominated for a Pushcart Prize, and a three-time recipient of a New Jersey State Council on the Arts Fellowship, he has won several awards for poetry and photography including the National Parks Calendar photography contest and the Soho Arthouse Gallery's "Captured! A Moment in Time" exhibition. His film documentary with collaborator Kevin Carey on the life of local Salem poet Malcolm Miller, titled *Unburying Malcolm Miller*, was released in 2017 and screened at the Massachusetts Poetry Festival. His book of poems and photographs titled *Between Frames* was published by Serving House Books.

H. L. Hix's poetry, essays, and other works have been recognized with an NEA Fellowship, the Grolier Prize, the T. S. Eliot Prize, and the Peregrine Smith Award, and been translated into Spanish, Russian, Urdu, and other languages.

Line-Maria Lång was born in 1982. She made her debut in 2009 with the short story collection *Rottekonge*. Her stylish and tantalizing exploration of themes such as childhood and sexuality has already garnered great acclaim. She is thus a favorite lecturer and has received several work grants from the Danish Arts Council.

Linda Lappin is the author of four novels: *The Etruscan* (Wynkyn de Worde, 2004), *Katherine's Wish* (Wordcraft, 2008), *Signatures in Stone: A Bomarzo Mystery* (Pleasure Boat Studio, 2013)—winner of the Daphne Du Maurier Prize for Mystery and Suspense Writing; and *Loving Modigliani: The Afterlife of Jeanne Hébuterne* (Serving House Books, 2020)—winner in the women's fiction category in the 2021 Indie Reader Discovery Awards, and finalist for the 2021 Daphne Du Maurier Award. She is also the author of a writing-craft book: *The Soul of Place: Ideas and Exercises for Conjuring the Genius Loci* (Travelers' Tales, 2015). She lives in Rome. (www.lindalappin.net).

Kerstin Lieff (www.kerstinlieff.com) earned her MFA in creative writing from Fairleigh Dickinson University. Her debut book, *Letters from Berlin* (Lyons Press: Random House), won the 2013 Colorado Book Award.

Roisin McLean writes fiction and creative nonfiction. She received her MFA in Creative Writing, Fiction, from Fairleigh Dickinson University, has been nominated five times for the Pushcart Prize, and was a semifinalist for The Katherine Anne Porter Prize in Fiction (Nimrod/Hardman). Her stories and essays appear in her collection *The Fifth Eye*, numerous online and print journals, and several anthologies. Her interviews with Thomas E. Kennedy appear in *The McNeese Review* and *Ecotone*.

Lars Movin was born in 1959. He is a director and writer, known for *Words of Advice: William S. Burroughs on the Road* (2007), *Onkel Danny—Portræt af en karma cowboy* (2002) and *The Misfits—30 Years of Fluxus* (1993).

Michael B. Neff worked in Washington, DC in managerial and budget-analyst job series from NASA to GSA. Always an avid writer, his work has appeared in such literary journals as *North American Review*, *Quarterly West*, *The Literary Review*, and *Conjunctions*. He now directs the Algonkian Conferences, helping new writers get published.

Sylvia Petter is an Australian, founding member of the Geneva Writers' Group, now based in Vienna, Austria. She has a PhD in Creative Writing (UNSW, Sydney, 2009) and was Co-Director Vienna for the 13th International Conference on the Short Story in English (2014). She has published four story collections, one of which is in German. Her debut novel, *All the Beautiful Liars*, was published in 2020/21 by Lightning Books, U.K. In June 2021, she launched her own imprint, Flo Do Books Vienna-Sydney, primarily to publish her own shorter bilingual works. Her antifa novelette in flash fiction, *Winds of Change*, was the first work of the imprint. She is contributing fiction editor of the online *WordCity Literary Journal*.

David R. Poe, born in Buffalo, has lived and written in France for thirty years. He continues to live in Paris and Normandy with his wife and son.

Dr. Azly Rahman grew up in Johor Bahru, Malaysia and holds a Columbia University (New York City) doctorate in International Education Development and six Masters Degrees in Education, International Affairs, Peace Studies and Communication, and Creative Writing (Creative Non-Fiction and Fiction). He has written more than five hundred analyses/essays on Malaysia and global issues. His twenty-five years of teaching experience in Malaysia and the United States span a wide range of subjects, from elementary to graduate education. He has edited and authored seven books, with five more forthcoming

(2018-19).

Lennox Raphael's work-in-progress, *Naipail's Country*, is a novel of human transformation. His writings include the play *Che!, Blue Soap* (musical direction by Archie Shepp), and *Waiting for Mick Jagger*, a *Harper's* Interview with Ralph Ellison, *Garden of Hope*, with Maryanne Raphael: and, of recent vintage, *Poetry*, (Medan Forlag); *Tears of the Soul, Nøyen Jøfru, Joy of Love, Art of Love*, special signed Finn Donsbæk limited editions: with drawings by LarsKræmmer; http://friktionmagasin.dk index.php/2016/12/15/utopia/ and several Kenn Clarke-designed BLURB books. He was a staff writer for *The East Village Other* (EVO) and wrote for *Evergreen Review*. He taught at City College of New York and The University of Rhode Island. He is co-curator of Berlin Soup International Arts Festival (www.berlinsoup.dk).

Sudeep Sen's prize-winning books include: *Postmarked India: New & Selected Poems* (HarperCollins), *Rain, Aria* (A. K. Ramanujan Translation Award), *Fractals: New & Selected Poems | Translations 1980-2015* (London Magazine Editions), *EroText* (Vintage: Penguin Random House), and *Kaifi Azmi: Poems | Nazms* (Bloomsbury). He has edited influential anthologies. Sen's works have been translated into over twenty-five languages. His words have appeared in many publications and on broadcasts. He is the editorial director of AARK ARTS, the editor of *Atlas,* and currently the inaugural artist-in-residence at the Museo Camera. Sen is the first Asian honoured to deliver the Derek Walcott Lecture and read at the Nobel Laureate Festival. The Government of India awarded him the senior fellowship for "outstanding persons in the field of culture/literature."

Martin Glaz Serup was born in 1978 and lives in Copenhagen. He has published seven children's books, most recently an illustrated collection of stories entitled *Yana and Eliah (and many other children)* (2013, illustrations by Lilian Brøgger), several chapbooks, as well as seven collections of poetry, most recently *Roman Nights* (2013, published in Sweden 2014)—of which excerpts in English are published in *Action Yes* and *Poetry Wales*—and the long poem *The Field* (2010), which was also published in the U.S.A. (2011), Sweden (2012) and Finland (2014). In 2013 Serup published his first book-length theoretical essay *Relationel poesi.*

Per Šmidl lived for two years in Wagon 537 at Christiania. Then he moved to Paris, then California, and when he got back to Denmark he wrote the bestseller *Chop Suey*. Many years as a political dissident in Prague followed after the publication in Denmark of his book *Victim of Welfare* in 1995. The book challenged the role and freedom of the individual in the welfare state. Some previous publications include the novel *Mathias Kraft*, 1999, and the essay "Ytringsfrihed," which means "Freedom of Speech," 2006.

The late Heather Spears was a Canadian-born poet, novelist, artist, sculptor, and educator. Residing in Denmark since 1962, she returned to Canada annually to conduct speaking and reading tours and to teach drawing and head-sculpting workshops. She published eleven collections of poetry, five novels, and three volumes of drawings.

Louise Stahl is a freelance proofreader and copyeditor, as well as a Contributing Editor to *The Literary Review*. She lives in NJ with her many critters, both two-legged and four.

René Steinke's most recent novel, *Friendswood*, was named one of National Public Radio's Great Reads, and Darin Strauss called it "a large-hearted, big-brained book." Steinke is the recipient of a 2016 Guggenheim Fellowship. Her second novel, *Holy Skirts*, a fictionalized biography of the Dada artist and poet, the Baroness Elsa von Freytag-Loringhoven, was a Finalist for the National Book Award. Her first novel is *The Fires*. Her essays and book reviews have appeared in *The New York Times*, *Vogue*, *O Magazine*, *Salon*, *4Columns*, *Bookforum*, and in anthologies. She is currently the Director of the MFA program in Creative Writing at Fairleigh Dickinson University, and she lives in Brooklyn.

Robert Stewart's books of poems include *Working Class* (Stephen F. Austin State UP, 2011) and *Plumbers* (BkMK P, 1998/revised 2nd edition 2017); his books of essays include *The Narrow Gate: Essays on Writing, Art & Values* (Serving House Books, 2014). He is a former editor of *New Letters* and lives in Prairie Village, Kansas.

Gladys Swan is a writer and visual artist, who taught in the Vermont MFA Program in Creative Writing, where she first met Tom. She has published eight collections of short fiction, and eight novels. The ninth, *Ceremony of Innocence,* is from Serving House Books. She is currently putting together a collection of essays.

Pia Tafdrup (www.tafdrup.com) was born on 29 May 1952 in Copenhagen. She made her literary debut in 1981 and has till now published seventeen collections of poetry. *Poems of Pia Tafdrup* has been translated into thirty languages. English translations of her poems have been published in more than fifty literary journals in the U.K., U.S., Canada, and Australia. Tafdrup has received the Nordic Council's Literature Prize in 1999 and the Nordic Prize in 2006 from The Swedish Academy.

Susan Tekulve's newest book is *Second Shift: Essays*. She is the author of *In the Garden of Stone*, winner of the 2012 South Carolina First Novel Prize and a 2014 Gold IPPY Award. She's also published two short story collections: *Savage Pilgrims* and *My Mother's War Stories*. Her nonfiction, short stories, and essays have appeared in journals such as *Denver Quarterly*, *The Georgia Review*, *The Louisville Review*, *Puerto del Sol*, *New Letters*, and *Shenandoah*.

Jayne Thompson teaches English and creative writing at Widener University. She is the director of The Chester Writers House in Chester, PA, a non-profit community writing center. She taught Accelerated Literature at Chester High School for one school year as a special project and has taught in many after-school programs for students as young as eight. In addition, she teaches at a prison in Pennsylvania, S.C.I. Graterford, and recently published an anthology of writings geared towards young people with her incarcerated students. Serving House Books published *Letters to My Younger Self: An Anthology of Writings by Incarcerated Men at S.C.I. Graterford and a Writing Workbook* in 2014.

Susan Tiberghien is an American-born writer living in Geneva, Switzerland. She holds a BA in Literature and Philosophy (Phi Beta Kappa) and did graduate work at the Université de Grenoble and the CG Jung Institute of Zurich. She has published three memoirs, *Looking for Gold, One Year in Jungian Analysis* (Daimon Verlag, 1997), *Circling to the Center: A Woman's Encounter with Silent Prayer* (Paulist Press, 2001), *One Year to a Writing Life* (Da Capo Press, 2007), and most recently, *Side by Side, Writing Your Love Story* and *Footsteps, In Love with a Frenchman* (both Red Lotus Studio Press, 2015) along with numerous narrative essays in journals and anthologies on both sides of the Atlantic.

Dan Turèll (March 19, 1946 – October 15, 1993), affectionately nicknamed "snittekongen" (Uncle Danny), was a popular Danish writer with notable influence on Danish literature. Influenced by the Beat Generation his work crossed a number of genres including autobiography, beat lit and crime fiction.

Timmy Waldron is the author of the short story collection *Stories for People Who Watch TV* from New Meridian Arts. His stories have been published in various print and online journals since the late '90s. His first short story collection, *World Takes*, was published by Word Riot Press. Timmy received an MFA from Fairleigh Dickinson University.

Christina Warren is a former Mississippian, living in Bern, Switzerland, where she works as an English teacher and translator.

CPSIA information can be obtained
at www.ICGtesting.com
Printed in the USA
BVHW011256231221
624772BV00007B/130

9 781947 175549